DECONSTRUCTION AND CRITICAL THEORY

DECONSTRUCTION AND CRITICAL THEORY

PETER V. ZIMA

Translated by Rainer Emig

continuum
LONDON • NEW YORK

CONTINUUM
The Tower Building, 11 York Road, London SE1 7NX
370 Lexington Avenue, New York, NY 10017-6503
www.continuumbooks.com
Originally published as *Die Dekonstruktion: Einführung und Kritik* © A. Francke Verlag,
Tübingen and Basel, 1994

English edition first published in 2002
© Continuum 2002

British Library Cataloguing-in-Publication Data
A catalogue record for this book is available from the British Library.
   ISBN 0-8264-5933-1 (hardback)
   ISBN 0-8264-5934-X (paperback)

Library of Congress Cataloging-in-Publication Data
Zima, P. V.
   [Dekonstruktion. English]
   Deconstruction and critical theory / Peter V. Zima; translated by Rainer Emig.
     p. cm.
   Includes bibliographical references and index.
   ISBN 0-8264-5933-1—ISBN 0-8264-5934-X (pbk.)
   1. Deconstruction. 2. Criticism – History – 20th century. I. Title

   PN98.D43 Z54 2002
   149–dc21   2001047580

Typeset by CentraServe Ltd, Saffron Walden, Essex
Printed and bound in Great Britain by MPG Books Ltd, Bodmin, Cornwall

CONTENTS

PREFACE

In its commercialized form, Deconstruction (both French and American) has been reduced, in a diversity of intellectual circles, to a mere catchphrase, a reduction that has removed this strand of thinking from the historical and intellectual context of its development. Many evaluate and condemn it without paying attention to this background and without considering Deconstruction's relevance for contemporary theoretical and philosophical debates. Like 'Existentialism' before it, Deconstruction has become an ideological provocation that polarizes the intellectual scene to this day.

Terminologically, then, it appears of little use to join either the advocates or enemies of Deconstruction by publishing a further argument for or against a unified concept of 'Deconstruction'. This is because the comprehension of this indeed heterogeneous philosophy, whose diversity is mirrored in the structure of the present book, is aided not by the ideological mechanisms of polarization, but rather by the theoretical procedures of *analysis* and *dialogue*.

Consequently, in what is to follow, the philosophical and aesthetic foundations of the various deconstructive approaches will be reflected upon and concretized – as in my earlier *The Philosophy of Modern Literary Theory* (London, 1999), to which the present book is linked. At the same time it strives for a dialogic presentation that derives in part from Critical Theory (Adorno, Horkheimer), yet does not use this theory mechanistically as a meta-discourse, but in a self-critical and reflexive way with regard to Deconstruction. The critique of deconstructive theories, therefore, ultimately leads to a self-critique.

The attempt to present Deconstruction from a philosophical and, more specifically, an aesthetic perspective is not only designed to counter the market-driven abstraction behind, say, the media's use of the term, but aims to do justice to the importance of literature and art in Derrida's thinking. This thinking, whose key concept of *dissémination* (dissemination, dispersion) was coined by Mallarmé, continually emerges from the literary, the poetic text and returns to it. Derrida himself confirms the orientation of his thinking towards literature: 'My interest lay primarily, even more strongly than with philosophy, if this is at all possible, with literature, the kind of writing that is labelled literary.'[1]

A further reason for approaching Deconstruction from a philosophical and aesthetic point of view, a perspective that generates a philosophical and aesthetic object rather than a linguistic or psychological one, is the thematic range of the present book. It has as its object not merely Derrida's work, but also the deconstructive literary theories developed in the United States. At Yale University authors such as Paul de Man, J. Hillis Miller and Geoffrey Hartman adopted some of Derrida's basic ideas and directed their attention to philosophers that have had a lasting impact on Derrida's thinking: Plato, Kant, Rousseau, Hegel, Nietzsche, Husserl and Heidegger. The Belgian-born Paul de Man in particular has developed a deconstructive theory of literature that derives from Nietzsche and questions some basic assumptions of German Idealism. Other Deconstructionists, such as Geoffrey Hartman, refer to Nietzsche and Derrida, but simultaneously align themselves with English Romanticism and the philosophy of Friedrich Schlegel. The latter will play an important part in the first chapter of the present study. It will become evident that, independent of direct influences, typological similarities (analogies) connect Deconstruction with German Romanticism.

The dialogue between Deconstruction and Critical Theory that is staged sporadically here is motivated by the assumption that linguistic, psychological and social manifestations are *ambivalent*. The critical discourse that has Deconstruction as its object is not radically different from the object itself, so that its critique at times becomes a self-critique. In the final chapter especially, it will become evident that Deconstruction and Critical Theory are facing similar problems that neither has been able to solve to date. For instance, Habermas' critique of Derrida, outlined in the last chapter, is justified in some of its aspects, but will also become the occasion for turning some of Derrida's and Adorno's insights against Habermas.

Generally speaking, it is not only the aim of the present study to describe Deconstruction critically through examples and model analyses, but also to make possible a dialogue between two different yet related theories. Such a dialogue presupposes not only reflexion and self-reflexion, but also an abandoning of the ideological dualism (which posits the correct position here, the incorrect one elsewhere) that inevitably leads to an intellectual monologue. Deconstruction and Critical Theory share a concern to perceive the Other in its alterity and not to incorporate it. For this reason alone they must reject every form of monologue.*

NOTE

1. J. Derrida, *Du droit à la philosophie* (1990), p. 443. All translations, unless otherwise stated, by R. Emig.

* The author has added two new sections to the present English translation: 'Derrida, Deleuze and the Critique of the Subject' (Chapter 2, section 4) and 'Feminist Deconstruction and Feminist Critiques: the Problem of Subjectivity' (Chapter 7, section 5).

1

AESTHETIC THEORY, DIALECTIC AND DECONSTRUCTION

At first sight one might consider *Deconstruction* as an attempt *to liberate critical thinking from institutionalized philosophy and to question in a radical way the dominance of concepts as well as systematic terminology.* Jacques Derrida defines it as a *systematic subversion of European metaphysics.*[1] In his view, Hegel's notion of totality and Saussure's linguistic system in particular are manifestations of a metaphysical structure of concepts that is closely related to the principle of domination. Derrida aims at dissecting these and other theoretical systems (see his critique of Kant below) by revealing their ambivalences and contradictions. His critique of idealist philosophy and Saussurean Structuralism cannot be understood outside the German philosophical tradition to which he refers in his polemics against metaphysics.

His attitude towards the German philosophers Immanuel Kant (1724–1804), Georg Wilhelm Friedrich Hegel (1770–1831), or Martin Heidegger (1889–1976) is characterized by a general ambivalence inasmuch as the French philosopher reiterates some of their theses in order to question the foundations of their systems. He develops 'a kind of *general theory of Deconstruction*'[2] and in doing so refers to some key terms and core arguments of Idealism in order to unveil its contradictory or, indeed, aporetic character.

In order to understand Derrida and the American literary theorists who have adapted and developed his ideas it is therefore important to address some basic problems of German Idealism in which the various modes of Deconstruction find their point of departure. Most of these problems concern the realm of aesthetics: the different notions of natural beauty, the work of art, and the literary text. They also affect the realm of semiotics and the competing definitions of the linguistic and the artistic sign. In contrast to a philosopher such as Hegel and to some of his Marxist followers – Georg Lukács, for instance – who believe that works of art can be identified with conceptual systems or clearly definable structures of signifieds, Immanuel Kant and his modern disciples regard all attempts to translate art and literature into concepts with scepticism. They tend to see the artistic sign as an ensemble of polysemic and interpretable signifiers that evoke ideas, yet cannot be tied to precise concepts.

Contemporary semioticians would claim, with reference to Louis Hjelmslev (1899–1965), that the Hegelian camp emphasizes the *level of content*, which can be defined broadly as the interplay of signifieds, while the Kantian privileges the *level of expression*, which entails the totality of signifiers. In this context, two completely different aesthetics might be at stake: an aesthetics of expression (of signifiers) and an aesthetics of content (of signifieds). Yet we shall see below that, in Derrida's view, even Saussure's distinction between *signifiant* and *signifié* is a dualistic relic of European metaphysics – as indeed is Hjelmslev's complementary distinction between the *level of expression* and that of *content*.

1 KANT, HEGEL AND DERRIDA:
THE (NON-)CONCEPTUAL BEAUTIFUL

One of the still unresolved problems of modern aesthetics (from Kant to Derrida) is the question whether it is possible to relate works of art to a concept and explain them in theoretical terms. The Kantian position, which is defended in modified form by the Anglo-American New Critics (who can be regarded in some respects as the precursors of Deconstruction), as well as by the Russian Formalists, and the Prague Structuralists, is well known and still informs academic debates on literature and the arts.

Kant regards the beautiful in nature and art as a phenomenon which 'pleases without a concept' and which ought to be perceived by the observer with 'disinterested pleasure'. Against the utilitarianism and rationalism of the Enlightenment philosophers Christian Wolff and Johann Christoph Gottsched, Kant proclaims the autonomy of art (the individual work) and rejects all attempts to subordinate the aesthetic sphere to aims that have nothing in common with it, such as didactics, religion, politics or commerce. For him, the beautiful is 'purposeful without purpose'.

For the present discussion, Kant's thesis on the non-conceptual beauty of nature is of particular importance since it derives from a theory of cognition that demarcates the limits of knowledge. The latter is limited in as much as the subject can only perceive objects in space and time, i.e. subjectively. The object as such, 'the thing in itself', escapes our comprehension and remains inaccessible.

Such a theory of cognitive limitation also affects the realm of aesthetics, where Kant refuses to dissolve the object of nature or art into conceptual thought in order to identify it with a particular concept. Although he emphasizes the importance of the beautiful in the cognitive process, he nonetheless distinguishes aesthetic ideas from rational ones in his *Critique of Judgement* (1790) and tries to demonstrate that these two basically distinct categories of ideas cannot be translated into one another. As in the general theory of knowledge, there are absolute limits here, since no rational concept can be adequate for an aesthetic idea, a creation of the imagination. 'But, by an aesthetic idea I mean that representation of the imagination which induces much thought, yet without the possibility of any definite thought whatsoever, i.e. a *concept*, being adequate to it, and which language, consequently, can never get quite on level terms with or render completely intelligible.'[3] The aesthetic object and the ideas that it evokes in us thus do not dissolve into conceptual thinking, 'for beauty is not a concept of the object, and the judgement of taste is not a cognitive judgement'.[4]

Consequently, each aesthetic phenomenon exceeds its conceptual representation, for it does not *designate* anything specific, and its relations to conceptual thought should rather be traced on the level of evocation or – as the semioticians would call it – the level of *connotation*. All attempts by the Hegelians (and later the Marxists) to relate works of art to concepts appear to the Kantians as dangerous chimerae and dogmas. R. Wiehl rightly emphasizes the fact 'that Kant's doctrine of reflexive judgement explicitly denies the possibility of a science of the beautiful . . . .'[5]

This view of the *Critique of Judgement*, a view that has subsequently become one of the commonplaces of institutionalized philosophy, is questioned by Jacques Derrida, who claims to have detected a basic contradiction in Kant's third Critique. What follows is not only meant to determine Derrida's position vis-à-vis Kant and Hegel, but also to give the reader a first taste of Deconstructionist argument. At this stage, this can only be a fleeting encounter with Deconstruction whose significance will perhaps become clearer after reading the second chapter.

In *The Truth in Painting* Derrida attempts to prove that Kant tries to apply 'an analytic of concepts on a process without concept'.[6] This attempt at a logical framing (*encadrement*) produces contradictions in Kant's discourse: in spite of its own attempt at framing, it also claims that the frame (*cadre, parergon*) of the work of art is secondary. Derrida concludes his critique with a deconstructive gesture when he presents Kant's linking of conceptual and aesthetic judgement as a contradiction, an aporia: 'The analytic of the beautiful thus gives, ceaselessly undoes the labor of the frame to the extent that, while letting itself be squared up by the analytic of concepts and by the doctrine of judgment, it describes the absence of concepts in the activity of taste.'[7]

In other words, Kant's own discourse on the beautiful undermines his attempt to connect – albeit indirectly – aesthetic with logical judgement. This first example already shows how the discourse of Deconstruction tries to reveal the contradictions and aporias in the discourses it comments upon and criticizes: Derrida accuses Kant of simultaneously wanting to understand the beautiful *with* and *without* concepts. Kant's description '*gathers together* without-concept and concept, universality *without* concept and universality *with* concept, the *without* and the *with*'.[8] In Derrida's opinion, this aporia demonstrates the failure of conceptualization in Kant.

In the chapters on Derrida, Paul de Man and J. Hillis Miller we shall see that detecting contradictions and aporias is a crucial element of deconstructive criticism, whose main function is to refute the claims of the concept and the rationality of the logos. Yet the

Deconstructionists will not be spared the critical question of whether the contradictions and aporias they reveal are perhaps their own constructions or distortions (see Chapters 3, 4 and 7).

In this context, Hegel's philosophy and aesthetics feature as general negations both of Deconstruction and of Kantian thinking. Hegel counters Kant's conception of a limited and self-demarcating cognition, whose conceptualization Derrida finds excessive, by a mode of thinking directed towards totality. The latter denies the basic non-comprehensibility of the object, the 'thing in itself', and culminates in an identification of subject and object.

The gap that separates subject from object and consciousness from Being in a first phase of the mind's development is eventually bridged in the context of a dialectic of totality which enables the subject to recognize the real world as its own creation. The turning points of this dialectic become visible in the *Phenomenology of Spirit* (1807), where Hegel attempts to show how the contradictions resulting from the confrontation of Spirit and reality are overcome by a general understanding culminating in absolute knowledge: 'In the *Phenomenology of Spirit* I have exhibited consciousness in its movement outwards from the first immediate opposition of itself and the object to absolute knowing.'[9]

This dialectical movement also underlies the *Philosophy of History* (1812) and the *Science of Logic* (1812–16) in which Hegel develops a dialectical logic of concepts (and not a propositional logic).[10] His dialectic can be called 'positive' insofar as it does not stop at the unity of opposites as negation and ambivalence, but, rather, overcomes the contradictions in increasingly complex syntheses, and eventually reaches the absolute idea which, in the same way as the absolute knowledge of the *Phenomenology*, confirms the complete identity of subject and object. In the *Science of Logic* this identity in the 'absolute idea' appears as truth itself: 'The absolute idea alone is *Being*, imperishable *life, self-knowing truth*, and is *all truth*.'[11]

The identity of subject and object brought about by Hegel on an historical, phenomenological and logical plane reappears in his aesthetics. In opposition to Kant, who emphasizes the originary character of the beautiful in nature and claims that it pleases 'without concept', Hegel endeavours to prove the superiority of art over nature. He insists on the 'insufficiency of the beautiful in nature' and believes with the rationalists of the Enlightenment that a science of the beautiful is possible. He regards a conceptual definition of art (and nature) as a reasonable aim, while the individual work of art appears to him as an object of philosophical and conceptual analysis.

The Spirit as subject recognizes in the aesthetic object its own domain: 'Thus the work of art too, in which thought expresses itself, belongs to the sphere of conceptual thinking, and the spirit, by subjecting it to philosophic treatment, is thereby merely satisfying the need of the spirit's inmost nature.'[12] Philosophical or scientific analysis (philosophy and science are synonymous in Hegel's system) thus overcome the alterity of the art object, because they recognize it as their own creation.[13] Deconstruction is consistently anti-Hegelian in as much as it not merely emphasizes the alterity of the work of art (or literature), but simultaneously highlights traces of this alterity in philosophical and scientific discourse. In doing this, it challenges Hegel's hierarchy of cognitive forms in which conceptual thought assumes the highest position.

Referring to this hierarchy, Gérard Bras aptly remarks that '[a]rt is transcended when the contradiction between the sensual and the spiritual is exhausted. This is the basic Idealist assumption which claims that eventually everything dissolves in the identity of the Spirit with itself.'[14] This identity forms the *telos* of historical development as conceived by Hegel in which the *Aufhebung*[15] (here: absorption) of art eventually leads towards philosophy and science.

Hegel and his Marxist heirs, such as Georg Lukács, might counter this argument with the claim that he does not really dissolve art in concepts, since he recognizes in its sensuous character the crucial element that distinguishes it from philosophical and religious thought. Indeed Hegel states that the work of art 'presents truth, the spirit as an object in a sensuous mode'.[16] Yet this 'sensuous mode of consciousness is the earlier one for man'[17] and is overtaken and replaced by philosophy and science. Ultimately, Hegel summarizes the aesthetic function as an auxiliary one and art as an *ancilla philosophiae*: it serves to make the ideas of philosophy accessible to sensual perception.

If one takes account of this subordination of art to conceptual thought, one is hardly surprised to learn from Hegel that religious consciousness is also more historically advanced than that of the artist. In view of this devaluation of the artistic and aesthetic sphere it is not altogether surprising that Adorno accuses the founder of modern dialectics of devising an heteronomous aesthetics, thus helping to advance the Marxist heteronomy which was later propounded in particular by Georg Lukács and Lucien Goldmann.[18]

Where do the advocates of Deconstruction stand in relation to Hegel? Which positions do they assume towards Hegel and Kant? What is important here is first and foremost to distinguish Derrida's Deconstruction from that of his American followers. In contrast to a literary theorist such as Geoffrey Hartman (who simply negates the Hegelian conceptual hierarchies by attempting to eliminate the distinctions between literature, science, and philosophy – very much in the tradition of the German Romantics), Derrida has recourse to some strategies of Hegelian dialectics in order to deconstruct the metaphorical system of the German philosopher even more thoroughly. He would like to turn the system-maintaining and system-generating dialectic against the system itself. In the third section and the second chapter it will become clear how much this procedure is related to the 'antimetaphysical' critique of the Young Hegelians (Feuerbach, Stirner, Vischer) and to Nietzsche's radical views on language. In this respect Paul de Man, a Nietzschean critic *par excellence*, can be regarded as Derrida's ally.

The Nietzschean vein in this type of American Deconstruction, however, often involves a return to Kant: to a thinking within limits which strictly refuses to dissolve the (aesthetic) object in concepts governed by the subject. In the posthumously published *The Resistance to Theory*, Paul de Man refers to Kant, who long before Nietzsche, and in contrast to Hegel, recognized the importance of the figure of speech, especially the metaphor, for 'our own philosophical discourse.'[19] From de Man's point of view, the figure of speech appears as the linguistic (rhetorical) element that steadfastly resists the domination of the concept criticized by Nietzsche.

Despite these affinities between Kant's philosophy and an American Deconstruction shaped by New Criticism (see Chapters 3–5), it would be a mistake, especially with regard to Derrida's critique of the Kantian position, to view the various theories of Deconstruction as attempts to restore Kantianism. Most of these theorists should rather be considered as anti-Hegelian and Nietzschean (Derrida, de Man, Hillis Miller) or Romantic (Hartman, Bloom). We shall see how the objections of the American Deconstructionists to the Hegelian system were influenced by Derrida, in a similar way as were their readings of Nietzsche and their conceptions of art and nature.

Hartman, Hillis Miller and de Man are clearly 'Derridean' where they demarcate the limits of conceptual thinking and emphasize the significance of the polysemic figure of speech, the signifier, and the entire level of expression of theoretical discourse. Like Derrida, Nietzsche and the German Romantics, they tend to reverse the Hegelian thesis that art should be subordinated to philosophical *logos* as an historically inferior mode of cognition.

2 FRIEDRICH SCHLEGEL'S ROMANTICISM: DECONSTRUCTION *AVANT LA LETTRE?*

Long before Nietzsche and his heirs, the authors of German Romanticism questioned Hegel's attempts to translate art into concepts. In addition to Wilhelm Schelling (1775–1854), of whom Manfred Frank claims that he conceived 'art as the space of presentation of that which is unrepresentable by means of concepts and reflexion',[20] the Schlegel brothers (August Wilhelm (1767–1845) and Friedrich (1772–1829)) emphasized the particularity and irreducibility of art. Their writings were reviewed by Hegel with the condescension of the professional philosopher who deigns to become involved with amateurs. Hegel's dislike of the Romantics is no personal idiosyncrasy, but testifies to the profound distrust with which dialecticians from Hegel to Lukács regard all forms of Romantic thinking, a thinking fascinated by the mysterious and the obscure aspects of language.

Friedrich Schlegel in particular points out the opaque character of the word in his well-known treatise 'On Incomprehensibility' and toys with the paradoxical idea that, besides art, philosophy and science especially turn out to be inexhaustible sources of linguistic opacity: 'I intended to show that one gains the purest and most precious incomprehensibility exactly from those sciences and arts that are most dedicated to communicating and making comprehensible, namely philosophy and philology . . . .'[21]

In Schlegel, the paradox and irony so characteristic of Deconstruction – especially that of Paul de Man and J. Hillis Miller –

emerge, possibly for the first time. The analyses of these literary theorists are continually concerned with revealing paradoxes and other contradictions. Paul de Man declares, for example, that Marcel Proust, despite his insistence on the superiority of metaphor, reveals that metonymy plays a key role in his own text. J. Hillis Miller pursues a similar strategy when he attempts to demonstrate that George Eliot wishes to ban figural language (metaphor and metonymy) from realist discourse, yet simultaneously confesses her indebtedness to these rhetorical figures in her argument (see Chapters 3 and 4). Derrida eventually takes the paradox to its extreme when he points to the irrational within rationality and the deconstructive elements in Hegel's own *system*.

By making the problems of paradox and irony central, Schlegel challenges Enlightenment rationalism, which must reject the heretical idea that science and philosophy actually increase the obscurity of the word rather than spreading the light of reason. But the Romantics did not only provoke the rationalists, whose philosophy had lost its fascination by the end of the nineteenth century. They also challenged the dialectician Hegel, who strove to make reality transparent by identifying subject and object. He reacted with biting irony and derided the dilettantism of the Romantic philosophers in his lectures on aesthetics.

The Romantic thinking of the Schlegels not only resists systematic discourse and Hegel's demand for an all-embracing reason; it also rejects all attempts to subordinate art to concepts. It starts from the thesis that fiction (poetry) will outlast all other genres and will eventually replace philosophy. It thus reverses the Hegelian argument according to which art merely retraces in the sensual realm – as a 'sensual glimmer of the idea' – the crucial steps of philosophical *logos*. In contrast to Hegel, who continues to insist on a dialectical science of art, Friedrich Schlegel starts from the idea that poetry can only be criticized by poets. He therefore anticipates the demands of the Deconstructionist Geoffrey Hartman who argues for a merger of literary criticism and the writing of fiction (see Chapter 5).

In his commentaries on 'Incomprehensibility' Schlegel freely admits 'that [he] considers art the core of humanity.'[22] In contrast to rationalists such as Gottsched, who reduce art to its didactic function, in contrast to the Hegelians, who turn it into a servant of philosophy, the Romantic upholds the superiority of poetry over conceptual discourse. He is the first to challenge the systematic thinking of rationalism and Hegel's Idealist dialectics at the beginning of the nineteenth century. In some respects he anticipates the critiques of Derrida and the American Deconstructionists. It is no coincidence that the latter (especially Hartman) continually refer to German and English Romanticism.

In their critique of language the Romantics oppose systematization, hierarchy and the dominance of the *level of content* (the *signified*). They privilege the fragment, the *level of expression*, the *signifier* and the polysemic figure of speech. 'The fragment', write Philippe Lacoue-Labarthe and Jean-Luc Nancy, 'thus constitutes the most "mimological" writing of individual organicity.'[23] The fragmentary and incomplete thinking of the Romantics, which flirts with a multiplicity of meanings, negates the rationalist and Hegelian assumption that reality as a whole can be made transparent with the help of clearly definable concepts. Long before the advocates of Deconstruction, it foregrounds the untameable productivity of language that, paradoxically, can be traced back to the very fact that it lacks complete transparency and is therefore also always at least partly opaque.

Friedrich Schlegel appears as a precursor of Deconstruction when he asks – not without an ironic wink – 'But is incomprehensibility really something so reprehensible and bad?'.[24] He replies to this rhetorical question (as is to be expected) by claiming that humanity owes its survival to the relative darkness in which it dwells: 'Truly, you would become very anxious if the whole world suddenly became totally comprehensible, as you demand.'[25]

Although Derrida's theory cannot be regarded as a wholesale systematic apology for opaque speech, it will be shown, particularly in Chapter 5, that Friedrich Schlegel's Romanticism anticipates crucial ideas of the Deconstructionists. Its modernity and topicality, upheld in conjunction with Paul de Man's arguments in a collection of essays edited by Volker Bohn,[26] is due to its discovery of one of the main difficulties of philosophy and science: the rationalist and Hegelian temptation to deny the limits of knowledge and to identify a dominating subject with the dominated objects.

In many respects Romantic thought is a return to Kant, whose idea of the limit of the subject's cognitive potential had a lasting influence on Friedrich Schlegel. Yet Schlegel goes very much further than Kant when he praises the opacity of language, advocates the 'merger of all forms of fictional creation',[27] especially in the novel, and eventually comes up with the radical demand that 'all nature and all science must become art.'[28] 'What Schlegel ... demands', comments Raimund Belgardt, 'is the destruction of all systems, categories and principles that no longer do justice to the new awareness of the eternal becoming of all phenomena that are determined by space and time. Only chaos itself can become fertile again; new creations can emerge only from there.'[29] With these demands Romanticism announces some aspects of Derrida's and de Man's Deconstruction, a Deconstruction aiming to overcome the opposition of literature and philosophy and to recruit rhetorical procedures such as allegory and irony for theory (see Chapters 2, 5 and 7: in the last particularly Habermas's pronounced criticism of this 'overcoming' of the borderline of literature and philosophy).

Despite all the affinities outlined here, the Romanticism of the Schlegels is no 'Deconstruction *avant la lettre*'. Their cult of the free subject, of genius, and of spirituality is irreconcilable with the Deconstruction of these metaphysical concepts in Derrida and the American theorists. By clinging to these concepts the Romantics continue the tradition of German Idealism. Moreover their elevation of nature, art and poetry, which distinguishes them from the rationalists and Hegel, belongs to a metaphysical Idealism which is alien to the exponents of Deconstruction. These turn towards pluralistic and multilayered writing (*écriture*), without respecting institutionalized hierarchies such as that of fiction and scientific prose.

Nonetheless, the Romantic critique of rationalism and Hegelian dialectics contains elements which recur in Derrida and his American followers: the rejection of conceptual domination and the corresponding rule of the metaphysical subject; the scepticism towards the rationalist claim that language is a transparent system of unequivocal signs; ultimately an essayistic thinking that strives towards a symbiosis of literature and theory.

This approach does not – like that of the rationalists – reject chaos, but accepts it as something which is part of its own substance. 'The properly romantic – poietic – task is not to dissipate or reabsorb chaos', write Philippe Lacoue-Labarthe and Jean-Luc Nancy, 'but to construct it or to make a *Work* from disorganisation.'[30] In this respect the 'Romantic task' can be compared to the programme of Deconstruction, not so much as an attempt to master the Babylonian chaos of languages but to make it eloquent.

3 THE YOUNG HEGELIANS:
DIALECTIC AND AESTHETICS OF MODERNITY

In some instances, Young Hegelians such as Max Stirner (1806–56), Ludwig Feuerbach (1804–72), and Friedrich Theodor Vischer (1807–1887) attack Hegelian dialectics and rationalism with arguments reminiscent of those put forward by the Romantics. Like Schelling and the Schlegels, some of them emphasize the ambiguity or ambivalence of all phenomena and refuse to accept the Hegelian system as a successful synthesis of subject and object, Spirit and reality. A Young Hegelian like Vischer approaches the Romantic position whenever he signals the importance of the dream (which had always been neglected by Hegel) and emphasizes the role of contingency or the autonomy of the object. Despite their critique of religion and their materialism (Feuerbach, Marx), their political engagement (Ruge) and their anarchist tendencies (Stirner), the Young Hegelians appear to be accomplices of the radical Romantics in attempting to dissolve the foundations of the Hegelian system. In this respect they anticipate some arguments of Derrida's deconstructionist project.

In contrast to the Romantics, however, their writings have not directly influenced Derrida and the American Deconstructionists. Still, their antisystematic and anti-Hegelian (and often anti-Idealist) modernity anticipates the *problematic* of Deconstruction in some crucial aspects. In its most general form this problematic coincides with the entire thinking of late modernity in its (neo-)Marxist, Nietzschean, psychoanalytic and Deconstructionist variants. Habermas comments on this in *The Philosophical Discourse of Modernity*: 'Today the situation of consciousness still remains the one brought about by the Young Hegelians when they distanced themselves from Hegel and philosophy in general . . . Hegel inaugurated the discourse of modernity; the Young Hegelians permanently established it, that is, they freed the idea of a critique nourished on the spirit of modernity from the burden of the Hegelian concept of reason.'[31]

At this point one might argue that the late modern era was perhaps initiated by this radical critique of Hegel in the works of the Young Hegelians, a critique which achieved its full realization in Marx and Nietzsche. This view is confirmed, at least in part, in Wolfgang Eßbach's thorough sociological study of the Prussian Young Hegelians. It shows, among other things, how Hegel's radical and rebellious disciples helped shape modern notions such as 'party', 'partiality' and 'individualism'.[32]

Yet their modernity, in which the Young Hegelians Marx and Engels also participate, cannot be narrowed down to the social sphere. Some Young Hegelian philosophers practise a materialist dialectic whose open character Ernst Bloch has commented on. Their critique of the philosophical system as a closed totality (Marx, Stirner, Feuerbach) not only made Adorno's negative dialectic possible, but also Derrida's Deconstruction. Both philosophers share the Young Hegelian dislike of Hegel's *Aufhebung* as synthesis and envisage an open dialectic which does not go beyond an encounter of opposites.

Manfred Frank remarks on the dissolution of the Hegelian synthesis in the discourse of the Young Hegelians: 'The emphasis on the negative revolutionary character of Hegelian dialectics common to all Young Hegelians deliberately departs from its synthetic structure that reduces every real change to mere "illusion".'[33] Hence both Adorno and Derrida are heirs of the Young Hegelians, since they participate in the 'negativism' that 'dominates post-Hegelian philosophy according to Theunissen.'[34]

In an experimental text on Hegel and the anarchist writer Jean Genet, which carries the ominous title *Glas. Que reste-t-il du savoir absolu?* [literally: Death Knell. What remains of Absolute Knowledge?], Derrida makes this debt to Young Hegelian ideas, indeed even to their style, evident. Like Feuerbach, Stirner and Bruno Bauer, he starts from a radical critique of religion in order to reveal its fundamental role in Idealist philosophy; like them he struggles with the Hegelian logocentrism and its link with the dominance of monotheism: 'The Hegelian dialectic, mother of the criticism, is first of all, like every mother, a daughter: of Christianity.'[35] With respect to Hegel's key concept of *Aufhebung*, *Glas* claims: 'God, if he is God, if one thinks what is being said when one names God, can no longer be an example of the *Aufhebung*. God is the infinite, exemplary, infinitely high *Aufhebung*.'[36] In other words: the construction of the Hegelian system via a dialectic of *Aufhebung* (the negation of negation as synthesis, as constructive positivity which Pierre Macherey contrasts with Spinoza's 'negativism'[37]) can only be envisaged within the framework of a Christian monotheism and patriarchy that simultaneously forms the basis of logocentrism, the rule of the concept.

In *Glas* and other writings, Derrida develops a post-Hegelian critique when he attempts to refute Hegel's thesis which holds that absolute knowledge leads to a complete identity of subject and object. Like some Young Hegelians (Vischer and Stirner for example), he attempts to demonstrate how the ambivalent and contradictory object of knowledge resists all idealist attempts to *define* (*delimit*) it and to adapt it to the will of an all-powerful subject. It should become clear in Chapter 2 that, for Derrida, not only the spoken or written text, but the entire world of objects appears as something that escapes conceptual definition.

In this respect he is a kindred spirit of the Young Hegelian Vischer, who emphasized the rule of the object as much as its tendency to escape the domination of the subject long before the advent of Deconstruction and Critical Theory. In his satirical novel *Auch Einer* [literally: Also One] of 1879 he stages the 'malice of the object' that, through its unpredictability and comic potential, debunks the 'cunning of reason' glorified by Hegel.

Regarding these differences between Hegel and the Young Hegelians, it is not surprising to find Vischer foregrounding other elements of modernity and accusing the master of having neglected them. Thus the 'malice of the object', for example, is governed by a fortuitous coincidence which is responsible for the object's escape from the system installed by the subject. These incongruities and gaps become particularly evident in the free-associative character of the dream.

Vischer states that Hegel attempted to dissolve chance in a necessity governed by the Spirit and tried to ban the dream from the philosophical system as a banality of everyday existence. In his review of Johann Volkelt's (1848–1930) study *Die Traumphantasie* [The Fantasy of the Dream], he accuses Hegel's systematic philosophy of striving towards a dissolution of nature in Spirit and of neglecting the dream as a trivial phenomenon. It is no coincidence that he refers to Schelling and the Romantics in order to re-establish the rights of nature, the object, chance and the dream.[38]

These four factors, rediscovered by Vischer, are also fore-grounded by Derrida. He sees in psychoanalysis not merely an analytical method with the dream as its object, but points out the ubiquity of the dream and of chance *at the heart* of Freud's and Lacan's discourses: 'The word transference reminds one of the unity of its metaphoric network, which is precisely metaphor and trans-ference (*Übertragung*), a network of correspondences, connections, switch points, traffic, and a semantic, postal, railway sorting . . . .'[39] In other words, the term transference is itself metaphoric and part and parcel of the often coincidental associations in the linguistic realm.

Another factor which links Derrida and his American followers with the Young Hegelians is the revaluation of the aesthetic sphere that both groups – each in its own way – defend against conceptual appropriation. Although the Deconstructionists are hardly inter-ested in the hierarchical relations between philosophy, religion and art that Hegel comments on, they would agree with Max Stirner's statements about the relation of art and religion: 'Thus art is the founder of religion and must not assume its place behind religion in a philosophical system such as Hegel's.'[40] Vischer confirms this re-evaluation of art when he emphasizes the non-conceptual character of art in his later works: 'When we turn towards the beautiful in a receptive manner, we do not want to comprehend it first.'[41] Some-times he goes even further than Stirner and revises the historical scheme of Hegelian aesthetics (Oriental antiquity: symbolic art – Greco-Roman antiquity: classical art – Christian-Romantic era), in order to make allowance for the 'great crisis, which separates the modern era from the Middle Ages'.[42]

Derrida continues this (in many respects modern) argument of the Young Hegelians and Nietzsche in a new context when he links the fate of philosophy to the literary figure of speech and refuses to subordinate art to any form of logocentrism, be it psychoanalytic, Marxist or Structuralist. Against Hegel and the rationalists he insists on the impossibility of a philosophical or scientific meta-language that would be able to explain works of art rationally. Like the Yale Deconstructionists he would like to topple the entire hierarchy of discourses.

In *Glas* and more recent writings, *Du Droit à la philosophie*, for example, he continues the philosophical arguments of Young Hegelian thought. He appears to follow Stirner's anarchist impulse, for instance, when he argues for the Deconstruction of a hierarchically structured teaching of philosophy. He seems to confirm the political engagement of Ruge, Feuerbach and even Marx when he advocates a deconstructive radicalization of democracy: 'Deconstruction ought to be inextricably linked with this political and institutional problematic . . . .'[43] In Chapter 7 it will become clear, however, that this Deconstructionist radicalism is a verbal one and never reaches the level of political and socio-economic analysis envisaged by Marx and Engels.

In general, Deconstruction – in all its variants – could be characterized as a 'Young Hegelian' discourse, since almost all of its exponents criticize Hegel's and Hegelian systematic thought, and instead find their orientation in Nietzsche's critique of metaphysics and in his anti-systematic essayistic style of writing. In this respect the attitude adopted by Geoffrey Hartman is also characteristic of the other Yale critics. In a commentary on Derrida's philosophy he remarks that the latter points in two directions: 'One is the past, starting with Hegel who is still with us; the other is the future, starting with Nietzsche who is once again with us, having been discovered by recent French thought.'[44] Looking towards the future therefore means turning towards Nietzsche's philosophy, a philosophy emerging from the critique of the Young Hegelians whose crucial arguments it coordinates and intensifies.

4   NIETZSCHE: AMBIVALENCE, DIALECTIC AND RHETORIC

Karl Löwith rightly dwells on the philosophical affinity between Nietzsche (1844–1900) and Young Hegelians such as Stirner, Ruge and Feuerbach. For Nietzsche, who was familiar with Stirner's anarchist study *Der Einzige und sein Eigentum* (The Ego and Its Own) (1845), had recourse to the critique of religion by Feuerbach and Bruno Bauer and incorporated elements of Feuerbach's materialism in his works – as Marx had done before him. Like the Young Hegelians, he attacked Idealist metaphysics, whose development had reached its climax in Hegel's systematic dialectics. Like Marx he questioned the foundation of Idealism: Christian monotheism. Löwith summarizes this development when he writes: 'The road which leads via the Young Hegelians from Hegel to Nietzsche can be characterized most plainly with reference to the idea of the death of God . . . .'[45]

His death is also that of a dialectics which hurries from *Aufhebung* to *Aufhebung*, until it reaches 'absolute knowledge', thus coinciding with the completion and closure (*clôture*, Derrida) of the system. In contrast to Hegel, who completed conceptual systematics, Nietzsche develops an open dialectics starting from a radical ambivalence, an irreconcilable unity of opposites which functions destructively rather than in a system-generating fashion.

In his critique of European metaphysics he stops at the unity of opposites and refuses to follow the Hegelian *Aufhebung* as a synthesizing movement: 'The metaphysicians' fundamental belief is *the belief in the opposition of values*. . . . For may there be no doubt . . . whether opposites even exist. . . .' He adds: 'It could even be possible that the value of those good and honoured things consists precisely in the fact that in an insidious way *they are related* to those bad, seemingly opposite things, linked, knit together, even identical perhaps. Perhaps!'[46] The spirit that Nietzsche sets free here no longer manages to believe in the metaphysical antinomies of the past. It explores the possibility of revaluing all values and of destroying the old metaphysical antinomy by joining opposites without synthesizing them in an Hegelian manner on a higher plane: 'Can *all* values not be turned round? and is good perhaps evil? and God only an invention and finesse of the Devil? Is everything perhaps in the last resort false?'[47] As a consequence of such questions the acknowledgement of radical ambiguity or irreconcilable ambivalence seems the only possible response: '*Total insight*: the *ambiguous* character of our modern world – exactly these symptoms might point towards *decline* and *strength*.'[48]

Nietzsche's critique of metaphysical antinomy and his notion of irreconcilable ambivalence are discussed in detail here, since they announce a late modern consciousness which is content neither with the old oppositions nor with their *Aufhebung* in Hegel's large-scale synthesis and which anticipates certain argumentative patterns of Deconstruction. Thus Derrida, for example, counters Jean-Pierre Richard by arguing that Mallarmé's key term *pli/fold* means virginity ('*virginité*') as much as that which violates it ('*ce qui la viole*') (see Chapter 2, section 4), and both Paul de Man and J. Hillis Miller attempt to prove that literary and philosophical texts contain contradictory meanings, i.e. that they are radically ambivalent and aporetic (see Chapters 3 and 4).

An Hegelian or Hegelian Marxist such as Georg Lukács (1885–1971) would object at this point that we are facing a 'blocked dialectics' in Nietzsche's philosophy and Deconstruction: a dialectics whose empty circulation is due to its inability to translate antinomy into a higher synthesis. From Nietzsche's (and Derrida's) position, however, the attempt to bring about a synthesis or *Aufhebung* appears as an act of violence marked by an air of arbitrariness: the subversive idea that good and evil might be inextricably 'connected' or 'entangled' does not generate a higher norm, an *Aufhebung* in Hegel's sense.

In this respect Nietzsche in particular appears as a precursor of Derrida and Paul de Man, both of whom emphasize the simultaneously ambivalent and aporetic character of linguistic, philosophical and literary phenomena. Hence the task of the translator, for instance, assumes an irreconcilably aporetic character for Derrida: 'YHWH simultaneously demands and forbids, in his deconstructive gesture, that one understands his proper name within language; he mandates and crosses out the translation, he dooms us to impossible and necessary translation.'[49]

Overcoming this basic contradiction is impossible for the post-Nietzschean philosophy emerging from the collapse of the Hegelian system. In this respect, Franco-American Deconstruction in its entirety could be conceived as a discourse of radical ambivalence leading to aporia. The aporias that Paul de Man highlights in philosophical and literary texts cannot be separated from this notion of ambivalence. Commenting on some of Nietzsche's writings in *Allegories of Reading*, de Man states, for example, that one can read them simultaneously 'as a glorification as well as a denunciation of literature.'[50]

In Chapter 3 it will become clear that the aporias pointed out over and over again by de Man cannot be made plausible in most cases, since they are in part arbitrary constructions or projections. His readings of Nietzsche nonetheless shed new light on the basic problem of a philosopher who contributed decisively to the destruction of the metaphysical *concept of truth* by revealing radical ambivalence (as a unity of opposites without *Aufhebung*).

Following Friedrich Schlegel, who rejected the demand of rationalist and Hegelian discourses to proclaim the truth, Nietzsche endeavours to dissect the metaphysical concept of truth. In a famous text he challenges the foundations of this concept: 'What is truth? A mobile army of metaphors, metonyms, anthropomorphisms, in short, a sum of human relations which were poetically and rhetorically heightened, transferred and adorned, and after long use seem solid, canonical, and binding to a nation. Truths are illusions about which it has been forgotten that they *are* illusions . . . .'[51] This passage, which is also quoted in Paul de Man's *Allegories of Reading*,[52] becomes the starting point of a rhetorical (figurative, tropological) Deconstruction of truth which does not surrender when faced with the truths of philosophy and science.

In Nietzsche, this rhetorical dissolution of the concept of truth is matched by a radical critique of the Hegelian concept of essence, a concept which other 'Nietzscheans', such as the later Barthes, Derrida and Deleuze, also question: 'The word "appearance" contains many seductions; and so I avoid it as much as possible. For it is not true that the essence of things appears in the empirical world.'[53] Perhaps it does not manifest itself at all, and Nietzsche's polemic against the metaphysics of essence could be interpreted as a swipe against Hegel, who believes it possible to locate essence behind appearances. One ought to remember his definition of art in this context: he assigns it the task of revealing the world of truth and Being hidden by appearance: 'Thus, far from being mere pure appearance, a higher reality and truer existence is to be ascribed to the phenomena of art in comparison with [those of] ordinary reality.'[54]

Nietzsche reverses the hierarchical relation of Being and appearance: not merely by diagnosing the rhetorical (metaphorical, metonymical) character of language, but by proclaiming the pre-eminence of appearance in art, which he defines, in opposition to Hegel, 'as the *good* will to appearance'.[55] Like the Romantics, but with subtler theoretical means, he dissolves the foundations of conceptual domination (logocentrism, as Derrida would call it) in philosophy and aesthetics. In this respect he seems the most important precursor of Derrida, de Man, Hillis Miller and Hartman, who all stress the rhetorical aspects of language. They thereby question the concept of truth and, together with it, the possibility of defining works of art on a conceptual plane, i.e. to reveal their 'truth contents' (Adorno), 'structures of meaning' (Goldmann), or 'depth structures' (Greimas).

In this context the *concept of rhetorics* should be examined more closely. J. Goth rightly reminds us in *Nietzsche und die Rhetorik* (Nietzsche and Rhetorics) that the German philosopher conceives rhetorics primarily as a figurative (metaphorical, metonymical) use of language whose complexity exceeds the classical definition of rhetorics as eloquence and art of persuasion.[56] Paul de Man, who quotes Goth's study, follows this line of argument when he claims that, for Nietzsche, the trope or figure of speech is not one form of language among others, 'but the linguistic paradigm par excellence'.[57] Elsewhere he adds by way of explanation: 'Nietzsche contemptuously dismisses the popular meaning of rhetoric as eloquence and concentrates instead on the complex and philosophically challenging epistemology of the tropes.'[58]

For the Nietzsche of the Deconstructionists, human thought cannot be separated from the particularities of language and is therefore entangled willy-nilly with the figure of speech, the trope. It is irrevocably 'rhetorical', and this insight explains why the author of *The Gay Science* describes truth as a 'mobile army of metaphors, metonyms, anthropomorphisms'. In his view no conceptual discipline can protect thinking from the effects of the trope, whose influence is often unconscious. In many cases the rhetorical figure produces unwanted shifts of meaning and polysemies – or indeed metaphysical Truths based on hidden misunderstandings or contradictions. From this perspective the whole of philosophy appears as a well-intentioned but futile attempt of purification from the trope as substance of philosophy.

Starting from this rhetorical re-interpretation of philosophy, Nietzsche abandons the established ideal of conceptual discipline and turns towards art: music and literature. Music in particular appears to him as the real model of artistic creation whose definition in terms of philosophical or even mathematical concepts he strictly rejects: 'how absurd would such a "scientific" estimation of music be! What would one have comprehended, understood, grasped of it? Nothing, really nothing of what is "music" in it!'[59]

This orientation towards the pure *phoné*, which also prevails in Nietzsche's early work *The Birth of Tragedy from the Spirit of Music* (1872), is accompanied by a re-assessment of the literary figure and the *level of expression*. Far from believing in the possibility of a scientific and conceptual explanation of art and literature, Nietzsche tends to reverse Hegel's argument – like the Romantics before him – and to search for answers to essential questions of philosophy in the language of poetry. The philosopher ought to abandon his futile hunt for univocal definitions and instead give in to the play of meanings to which art and literature invite him.

Ernst Behler rightly reminds us of the role of *play* in Nietzsche's notion of reality, which also announces Derrida's Deconstruction that playfully dissects the concept of truth. Behler writes about Derrida: 'Nietzsche's approval of the world as play and the innocence of the future [is] for him the "acceptance of a world of signs without fail, without truth, without origin" that is open to our active interpretation.'[60]

In Chapter 2 it will appear that Derrida refers to Nietzsche when he replaces the metaphysical concepts of *Being* and *Truth* by *play*. In contrast to the philosophers of the metaphysical tradition who pretend to attain the final concept, the signified on the level of content, Nietzsche, Derrida and the Yale Deconstructionists trigger the play with polyvalent signifiers and thereby shift the entire aesthetic and literary problematic to the *level of expression*. Like Nietzsche they attempt to transgress institutional barriers, separating the philosophical from the literary realm, in order to make the freedom of unrestricted textual play possible. We shall see that Geoffrey Hartman especially, starting from Anglo-American New Criticism, redefines the role of the literary critic whom he would like to turn into an author equal to the literary writer. Following Nietzsche, he rejects the institutional distinction of primary and secondary literature and argues in favour of acknowledging the critic's text as a literary product *sui generis*.

It would certainly be impossible to label the exponents of Deconstruction Romantics or successors of the Young Hegelians without simplifying matters unduly. Yet it is quite possible to recognize in them Nietzsche's late modern or post-modern heirs, successors of an anti-systematic philosopher who was the first to systematically challenge logocentrism and the *esprit sérieux* of European metaphysics.

5 FROM HEIDEGGER TO DERRIDA:
CRITIQUE OF METAPHYSICS

The impact of Nietzsche's philosophy on the work of Martin Heidegger (1889–1976) has been the object of several comprehensive studies. At the close of the present chapter there is only scope to touch on the philosophical problems relating Nietzsche to Heidegger and the latter with Derrida. Jacques Taminiaux talks about the 'most intimate affinity' ('*l'affinité la plus intime*') between Nietzsche and Heidegger in this respect and refers to statements by the Freiburg philosopher.[61] What does this affinity consist of?

It surfaces especially in the critique of Western metaphysics, a critique continued and radicalized by Derrida, de Man and other Deconstructionists. In an initial step Heidegger refers to Nietzsche when he states that he was the first to reveal the real foundations of metaphysics: the 'will to power' that, according to Heidegger, presupposes the 'will to will'.

Metaphysics is completed in Hegel's system, whose absolute knowledge is understood as the 'will of the Spirit'.[62] Yet this 'Spirit of will' does not know its real character, whose essence is the domination of the subject over the object, over nature: 'Metaphysics in all its guises and historical stages is one single, but probably necessary, fate of the West and the condition of its planetary rule.'[63] According to Heidegger, Nietzsche was the first to recognize the predestined character of this – technical and technological – rule when he constructed the essential link between religious, philosophical and scientific thought on the one hand and the 'will to power' on the other. The 'eternal return' of the will to power highlights the repetition which forms the basis of the principle of domination. 'Hence, the basic character of being as will to power is also defined as the "eternal recurrence of the same".'[64]

Despite this crucial insight, Heidegger accuses Nietzsche of not having left the realm of European metaphysics, since his reversal of Platonic Idealism, along with a materialism influenced by Feuerbach and some nineteenth-century positivists, ultimately contributes to a strengthening of the metaphysical order: 'The reversal of Platonism, according to which the sensuous becomes the true world and the transcendental the untrue one for Nietzsche, still remains within metaphysics.'[65]

In contrast to Nietzsche, who turns towards the sensually perceptible world, Heidegger proposes overcoming metaphysics on an ontological level: 'Overcoming metaphysics is conceived in terms of the history of Being.'[66] It is important first and foremost to recognize in the 'history of Being' the basic distortion of Western thinking.

It is obvious that Derrida, as Nietzsche's heir, as heir of the Young Hegelians, cannot make this ontological and idealist approach his own. Jean-Pierre Cometti may be right in principle when he remarks that Heidegger succeeds in 'fundamentally questioning what he later calls the language of metaphysics'.[67] Yet a deconstructive critique is not the issue here, but a search for the authentic truth of Being that is indeed metaphysical. 'His "destruction" of metaphysics', comments Christopher Norris, 'is intended not, like Derrida's, to release a multiplicity of meanings but to call meaning back to its proper, self-identical source.'[68]

From this perspective Heidegger's ontology appears as the very opposite of Derrida's Deconstruction. Yet the two philosophers agree that the transcendental realm of philosophy must be linked to Nietzsche's 'will to power'. In other words: metaphysics is a manifestation of the 'will to will' (Heidegger) and the principle of domination. We shall see that Derrida's critique of *logocentrism* and *phallogocentrism* (phallus + logos) cannot be separated from his Nietzschean and Heideggerian critique of metaphysics. Like the two German philosophers, he seems to recognize in Western Idealism an instrument of domination.

The term *Deconstruction*, which he introduces into the philosophical and philological debate, goes back to Heidegger's task of 'Destroying the History of Ontology'.[69] This Deconstruction does not seek to be a destruction, but a dissection and critical reappraisal. Heidegger describes the process of Deconstruction planned by himself in the following terms: 'this hardened tradition must be loosened up, and the concealment which it has brought about must be dissolved.'[70] He adds: 'But this destruction is just as far from having the *negative* sense of shaking off the ontological tradition. We must, on the contrary, stake out the positive possibilities of that tradition, and this always means keeping it within *limits* . . . .'[71]

Derrida also conceives his Deconstruction not as destruction, but as a transgression of boundaries, a revelation of contradictions, and a dissection. He refers to the post-Hegelian tradition when he describes his approach as follows: 'It is thus a reflexion on the system, on the closure and opening of the system. Of course, it was also a kind of active translation that displaces somewhat the word Heidegger uses: "Destruktion", the destruction of ontology, which also does not mean the annulment, the annihilation of ontology, but an analysis of the structure of traditional ontology.'[72] Deconstruction, Derrida adds, is no 'critique', but rather an '*Abbau*' [German in the original: *mining*, but also *gradual removal* (translator's note).][73] This still means that it contains a destructive, 'annulling' element, reminiscent of Heidegger's 'loosening' and 'removal'. For it is hardly imaginable that something should be loosened, removed or mined and yet remain intact *in toto*. In any case, Deconstruction is more than 'structural analysis': it is a radical doubting of the concept of structure (see Chapter 2).

At this point it seems sensible to engage with Heidegger's critique of metaphysics in greater detail. For his starting point and his deployment of an ontological argument geared towards *Being* are both primarily responsible for obscuring the basic problematic of the 'will to will' and the principle of domination: the interpersonal relationships in a social system based on the exploitation of nature and political repression.

This problem was examined comprehensively by Adorno and Horkheimer in *Dialectic of Enlightenment* (1947), where the principle of domination is not merely identified with capitalism (their critique also applies to so-called Socialist societies) but also conceived as an economic, social and historical phenomenon. The great metaphysical systems of rationalism, positivism and neopositivism are simultaneously linked to specific historical and political situations in which they articulate *concrete and particular interests*. The metaphysical, rationalist or positivist principle of domination cannot, therefore, be separated from particular socio-historical constellations and should not be reduced to an ontological problem of *existential philosophy* – as it is in Heidegger – which is itself a social phenomenon. By ignoring the entire economic, social and political problematic and by positioning his ontology outside the social sciences, Heidegger succumbs to a mystification later criticized by Adorno.[74]

Despite his critique of Heidegger in *Margins of Philosophy* and other commentaries[75] (he spots a remainder of metaphysics in Heidegger's opposition between the authentic and the derivative), Derrida tends, with Heidegger, to separate the philosophical and linguistic problematic from the questions of the social sciences which he, in turn, considers to be metaphysical.[76] In Chapters 2 and (especially) 7 of the present study it will be shown that this view often prevents him from giving the social context of philosophy its due and from recognizing in language (that is to say, discourse as a semantic and narrative structure) the expression of collective interests. This does not mean, however, that his linguistic critique must be rejected or that it can be ignored – especially since it converges with Adorno's in crucial points.

Like Adorno, Derrida detects the paradoxes and aporias of linguistic communication, for instance the fact that translation is at the same time necessary and impossible, that metaphysics can only be criticized with metaphysical concepts, etc. With regard to this latter point, he also takes recourse to Heidegger, who makes the participants of a fictional philosophical dialogue exclaim that '[t]he language of the dialogue constantly destroyed the possibility of saying what the dialogue was about'.[77] In a sense, this remark summarizes the entire linguistic situation of Adorno and Derrida: that of expressing critical ideas within the framework of dominant discursive patterns. This explains why the two philosophers ceaselessly attempt to develop discursive forms such as essay, parataxis, collage outside the hegemony of institutionalized linguistic schemes.

Heidegger's critique of metaphysics leads to a subversion of established aesthetics. In a brief (but important) text, ' "Metaphysics" and the Origin of the Work of Art', Heidegger links Western aesthetics to the problems of metaphysics and argues in favour of overcoming aesthetics which he relates to the 'will to will', technical achievement and the 'art industry.'[78] In his essay *The Origin of the Work of Art* and his commentaries on Hölderlin he ascribes to art the non-metaphysical and non-aesthetic role of disclosing Being: 'The work of art discloses in its own manner the Being of Existence.'[79]

Derrida's view of art matches Heidegger's in as much as he – like the Freiburg philosopher – doubts the metaphysical dichotomies of institutionalized aesthetics: for instance the established opposition between content and form, technique and material, etc. At the same time, however, the philosopher of Deconstruction opposes existential philosophy, since he does not perceive art to be the dutiful guardian of Being, but the source of unlimited plurality and a never-ending interplay of signifiers. No essentialist or ontological definition can tame or limit this plurality. In the next chapter it will be shown, among other things, how Derrida imagines the plural or 'writerly' (as Roland Barthes would call it) character of the philosophical and literary text.

NOTES

1. *Subversion* signifies not so much political revolution as a '*bouleversement des idées et des valeurs reçues*' [re-evaluation of established ideas and values]; *Petit Robert*.
2. J. Derrida, *Positions* (1981), p. 41.
3. I. Kant, *Critique of Aesthetic Judgement* (1911), pp. 175–6.
4. Ibid., p. 147.
5. R. Wiehl, 'Prozesse und Kontraste', in *Kant oder Hegel? Über Formen der Begründung in der Philosophie* (1983), p. 562.
6. J. Derrida, *The Truth in Painting* (1987), p. 75.
7. Ibid.
8. Ibid., p. 76.
9. G. W. F. Hegel, *Science of Logic* (1969), p. 48.
10. Compare D. Dubarle and A. Doz, *Logique et dialectique* (1972), p. 82.
11. Hegel, *Science of Logic*, p. 824.
12. G. W. F. Hegel, *Aesthetics: Lectures on Fine Art*, vol. 1 (1975), p. 13, 16.
13. On the problem of recognition as *anamnesis*, see E. Bloch, 'Hegel und die Anamnesis; contra Bann der Anamnesis', in *Auswahl aus seinen Schriften* (1967), pp. 117–19.
14. G. Bras, *Hegel et l'art* (1989), p. 90.
15. *Aufhebung* is a crucial term in Hegel's thinking, yet also one that is notoriously difficult to translate. It signifies sublation or elevation, but can also mean abolition or even reversal [translator's note].
16. Hegel, *Aesthetics*, vol. 1, p. 103.
17. Ibid., p. 104.
18. T. W. Adorno, *Aesthetic Theory* (1997), pp. 134–5 and 209–10.
19. P. de Man, *The Resistance to Theory* (1986), p. 75.
20. M. Frank, *Der unendliche Mangel an Sein: Schellings Hegelkritik und die Anfänge der Marxschen Dialektik*, 2nd ed. (1992), p. 112.
21. F. Schlegel, 'Über die Unverständlichkeit', in *Kritische Ausgabe*, vol. 3 (1967), p. 364.
22. Ibid., p. 366.

23. P. Lacoue-Labarthe and J.-L. Nancy, *The Literary Absolute: The Theory of Literature in German Romanticism* (1988), p. 44.
24. Schlegel, 'Über die Unverständlichkeit', p. 370.
25. Ibid.
26. V. Bohn (ed.), *Romantik: Literatur und Philosophie* (1987). It contains essays by de Man and Derrida.
27. F. Schlegel in R. Belgardt, *Romantische Poesie: Begriff und Bedeutung bei Friedrich Schlegel* (1969), p. 24.
28. Ibid.
29. Ibid., p. 25.
30. Lacoue-Labarthe and Nancy, *The Literary Absolute*, p. 51.
31. J. Habermas, *The Philosophical Discourse of Modernity: Twelve Lectures* (1987), p. 53.
32. W. Eßbach, *Die Junghegelianer: Soziologie einer Intellektuellengruppe* (1988), ch. 2, 4: 'Zum Begriff politische Partei'. For Eßbach's critique of Habermas, see especially pp. 58–9.
33. Frank, *Der Unendliche Mangel an Sein*, p. 390.
34. G. Lohmann, 'Fragmentierung, Oberflächlichkeit und Ganzheit indivi- dueller Existenz: Negativismus bei Georg Simmel', in *Dialektischer Nega- tivismus* (1992), p. 343.
35. J. Derrida, *Glas* (1986), p. 202.
36. Ibid., p. 30.
37. P. Macherey, *Hegel ou Spinoza?* (1979), pp. 253–4.
38. F. T. Vischer, 'Der Traum', in *Kritische Gänge*, vol. 4 (1922), pp. 482–3.
39. J. Derrida, *The Post-Card: From Socrates to Freud and Beyond* (1987), p. 383.
40. M. Stirner, 'Kunst und Religion', in *Kleinere Schriften und seine Entgeg- nungen auf die Kritik seines Werkes 'Der Einzige und sein Eigentum'* (1976), p. 264.
41. F. T. Vischer, *Das Schöne und die Kunst: Einführung in die Ästhetik*, 2nd ed. (1898), p. 43.
42. F. T. Vischer, 'Plan zu einer neuen Gliederung der Ästhetik', in *Kritische Gänge* (1922), vol. 4, p. 175.
43. J. Derrida, *Du Droit à la philosophie* (1990), p. 424.
44. G. H. Hartman, *Saving the Text: Literature/Derrida/Philosophy* (1981), p. 28.
45. K. Löwith, *From Hegel to Nietzsche. The Revolution in Nineteenth Century Thought* (1984), p. 188.
46. F. Nietzsche, *Beyond Good and Evil: Prelude to a Philosophy of the Future* (1998), p. 6.
47. F. Nietzsche, *Human, All Too Human* (1996), p. 7.
48. F. Nietzsche, *Aus dem Nachlaß der Achtzigerjahre*, in *Werke*, vol. 6 (1980), p. 624.
49. Derrida, *The Post-Card*, p. 165 (YHWH = God's name in the Old Testament).

50. P. de Man, *Allegories of Reading: Figural Language in Rousseau, Nietzsche, Rilke, and Proust* (1988), p. 110.
51. F. Nietzsche, 'On Truth and Lying in an Extra-Moral Sense', in *Friedrich Nietzsche on Rhetoric and Language* (1989), pp. 246–57 (p. 250).
52. de Man, *Allegories of Reading*, p. 110.
53. Nietzsche, 'On Truth and Lying', p. 252.
54. Hegel, *Aesthetics*, vol. I, p. 9.
55. F. Nietzsche, *The Gay Science* (1974), p. 163.
56. J. Goth, *Nietzsche und die Rhetorik* (1970).
57. de Man, *Allegories of Reading*, p. 105.
58. Ibid., p. 130.
59. Nietzsche, *The Gay Science*, p. 336.
60. E. Behler, *Derrida-Nietzsche/Nietzsche-Derrida* (1988), p. 86.
61. J. Taminiaux, 'La Présence de Nietzsche dans *Sein und Zeit*', in *Etre et temps de Martin Heidegger, Sud* (May 1989), p. 75.
62. M. Heidegger, 'Überwindung der Metaphysik', in *Vorträge und Aufsätze*, vol. 1, 6th ed. (1990), p. 72.
63. Ibid., p. 73.
64. M. Heidegger, *Nietzsche* (1982), pp. 7–8.
65. Heidegger, 'Überwindung der Metaphysik', p. 75.
66. Ibid., p. 74.
67. J.-P. Cometti, 'Situation herméneutique et ontologie fondamentale', in *Etre et temps de Martin Heidegger*, p. 95.
68. C. Norris, *Deconstruction: Theory and Practice*, 2nd ed. (1991), p. 70.
69. M. Heidegger, *Being and Time*, 10th ed. (1992), p. 41.
70. Ibid., p. 44.
71. Ibid.
72. J. Derrida, *Points . . . Interviews, 1974–1994* (1995), p. 212.
73. Ibid.
74. T. W. Adorno, *The Jargon of Authenticity* (1973).
75. J. Derrida, *Margins of Philosophy* (1982).
76. See Derrida, *Points . . .*, p. 284: 'However, an ethnology or sociology of religions would only be up to these questions if it were no longer itself dominated, as regional science, by a conceptuality inherited from these metaphysics or onto-theologies.'
77. M. Heidegger, *On the Way to Language* (1982), p. 5.
78. M. Heidegger, 'Die "Metaphysik" und der Ursprung des Kunstwerks', in *Beiträge zur Philosophie (Vom Ereignis), Gesamtausgabe* (1985), vol. 65, p. 505.
79. M. Heidegger, 'Der Ursprung des Kunstwerks', in *Gesamtausgabe* (1985), vol. 5, p. 25.

2

DERRIDA

DECONSTRUCTION, PHILOSOPHY AND LITERARY THEORY

It is not the aim of this chapter to reduce Derrida's Deconstruction to the problems of literary theory or to present it as a method of literary analysis that it never set out to be. Although Deconstruction plays an important role in the debates on literary analysis, and has rightly been taken into account in this context,[1] it expresses a nagging doubt concerning every methodology rather than a methodological awareness. In what follows, this doubt will be outlined on a philosophical as well as a literary level, and the practice of a critical and rebellious strand of thought which is frequently isolated from its cultural context and caricatured will be made concrete.[2]

If one follows the individual arguments put forward by Derrida against Structuralism or Austin's and Searle's Speech Act Theory, one might hope to overcome the high level of abstraction which characterizes most debates about Deconstruction and to achieve a concrete understanding and critique of deconstructive practice and its theoretical premises. It will become clear, however, that the critique of Deconstruction can turn against the criticizing agencies themselves, an observation that fully confirms some of Derrida's own arguments (for instance in *Limited Inc.*). Their critical appraisal only appears possible in a dialogical argument that stays true to its own theoretical premises without annexing the opposite position in a monological (rationalist or Hegelian) manner. In this dialogical context, Deconstruction appears neither as philosophical irrationalism nor as fashionable obscurantism, but as a theoretical approach that often subverts the prejudices and received ideas of rationalist ideologies which are firmly rooted in everyday consciousness.

The comments on Derrida's literary analyses will show why each rationalist or Hegelian attempt to turn an ambivalent text into a conceptual structure is doomed to fail. Moreover, they will outline the limits which each Deconstructionist interpretation will reach sooner or later: limits that coincide with the phonetic, semantic and syntactic structures of texts – no matter how these are defined. In this respect the critique of Derrida's strategy of interpretation will be related to the problems of Chapter 1: the question of the conceptual definability of art and literature.

Before this crucial semiotic and aesthetic problem is approached, however, it is necessary to return to Derrida's critique of the metaphysical tradition in order to explain to which extent such a critique expresses radical doubts concerning the metaphysical and onto-theological conception of language.

1 *PAROLE* AND *ÉCRITURE*: CRITIQUE OF METAPHYSICS, CRITIQUE OF HEGEL

By the end of the previous chapter a basic difference between Heidegger and Derrida emerged. Despite his claim that '[w]hat I have attempted to do would not have been possible without the opening of Heidegger's questions',[3] Derrida points out the metaphysical residues in the work of the Freiburg philosopher. At the same time, he continues Heidegger's (self-)critique of metaphysics when he explains that, despite the relatedness of Deconstruction and Heidegger's ontology, he is 'attempt[ing] to locate in Heidegger's text . . . the signs of a belonging to metaphysics, or what he calls onto-theology'.[4] This concerns, among other things, the presence of Being which the author of *Being and Time* (1927) wishes to detect in his ontological explorations as well as in his commentaries on Hölderin and literature in general. Discussing Hölderlin's poems, he comments on the apparition of 'essence' and the 'approximation [of poetry] to the origin', thereby emphasizing the affinity of poetry and Being.

Chapter 1 already mentioned the (at least partial) irreconcilability of the philosophy of Being and Deconstruction, since the latter strictly refuses to acknowledge a 'truth of Being' or 'present truth', whose concept Heidegger derives from Husserl's ontology. The crucial argument that Derrida directs against Heidegger concerns language, or, more precisely, the presence of metaphysics in the linguistic realm. In a treatise where he tackles Heidegger's philosophical and political position, Derrida holds the philosopher of Being responsible for a discourse governed by 'logocentrism' and 'phonocentrism': 'Whatever lateral and marginal motives may work together in it, a specific and strictly sustained Heideggerian discourse is ruled by logocentrism and phonocentrism . . . .'[5] Despite the importance which Heidegger's distinction of Existence and Being, the ontic and the ontological sphere, holds for him, Derrida does not hesitate to label the philosophy of Being part of the metaphysical and logocentric tradition. He makes it his aim to pinpoint the 'metaphysical claims' of this philosophy: 'Now, among these holds, the ultimate determination of difference as the ontico-ontological difference . . . still seems to me, in a strange way, to be in the grasp of metaphysics.'[6] Following Nietzsche, Derrida undertakes to dissolve this metaphysical difference marked by Heidegger into an open *différance* (see further below).

At this point logocentrism, hitherto merely mentioned in passing, can be defined in the linguistic context outlined by Derrida and other exponents of Deconstruction. As the foundation of Western metaphysics logocentrism or phonocentrism is, according to Derrida, *the domination of the spoken word* (*parole* or *phoné*) which is meant to guarantee the presence of meaning (*présence du sens*). The most influential philosophical discourses from Plato to Heidegger tend to privilege the spoken word (*parole*) and to regard writing (*écriture*) with suspicion or even to suppress it.

In a commentary on Plato's *Phaedrus*, Derrida attempts to show to what extent the Greek philosopher perceives writing or the written text as a drug whose advantages he considers dubious: 'Only a little further on, Socrates compares the written texts Phaedrus has brought along to a drug (*pharmakon*).'[7] Like all drugs writing combines immediate advantages with partly devastating effects: on the one hand it supplies our memory with aids and crutches; on the other hand it can lead to an atrophy of memory, because it prevents us from exercising our memory regularly.

In the same way as his heirs, and like all idealist philosophers, Plato eventually condemns writing, which he considers divorced from real life and even hostile towards it. It is ambivalent and transient, since it can be read in several contradictory and changing contexts. Far from guaranteeing the presence of truth and the presence of meaning as a living and immediately effective word in the manner of *parole*, writing depends on unstable opinion. According to Derrida, Plato holds the position 'that writing is essentially bad, external to memory, productive not of science but of belief, not of truth, but of appearances.'[8]

At this stage it is important to bear in mind that writing is by no means condemned for mere technical reasons (for instance as an inadequate aid), but on moral, psychological and social grounds. It appears harmful to the philosopher because it displays a basic weakness: the instability of meaning. It questions the immediate presence of truth that, according to Plato, can only be guaranteed by the definiteness of the spoken word.

Derrida holds the slightly unusual position that the most important exponents of the metaphysical philosophical tradition adhere to the unequivocal *parole*, which they relate to the authority of the *logos* and the presence of meaning. They thereby contradict – like, for instance, Rousseau or Hegel – their own literary practice which challenges the presence of sense and the concept of truth as writing. In their eyes, Derrida claims, writing has always been suspect because it is subject to interpretation and – by functioning in diverse contexts – evades an unequivocal definition. For these reasons it has to be guarded by the conceptual logos which Derrida associates with the authority of the metaphysical philosopher and that of the father, the paternal agency: 'The father is always suspicious and watchful towards writing', states *Dissemination*.[9]

He retraces the pathways of Western metaphysics in order to show how the philosophers of the eighteenth century – for example Jean-Jacques Rousseau and Etienne Bonnot de Condillac – have contributed significantly to the consolidation of Platonic logocentrism and phonocentrism. Thus we read in Derrida's *Of Grammatology*, 'Rousseau belongs therefore . . . to the tradition which determines literary writing in terms of the speech present in the story or song; literary literality would be a supplementary accessory fixing or coagulating the poem, representing the metaphor.'[10]

Derrida expresses fundamental doubts concerning the metaphysical opposition between 'main object' and 'accessory object' ('supplément'), 'original' and 'imitation', 'ergon' and 'parergon'. He eventually reverses the hierarchical relation of word (*parole*) and writing (*écriture*) and claims that writing, far from being a supplement of the spoken word in Rousseau's sense, forms the precondition of every oral statement as *Urschrift* or *archi-écriture*. This *Urschrift* appears to Derrida as an '*archi-synthèse irréductible*' ('irreducible arche-synthesis') and '*condition de tout système linguistique*' ('condition of all linguistic systems').[11] This is the reason, he explains, why linguists such as Hjelmslev have failed to pay tribute to *archi-écriture* within their systems.

This, however, does not mean that Derrida postulates an historical pre-eminence of writing. He rather starts from the assumption that even the spoken word, considered unequivocal by metaphysical philosophers and linguists, is subject to the effects of ambivalent writing – despite the repressive measures of logocentrism that demands conceptual definiteness (see Chapter 2, section 3). In other words, *écriture* as writing always already inhabits the spoken word with all its shifts of meaning and ambivalences and cannot be neutralized by *parole* in its striving for truth and presence of meaning.

It is no coincidence that Derrida links *écriture* with the dream at the close of his treatise on Rousseau: 'And if the scene of dream is always a scene of writing?' ('*Et si la scène du rêve est toujours une scène d'écriture?*').[12] Like some Young Hegelians and like Nietzsche, the discoverer of the Dionysian, Derrida explores in a post-Freudian context the link between text, dream and the unconscious in an attempt to show that Rousseau may consciously strive to prove the secondary and derivative (*supplément*) character of writing, but unconsciously exposes the metaphoric centre of language as well as the 'writerly' and literary character of his own works – especially in his *Discours sur l'origine et les fondements de l'inégalité* (Discourse on the origin and foundations of inequality) (1754) and in *Emile* (1762). The philosopher of the metaphysical tradition thus betrays his own aim of proving the priority of *parole*.

More dogmatically and severely than Rousseau, Condillac, according to Derrida, argues for a systematic and methodical supervision of philosophical *écriture*. Different from the poets and orators, of whom Condillac claims that they already 'realized the use of method in an early stage', the philosophers fell victim to the frivolity of ambivalent writing. Derrida dwells upon the link between frivolity and writing in Condillac's text: 'The root of evil is writing. The frivolous style is the style that is written.'[13] It requires a paternal agency to supervise philosophical writing, the frivolous style, and to compel it to a methodical approach. This agency is logocentrism or *phallogocentrism* (phallus + logos) which Derrida detects in such different philosophers as Condillac, Hegel and Husserl. Similar to Rousseau, Condillac betrays, equally despite himself, his logocentric project when he locates the origin of language in the metaphor and eventually admits that he himself cannot make do without rhetoric and the shifts of meaning in writing.

The critique of logo- and phonocentrism in the works of Edmund Husserl (1859–1938), the founder of modern phenomenology who insists, more than anyone else, on presence of sense and truth, is of particular importance for Derrida's Deconstruction. In his treatise *Philosophy as a Strict Science* (1911) Husserl envisages 'a definitive fixation of scientific language'[14] as a distant goal and mentions the 'strict concepts' that are to be defined.[15]

It is therefore hardly surprising that Derrida counts Husserl among the most important heirs of European metaphysics, among those philosophers who are keen to strengthen the domination of logos, i.e. the spoken word, and to bring about the presence of meaning (*présence du sens*). In *La Voix et le phénomène* Derrida sums up Husserl's position within the metaphysical tradition: 'The necessary privileging of *phoné* that is implied in the entire history of metaphysics is radicalized even further by Husserl when he exploits with utmost critical subtlety its means and possibilities.'[16]

More pronouncedly than in his commentaries on Rousseau and Condillac, Derrida emphasizes in *La Voix et le phénomène* the link between the principle of domination and logocentrism/phonocentrism. He thereby continues Heidegger's critique of metaphysics and of the 'will to will' as an expression of technocracy. Criticizing Husserl, he speaks of an 'era of the voice as the *technical* domination of the being of the object' and of the 'unity of *techné* and *phoné*'.[17] How does this technical principle of domination emerge in Husserl? In a systematic attempt, says Derrida, to eliminate the 'excesses of meaning' which appear on the level of expression (Saussure's level of the signifier) and to retain the 'layer of pre-expressive meaning' ('*la couche de sens pré-expressif*') as well as the 'ideal of the conceptional and universal forms' ('*l'idéalité de la forme universelle et conceptuelle*').[18] In other words: what is at stake is the perfection of the Platonic (metaphysical) ideal of pure forms which is not blurred by the vagaries of ambivalent expression. Only in this way can the presence of meaning be guaranteed, according to Husserl. Postulating a 'scientific fixation' of terms and 'conceptual rigour', Husserl advocates a new foundation of philosophy on the basis of a strict terminology.[19]

Derrida nonetheless believes that Husserl is forced to acknowledge the autonomy of the signifier within the framework of his argument and to deconstruct his own discourse. For the sign is historical, and the presence of meaning (*présence du sens*) that is 'pre-expressive' and divorced from signifiers is an illusion that dissolves as soon as the temporal and spatial variability of all signs is taken into account. Crucial is 'what Husserl believed to be able to isolate as a particular, coincidental, dependent and secondary experience: the experience of the infinite derivation of signs that wander about aimlessly, change their locations, and continue to mystify their own realisation without beginning and end'.[20] In other words: the presence of meaning cannot be achieved because the historical shifts of meaning prevent the fixing of signifiers onto particular signifieds.

The above passage is important not only because it contains Derrida's decisive argument against Husserl's attempt to realize and fix meaning, but also because it shifts a phenomenon such as the variability of meaning, which phenomenology considers marginal or secondary, into the centre of the analysis. It will become clear – especially in Derrida's critique of Speech Act Theory – that this re-evaluation of the seemingly marginal, secondary or supplementary as the main object is a favoured strategy of Deconstruction.

Although he regards Heidegger's ontology in many respects as a continuation of logocentric metaphysics and although he holds against the author of the philosophy of Being his belief in the 'presence of the voice',[21] Derrida relies on the Freiburg philosopher in order to challenge the concept of identity. He takes as his starting point Heidegger's *Identity and Difference* of 1957, where the philosopher of Being accuses metaphysics of not having defined its stance towards the ontological difference between Being and Existence. Since it has always regarded Being as the foundation or condition of Existence, metaphysics is seen as incapable of getting to the bottom of the problem that difference poses. For Existence and Being mutually determine each other and can therefore not be defined independently of their difference. Heidegger conceives of the latter as a temporalized negativity, as 'that which differs by virtue of the difference' whose identity metaphysics has been unable to fix.[22]

By driving further this argument which tends towards the negative, towards the conceptually indeterminable, Derrida characterizes Heidegger's philosophy negatively as a thought which does not look towards something definite located beyond metaphysics: 'Another centre would be an other now; on the contrary, this *displacement* would not envisage an *absence*, that is an other presence; it would *replace* nothing.'[23] In other words, Heidegger's discourse focuses on the negative, on that which cannot be grasped conceptually, that which differs ceaselessly and shifts into the infinite. Inside this Heideggerian negativity, Derrida will eventually develop his non-concepts of *écriture* (writing), *différance* and *trace* (see Chapter 2, section 3).

Hegel is another philosopher who anticipates the negativity of Deconstruction, the non-presence of meaning and writing, despite his logocentrism and his preference for the spoken word (*parole*). Although his philosophy belongs to the nineteenth century, its importance for Derrida's critique is only discussed towards the close of the present chapter for the following reason: it is a philosophy whose extreme Idealism announces Young Hegelian and Marxian materialism and whose logocentrism turns into Deconstruction – according to Derrida – since it repeatedly evokes writing.

Derrida attempts to show how much Hegel enhances the spoken word in order to ascertain the presence of meaning, against which he 'had to debase or subordinate writing' ('*a dû abaisser ou subordonner l'écriture*').[24] Chapter 1 has already dealt with Hegelian logocentrism, which also manifests itself in the realm of aesthetics, where Hegel privileges the concept. One could claim with Hjelmslev that his aesthetics is geared towards the level of content and thereby neglects the level of expression as well as the ambivalence of its signifiers. 'Yet', Derrida remarks, 'all that Hegel thought within this horizon, all, that is, except eschatology, may be reread as a meditation on writing. . . . Hegel is the last philosopher of the book and the first thinker of writing.'[25]

One should pay attention to the 'Young Hegelian' bias of this statement: like Feuerbach, like Marx and Engels, who believed that the fulfilment of Hegelian Idealism announced the contours of a coming revolution that would translate Hegel's conceptual over-coming of alienation into social practice, Derrida believes that he can trace within the extreme forms of logocentrism signs of its overcoming by writing (*écriture*) and Deconstruction. How should one imagine this overcoming? Can one imagine Hegel as a precursor of Deconstruction?

In *Dissemination* Derrida quotes many of Hegel's texts in order to prove that the total or absolute knowledge which the German philosopher focuses on in fact excludes the definiteness of the voice and the presence of the concept. In doing so he refers to Hegel's idea that dialectical thinking which aims to comprehend the totality of relationships cannot be summarized in an abstract way in a preface. For the preface in many respects presupposes that the main body of the text to which it refers is already known. It assumes that the basic ideas of the main text can be made present (presence of meaning, *présence du sens*). Yet a realization of this kind which would make the main text superfluous is an illusion, since the basic ideas of the *Phenomenology of Spirit* or *Science of Logic* only unfold in the context of totality, in the argument as a whole, and therefore cannot become present in isolation.

The question 'What is science?' can only be answered at the close of the treatise, according to Hegel, when one has succeeded in elaborating the entire context: 'What logic is cannot be stated beforehand, rather does this knowledge of what it is first emerge as the final outcome and consummation of the whole exposition. Similarly, it is essentially within the science that the subject matter of logic, namely, thinking or more specifically *comprehensive* think-ing is considered; the Notion of logic has its genesis in the course of the exposition and cannot therefore be premised.'[26]

Yet what happens, Derrida asks, when the context as a whole remains open and 'the finale' or 'the conclusion' cannot be reached? In this case only negations and shifts of meaning can be discussed, not, however, a presence of meaning or a present truth. At the same time he questions – with the Young Hegelians and Nietzsche – Hegel's syntheses which lead to the closure (*clôture*) of the system and are driven by the concept of *Aufhebung*. In *Glas* he attempts to show how much the mechanism of *Aufhebung* turns into an act of force emerging from the principle of domination: '*Aufhebung* is also a suppressive counterpressure.'[27] On the semiotic level it appears as a metaphysical idealization to Derrida: 'The concept relieves the sign that relieves the thing.'[28]

One must stop conceiving the unity of opposites as *Aufhebung* or synthesis in order to rediscover the negativity of the Hegelian dialectic. For the term *Aufhebung* not only means 'preservation', but also 'annulment': a resolution is *aufgehoben* (reversed). Faced with this ambivalence, which characterizes the central concept in Hegel's dialectic, Derrida can attempt to deduce his counter- or non-concept of *différance* (see section 3) from the deconstructive negativity of this very dialectic. For it seems indeed possible to think the unity of opposites without synthesis, without *Aufhebung*, as a radical ambivalence or as an aporia. In this context Derrida can characterize Deconstruction generally as 'that singular aporia called "deconstruction" '.[29]

In this and the next chapter it will become clear that Derrida and the Yale Deconstructionists spare no effort to bring out the *negativity* of the philosophical, literary or other text: its ambivalences, aporias and polysemies; everything that resists conceptual and unequivocal definition.

2 DERRIDA AS A NIETZSCHEAN: *ÉCRITURE*

From the outset Nietzsche has figured as a thinker of radical ambivalence and of writing. In contrast to Heidegger, who tends to regard Nietzsche's entire philosophy as deriving from the principle of the 'will to power', Derrida emphasizes the ambiguities and antinomies of Nietzsche's text. At the same time he follows in his deconstructive strategies the playful and undefinable experiments in Nietzsche's writings, which announce a language liberated from the authority of the spoken word and metaphysical truth. In *Writing and Difference* he refers to Nietzsche, of whom he claims that he has replaced the metaphysical terms of essence and truth by the experience of play: 'We doubtless would have to cite the Nietz-schean critique of metaphysics, the critique of the concepts of Being and truth, for which were substituted the concepts of play, interpretation, and sign (sign without present truth).'[30]

The problematic of ambivalence comes to the fore in his text *Spurs. Epérons. Nietzsche's Styles*, which can be read as a decon-structive commentary on Hegel's dialectic or even as a parody of it. According to Derrida Nietzsche's discourse incessantly combines thesis and antithesis, without ever permitting *Aufhebung* in the Hegelian sense. Nietzsche at one point condemns woman as the 'advocate of untruth', sometimes as the 'advocate of truth' (as a philosophical and Christian being); eventually 'woman is acknowl-edged, outside this double negation, and accepted as the affirmative, resisting, artistic, Dionysian force.'[31] Does Nietzsche's argument suggest that we are facing an Hegelian synthesis or a construction of a system on the basis of dialectics? Derrida responds: 'But if these three types of statement are to form an exhaustive code, if their systematic unity is to be reconstructed, the parodying hetero-geneity of the style, the styles, should itself be masterable and reducible to the content of a single thesis.'[32] Such a reduction turns out to be impossible when one takes into consideration all the excesses of meaning and contradictions of Nietzsche's text. Eventu-ally one must realize that the text is heterogeneous and that its heterogeneity is not even intended by its author. It can therefore not be explained in the context of his 'inscrutable genius' which is an integral part of the Nietzsche-cult.

The heterogeneity of the text should rather be regarded as the symptom of a negative dialectic that on the one hand permits the unity of opposites, yet on the other hand replaces the Hegelian *Aufhebung* by irreconcilable ambivalence, thus providing every form of system formation. Derrida adopts this Nietzschean concep-tion of extreme ambivalence when he claims that Kant defines the beautiful 'without concept and with a concept' ('*sans et avec* concept', see Chapter 1, section 1), when he asserts that translation is at the same time 'necessary and impossible' ('*nécessaire et impos-sible*', see Chapter 1, section 4) and that Hegel's philosophy announces the birth of writing – despite all attempts of the thinker of systems to strengthen the authority of *parole*.

As a consequence, Derrida can write about Nietzsche elsewhere that '[t]he future of the Nietzsche text is not closed.'[33] For the ambivalences and polysemies of this text safeguard its 'caractère scriptible' (Barthes), its capacity to signify in new contexts and to be re-written. Derrida explains: 'Next, the effects or structures of a text are not reducible to its "truth", to the intended meaning of its presumed author, or even its supposedly unique and identifiable signatory.'[34] At this point it becomes obvious that the doubt concerning the unity and univocity of texts leads to the complementary doubt concerning the concept of subject which Derrida deconstructs as a metaphysical entity.

For the antinomies of texts make the search for autonomous author subjects appear illusory. Derrida has never denied the existence of a myth of the subject which amounts to closing one's eyes to the heterogeneity of the subject's position. Part of this ideological deception is the entanglement of subjectivity in the principle of domination highlighted by Derrida in *Points de suspension*: 'The virile strength of the adult male, the father, husband, or brother . . . belongs to the schema that dominated the concept of subject.'[35] The Deconstruction of the text and the subject is intended to dissolve the violent and illusory unity which makes the two poles of power what they are.

If, however, Nietzsche's text is recognized as a polysemic and 'writerly' construct, then Derrida's interpretation appears contingent. For this very reason the Deconstructionist feels obliged to defend it against Heidegger's reading (see Chapter 1, section 5). 'Nietzsche, far from remaining *simply* (with Hegel and as Heidegger wished) *within* metaphysics, contributed a great deal to the liberation of the signifier from its dependence or derivation with respect to the logos and the related concept of truth or the primary signified, in whatever sense that is understood.'[36] This defence of Nietzsche's philosophy indicates that the development of metaphysics can be interpreted differently in the context of various historical discourses and that Derrida's reading of Nietzsche presents the liberation of the signifier and of writing (*écriture*) in a somewhat teleological fashion.

Sarah Kofman remarks that writing is quite ambivalent, since it is situated beyond all institutionalized dichotomies: 'Writing belongs to an indefinite gender, since it is an hermaphrodite and precedes the differentiation into masculine and feminine. Like

Nietzsche's Dionysos.'[37] This commentary highlights the close link between Nietzschean ambivalence and Derrida's conception of writing: the latter evades the authority of the unequivocal, the spoken word (*parole*) which emerges from non-dialectic opposites such as *signifier/signified*, *original/derivative*, *main object/marginal object* (*supplement*). What is at stake for Derrida – as for Nietzsche – is the undermining of these oppositions, their dissolution. In this context, however, the question crops up whether Derrida does not contribute to the revival of the metaphysical tradition when he introduces new value-ridden and hierarchical oppositions such as *parole/écriture* or *logocentrism/Deconstruction* (see Chapter 2, section 3).

Another crucial aspect of Derrida's writing is its orientation towards the rhetoric of tropes, towards metaphor. In a well-known text on truth (see Chapter 1, section 4), Nietzsche paves the way for the 'Deconstruction' of the concept of truth by dissolving it into a 'mobile army of metaphors'. Derrida takes up this Nietzschean idea when he conceives the entire history of philosophy as a process of metaphorization and claims that it is impossible to think or argue outside metaphor and rhetoric. Metaphor cannot be defined or tamed by the concepts that it has itself brought into being: 'It cannot dominate itself, cannot be dominated by what itself has engendered.'[38] The concept of metaphor is itself metaphorical: *metapherein* (carry over). In this way the metaphysical opposition between concept and metaphor is deconstructed by Derrida who develops a rhetorical writing, geared towards the trope and meant to replace metaphysical concepts with figures of speech such as *trace* or *dissémination* (see Chapter 2, section 4).

It is a non-conceptual and in part anti-conceptual writing determined to topple all hierarchies established by the philosophical logos and to straddle the boundaries between literature and philosophy. Yet this does not mean, as will become clear in the final chapter, that Derrida argues for a dissolution of philosophy in literature, as Habermas has claimed. Nevertheless, Michel Haar is right when he stresses the importance of Nietzsche's philosophy for Derrida, an influence which becomes apparent not only in the rhetoric of tropes but also in a taste for parody, aphorism and fragment: 'Derrida adopts Nietzsche's poetic of writing, a poetic of reformulation and parody, of aphorism and fragment . . . a thoroughly reflexive and calculated politics of discipline concerning language, without, however, making Nietzsche's motivations his own and without agreeing with Nietzsche's main thesis.'[39]

What are these motivations, and what is Nietzsche's main thesis? It is the 'artistic will to power' which Derrida rejects, since he sees in it the basic principle of Western metaphysics criticized by Heidegger. In order to escape from this metaphysic he follows the path of writing cleared by Nietzsche.

In the past Derrida's critique of metaphysics has often been exposed to criticism as a rhetoric of overcoming, since it seemed to many that Deconstruction gave in to the modern or post-modern pressure to distance itself from all varieties of Platonism and from Hegel's absolutism. This impression was not completely false, and Richard Rorty might not be wrong when, commenting on Derrida, he mentions 'this somewhat farcical attempt to be ever more un-platonic'[40] and adds that Platonic Idealism, which had been valued as the highest virtue not so long ago, is now avoided as the greatest vice.

Rorty might have – as Gellert once did – a sensitivity for the fashionable detours of philosophy, yet he overlooks that the Nietz-schean play of Deconstruction is not simply one of words or tropes, but a game against the principle of domination within language, within discourse, i.e. a critique. This critical component, which relates Deconstruction to Adorno's theory, has escaped Rorty. He does not recognize it because he does not investigate the domination of the object by the subject or the complementary question of the domination of nature by society.

3   CRITIQUE OF STRUCTURALISM AND SPEECH ACT THEORY: *DIFFÉRANCE* AND *ITÉRABILITÉ*

In many respects one could regard Structuralism in the Saussurian sense as an antipode of Deconstruction. In contrast to the latter Saussure assumes fixed phonetic or semantic opposites such as b/p, d/t, z/s, male/female, signifier/signified which he considers unproblematic. The differences and oppositions which Derrida attempts to deconstruct are treated as the bases of language and of linguistics by Saussure and his Structuralist heirs (Emile Benveniste, Algirdas Julien Greimas).

Saussure himself sees the differences between phonetic and semantic units as basic conditions for the proper functioning of language. The individual functions of the linguistic system cannot be defined in isolation, but only with reference to their mutual relations. Hence Saussure can claim that 'there are only differences within language'. He explains: 'Within the same language, all words used to express related ideas limit each other reciprocally; synonyms like French *redouter* 'dread', *craindre* 'fear', and *avoir peur* 'be afraid' have value only through their opposition: if *redouter* did not exist, all its content would go to its competitors.'[41]

Although Derrida accepts Saussure's thesis concerning the mutual conditioning of the linguistic units, he rejects the complementary thesis of the Geneva linguist according to which a word such as 'thinking' can be determined unequivocally in the context of the differing units that form its semantic field. This thesis appears to the Deconstructionists both as a rationalist and a logocentric attempt to rescue the presence of sense as a transcendental *signified* (*signifié transcendantal*, Derrida).

Derrida believes that the presence of meaning cannot be achieved, an opinion that is quite troubling for most rationalists, since each sign continually points towards other preceding or subsequent signs, thus precipitating the dissolution of its own identity and of the presence of meaning. In other words: meaning can never be present, since it develops in a continually open context of reference and thus becomes subject to a change which Derrida labels, in accordance with the French verb *différer*, *différance*. This *différance* inhabits each difference based on the illusory idea that each of the two terms – for example in Saussure's opposition of *signifier/signified* – can be unequivocally determined and identified: 'The differences are thus generated – deferred (*différées*) – by *différance*.'[42] Derrida adds as an explanation: '*Différance* is responsible for the fact that the shift of signification is only possible when each of the so-called "present" elements that appear in the sphere of the present refers to something other than itself, thereby retains the mark (*marque*) of the preceding element and already permits itself to be shaped by its relation to the subsequent element.'[43] He calls this marking by past or future elements *trace*, and claims that it prevents identification, definition or the 'becoming present' of a linguistic sign.

In the philosophical context *différance* appears as an aspect of the extreme, the irreconcilable ambivalence derived from the dialectic unity of opposites without synthesis. Derrida remarks on the relation of Hegelian *Aufhebung* and *différance*: 'If there were a definition of *différance*, it would be precisely the limit, the interruption, the destruction of the Hegelian *relève* wherever it operates.'[44] In the philosophical as well as the semiotic and linguistic context *différance* appears as the negative, the inconclusive that can neither be tamed by dialectic syntheses nor by rationalist definitions. This negativity is related to the well-known fact (also known by linguistics, especially in semantics and pragmatics) that within a particular discourse or in pragmatic contexts shifts of meaning within the same word (lexeme) can occur (see opposite: *iterability*). Yet this fact has neither prompted linguists nor philosophers to doubt in principle the definability of lexical units.

Derrida accuses Saussurean linguistics, whose rationalism-based logocentrism and phonocentrism he criticizes, of continuing the metaphysical tradition and of privileging the spoken word that guarantees the presence of meaning and the transcendental signified, i.e. the Platonic idea. In his polemic against all linguistics of the signified (the level of content, as Hjelmslev would call it), Derrida emphasizes the polysemic signifier and the level of expression.

He seems to approach the style of the later Barthes, who also took recourse to Nietzsche in order to liberate the interpretable and 'writerly' signifier from the yoke of the defined concept, and creates the neologism *différance*, thus evoking the endless deferral of the presence of meaning. It features, at least indirectly, in Heidegger, who writes about 'a clearing of what veils and closes itself off' in *Identity and Difference*.[45] In a semiotic context *différance* can therefore be understood as an open interplay of signifiers described by Derrida in his critique of Jean Rousset's 'Structuralism': 'And that the meaning of sense (in the general sense of meaning and not in the sense of signalization) is an infinite implication, the indefinite referral of signifier to signifier? And that its force is a certain pure and infinite equivocality which gives signified meaning no respite, no rest, but engages it in its own *economy* so that it always signifies again and differs? Except in the *Livre irréalisé* by Mallarmé. That which is written is never identical to itself.'[46] *Différance* could therefore be defined generally (and against Derrida's intention) as the 'endless deferral of meaning or presence of meaning and as the negation of the identity of the sign' (see *iterability*).

Derrida's final sentence refers both to Mallarmé's negative utopian project (Greek *ou topos* = no place) and to two complementary problems of Deconstruction already touched on above (see Chapter 2, section 1): the problem of writing (*écriture*) and that of identity. They complement each other in so far as, according to Derrida, writing has been accused by 'logocentric' philosophers of weakening or indeed dissolving meaning. This dissolution of the presence of meaning is due to the fact that the written text can be read in several contexts, each of which produces a shift of meaning that in turn produces the *différance* described by Derrida. In other words, writing brings about the dissolution of the semantic identity of the sign. Its repetition in heterogeneous communicative contexts yields irreconcilable relations of meanings which can destabilize the identity of a word or concept.

Derrida calls this deconstructive repetition *iterability* (*itérabilité*) and contradicts Anglo-American Speech Act Theory as well as French Structuralism (Martinet, Greimas) who tend to agree that the repetition of a sign consolidates meaning along with the semantic context of a sign as *recurrence* or *iterativity* and hence is far from dissolving these two components. Derrida reverses this thesis when he criticizes Austin's Speech Act Theory in his famous article 'Signature, Event, Context' and introduces 'unities of iterability' ('*unités d'itérabilité*'), 'unities separable from their internal or external context, and separable from themselves, to the extent that the very iterability which constitutes their identity never permits them to be a unity of self-identity'.[47] Manfred Frank summarizes the process of iterability most concisely: 'The meaning of a sign/an utterance is severed from itself by each use; it becomes displaced (*déplacé*).'[48]

In other words, *iterability* as the repetition or recurrence of a sign dissolves the semantic identity of this very sign: first for pragmatic reasons (because of the difference between communicative contexts), secondly for semantic reasons (because of the change of meaning that occurs within the discursive context: within a *cotext*, as some linguists would call it in order to distinguish the pragmatic communicative context from the intratextual cotext). Derrida only implicitly considers these two levels when he mentions an 'interior or exterior context' ('*contexte interne ou externe*'). Yet it seems important to distinguish them explicitly at this point, since Austin's and Searle's Speech Act Theory is geared mainly towards the pragmatic communicative level, while Greimas's semiotic focuses on the semantic level.

John R. Searle, the contemporary exponent of Speech Act Theory, felt challenged by Derrida's critique, especially since he could neither accept Deconstruction's heretic idea that the author's *intention* is never fully present in his or her text nor the argument that John L. Austin (1911–60) mapped out a theory founded on illusory abstractions. Indeed, Derrida accuses Austin of neglecting the 'citation functions' ('*fonctions citationelles*') of language (e.g. parody, pastiche, irony) and of assuming *the transparency of the authorial intention, the definiteness of the utterance*, as well as *the presence of a contextual totality*.

Yet this complete context – we are dealing here with an Hegelian problem *par excellence* – cannot be grasped, or be realized, for the understanding has prevailed since the foundering of 'absolute knowledge' that all contexts are principally open. As Jonathan Culler puts it, 'meaning is context-bound, so intentions do not in fact suffice to determine meaning; context must be mobilized. But context is boundless, so accounts of context never provide full determinations of meaning.'[49]

Derrida himself remarks in *Mémoires – Pour Paul de Man* that 'everything depends upon contexts which are always open, non-saturable'.[50] In the article commented on by Searle he explains: 'For a context to be exhaustively determinable, in the sense demanded by Austin, it at least would be necessary for the conscious intention to be totally present and actually transparent for itself and others, since it is a determining focal point of the context.'[51] However, one could reverse this argument and claim that conscious intention can never be completely present and really transparent as long as the complete context has not been determined exhaustively.

In short, Speech Act Theory appears to Derrida as a phonocentric idealization of communicative circumstances which can only postulate the *presence* of authorial *intention* and the *identity* of a recurring speech act because it ignores open and inconclusive contexts and at the same time brackets off the citational functions of language as anomalies. Only by relying on this abstraction or idealization can Austin situate the so-called *infelicities* or failed speech acts at the periphery of his communicative system. Derrida, however, who has always attempted to deconstruct the metaphysical oppositions between *central* and *marginal, main* and *derived*, focuses his entire attention on these *infelicities* or 'failed' speech acts, which he believes to be behind the shifts of meaning in the sense of iterability. Far from being anomalies, they dominate the events of everyday language. Ultimately, Derrida concludes, Austin deconstructs his own theory by presenting a long list of exceptions or *infelicities* that occupy the centre of attention and cannot be considered as peripheral.

One must add here, however, that Derrida hardly succeeds in deconstructing the metaphysical hierarchy of main and marginal, central and peripheral elements. He merely reverses it by declaring that which Austin took to be a marginal phenomenon, namely the *infelicities*, the main thing. This reversal might have a carnivalesque and critical effect in the Bakhtinian sense,[52] yet it does not destroy the hierarchical order. Like most revolutions it merely produces a new one.

Perhaps more important than this attempt to overcome linguistic hierarchies is Derrida's critique of Austin's distinction between *constative* (statements) and *performative* (promises, warnings and threats) speech acts. How far constative and performative speech acts can melt into one another is demonstrated by Culler: 'The distinction between *performative* and *constative* has proved very fruitful in the analyses of language, but as Austin presses further in his description of the distinctive features of the performative and the various forms it can take, he reaches a surprising conclusion. An utterance such as "I hereby affirm that the cat is on the mat" seems also to possess the crucial feature of accomplishing the act (of affirming) to which it refers.'[53] Culler's example takes the form of a performative utterance, since 'I affirm' is analogous to 'I promise' in that it performs an action. At the same time the sentence 'The cat is on the mat' can be regarded as the shortened form of the sentence 'I hereby affirm that the cat is on the mat' and thus be defined as a performative utterance. Derrida refers to these difficulties of distinguishing types of speech acts neatly and comments: 'Austin has not taken into account that . . . which therefore confuses all the ulterior oppositions whose pertinence, purity, and rigor Austin sought to establish in vain.'[54] What Austin has neglected is *iterability*, that which causes one (and the same?) speech act to be constative in context A and performative in context B.

Searle's reply to Derrida's critique is long, and a comprehensive commentary is outside the scope of the present exposition. Its gist, however, can be put in a few sentences: the intentionality of the written text does not differ in essence from the intentionality of the spoken word, and the presence of meaning is guaranteed by both forms of communication; speech acts or sentences articulate unambiguously the intentions they are based on, and '[i]n as much as the author says what he wants to say, the text expresses his intentions'.[55]

In his core argument, Searle reverses Derrida's claim according to which iterability dissolves the identity of the sign along with semantic coherence of discourse and concludes: 'Thus the diverse characteristics of intentionality that we observe in speech acts presuppose an iterability that not only concerns the one type that we have analysed, namely the repetition of one and the same word in different contexts, but also the iterability of the application of syntactic rules.'[56] This argument is doubtlessly plausible, in so far as it confirms the linguistic rule that redundancy or recurrence strengthens the semantic and syntactic coherence of discourse. Nonetheless a certain common-sense reductiveness becomes noticeable when Searle states that a text generally expresses the author's intentions. If this was the case, Kant's, Hegel's, Marx's, Proust's, Kafka's and Mallarmé's works would not have become objects of endless controversies – and there would not have been so many misunderstandings between Searle and Derrida.

Derrida himself refers to some of those misunderstandings in his 130-page reply to Searle. It bears the polemical title *Limited Inc.*, which implies that John Searle's authorship is uncertain since, in his response 'Reiterating the Differences: A Reply to Derrida', the American theorist refers to H. Dreyfus and D. Searle, with whom he has discussed Derrida's essay. Since Derrida does not seem to appreciate a dialogical approach to philosophy, he dislikes such a strategy and accuses Searle of hiding behind an anonymous collective. He playfully alters his name to *Sarl: Société à responsabilité limitée* ('Limited Inc.').

Although this simultaneously deconstructive and playfully rhetorical gesture produces a whole range of allusions, puns and figures of speech in *Limited Inc.*, which a sober reader searching for clarity notices with a mixture of amusement and consternation, the polemic poses a question not present in Searle: is iterability not a simultaneously constructive and deconstructive process? Derrida remarks: 'Iterability alters, contaminating parasitically what it identifies and enables to repeat "itself"; it leaves us no choice but to mean (to say) something that is (already, always, also) other than what we mean (to say), to say something other than what we say *and* would have wanted to say, to understand something other than . . . etc.'[57]

Derrida is probably right when he claims that each utterance says 'more' than the speaking subject intends, and that each sign (each and every concept) *can* undergo a change of meaning with each repetition. Almost every author has made the partly unpleasant, partly surprising and creative experience that his statements were not received and understood in accordance with his intentions. Yet that does not mean in every case that he has been *mis*understood. He was only understood differently from how he understands himself.

The intention, the univocity and transparency (presence of meaning) Searle does not seem to doubt is in reality a complex phenomenon directly related to *iterability* which at one point strengthens the semantic coherence of discourse and weakens it at another. Derrida is right in every respect when he points out this ambivalence of linguistic repetition (of semantic redundancy), thus challenging the entire rationalist Cartesian tradition from Port Royal to Saussure and Greimas with the claim that redundancy or recurrence creates coherence while simultaneously dissolving it: 'Iterability supposes a minimal remainder . . . in order that the identity of the *selfsame* be repeatable and identifiable *in, through*, and even *in view of* its alteration. For the structure of iteration – and this is another of its decisive traits – implies *both* identity *and* difference.'[58] In other words, there is no repetition without shifts of meaning, without *différance*, without a subversion of the metaphysical presence of meaning. Derrida elaborates this idea in 'Vers une éthique de la discussion' (the postscript to *Limited Inc.*): 'Let us not forget that "iterability" does not signify simply, as Searle seems to think, repeatability of the same, but rather alterability of this same.'[59]

At this stage it becomes clear why Derrida conceives iterability – in a similar way as *différance* – as 'an aconceptual concept or another kind of concept, heterogeneous to the philosophical concept of the concept, a "concept" that marks both the possibility and the limit of all idealization and hence of all conceptualization.'[60] What is at stake are provisional or heuristic labels which are meant to denote borderline cases of terminology. They are meant to explain, for instance, why almost all key terms of philosophical or social theory are multifaceted and are endlessly debated and interpreted. Not only Thomas Hobbes's 'moral obligation' and Karl Marx's 'surplus value', but also Max Weber's concept of 'charisma', and Niklas Luhmann's concept of 'differentiation' can become the topic of discussions, differentiations and 'differences' in the sense of 'différance'. Their conceptual fixing in philosophical and sociological dictionaries might be useful idealizations, but cannot do justice to their polymorphous dynamic.

In this context Deconstruction does not appear as a philosophical iconoclasm that is primarily concerned with offending the exponents of institutionalized philosophy, but as a corrective of the philosophical mainstream founded on the naive assumption that its concepts have been fixed once and for all. One must ask, though, if only Deconstruction is able to pay tribute to the historicity and the changing meanings of concepts. As an alternative to the deconstructive approach a meta-theory is conceivable. It is based on the idea that all theoretical discourses emerge in dialogical contexts and that concepts can undergo a change of meaning both between heterogeneous discourses and within one and the same discourse that always displays a dialogical structure (see Chapter 7).

Now an exponent of Critical Rationalism might point out that one only needs to turn one's back on 'obscure' thinkers such as Hegel, Heidegger or Derrida in order to feel once again firm – i.e. conceptual – ground under one's feet. That this reaction is based on illusory assumptions is illustrated by another discussion which is as famous as the dispute between Derrida and Searle. It took place between Karl R. Popper, Thomas S. Kuhn and other theorists of science who were interested in the term 'paradigm' that Kuhn had introduced and that Popper heavily attacked. We are neither concerned with the problems of this debate here nor with the term *paradigm* as such, but with the fact that the definition of this term in Kuhn's book *The Structure of Scientific Revolutions* appeared unsatisfactory to most participants in the debate, in particular to Margaret Masterman. She discovered twenty-one *diverging* definitions ('inconsistent with one another'[61]) of *paradigm* in Kuhn's study, i.e. on the level of the *cotext*.

Were such divergences intended? Certainly not. Yet one can also assume that these divergences or differences are not simply deficiencies an author ought to eliminate in later editions, but that the stimulating versatility of Kuhn's book is increased by them and that this philosophical classic would be quite turgid if Kuhn had defined his key concept unequivocally and once and for all. The Deconstructionist is not entirely wrong when he relates the productivity of language and the fertility of thinking as such to iterability and to différance as a phenomenon related to this iterability.[62]

Derrida analyses the situation correctly when he stresses the disruptive effects of iterability in his debate with Searle, but emphasizes its productiveness elsewhere. Yet he exaggerates the semantic obstacles which the subject of a discourse must overcome. Greimas and Courtés, dyed-in-the-wool Structuralists, are not completely wrong when they define *semantic isotopy* (the semantic level on which textual coherence happens) as the 'iterativity along a syntagmatic chain of classemes which assures the homogeneity of the utterance-discourse'.[63] They emphasize therefore homogeneity and not its dissolution or Deconstruction; for them *iterativity* acts as the guarantor of meaning and coherence. Derrida, on the other hand, stresses *iterability* as the dissolution and deferral of meaning. Where does the truth lie?

It is not 'somewhere in between', but is to be found dialogically between the two extreme positions: between Structuralism and Deconstruction. On the one hand it is obvious that recurrence or iterativity of semantic elements safeguards textual coherence. Otherwise every didactic attempt to explain something by way of definitions and examples would be nonsensical, and even Derrida's own endeavours to explain the aims of Deconstruction in numerous interviews would be in vain. On the other hand one must take account of the fact that recurrence *or* iterativity (are they really *synonyms*?) can produce unintentional shifts of meaning. Even *falsification*, a key term of the critical rationalist Popper, has in the meantime acquired meanings that do not square with the original definition of the year 1936 – as have Greimas's terms *isotopy* and *actant* which today no longer match those of his *Structural Semantics* of 1966. A paradoxical conclusion emerges from this: theories owe their chance of survival to the impossibility of final definitions, i.e. to the failure of the presence or persistence of meaning.

Greimas's remark in his *Structural Semantics* that 'there are no mysteries in language' ('*il n'y a pas de mystères dans le langage*'[64]) is probably a rationalist illusion. Yet Derrida's idea that each discourse deconstructs itself, since Deconstruction is not a procedure external to the texts but 'always already at work in the work',[65] is undercut by his own works.

For Deconstruction itself is founded on a relatively stable semantic taxonomy structured by primary oppositions such as *parole/écriture*, *présence du sens/différance* and *logocentrism/Deconstruction*. If this taxonomy were lacking, Deconstruction as a theory could neither be represented nor criticized. Moreover, Derrida presupposes in all his commentaries the possibility of identifying texts such as *Limited Inc.* or *Writing and Difference* unambiguously. Were these works not *identifiable* and *repeatable* as particular texts expressing certain definable ideas, it would be impossible to refer to them, to quote them and to translate them. Derrida does assume the identifiability of works, for example when he attempts to counter Searle's accusation that he has completely misrepresented Austin's text with the rhetorical question of how Searle succeeded in identifying Austin's misfigured and wrongly interpreted text.[66]

The fact that Deconstruction cannot avoid postulating relatively stable structures and identities was noticed by Bertil Malmberg in his commentary on Derrida's concept of language: 'In reality, it is the principle of general structures (deep structures) and linguistic universals which explains both the possibility of translation and of transformation within individual languages.'[67] In the final section of this chapter it will become clear that Derrida also opposes the rationalism of deep structures in translation theory and takes up a position not very distant from that of Walter Benjamin.

Like Kafka, Derrida is fascinated by the untranslatable, the inaccessible. This might be the reason why he has commented

extensively on the parable *Before the Law* that can also be interpreted as a story about *différance*. Derrida reads Kafka's parable as
a 'tale of inaccessibility': '*récit de cette inaccessibilité, de cette
inaccessibilité au récit.*'[68] At the same time it appears to him as a
search for the essence or the law which continually evades the grasp
of the searcher. 'What is forever deferred, until death, is the entry
into the law itself . . .' ('*Ce qui est à jamais différé, jusqu'à la mort,
c'est l'entrée dans la loi elle-même . . .*').[69] Endlessly deferred is also
the truth of Kafka's text whose reader hurries with its protagonist
K. from interpretation to interpretation without ever discovering
the true meaning, without ever penetrating into the law of the text.
For Derrida this law is without essence: 'It evades the essence of
Being that would be presence. Its "truth" is thus non-truth of which
Heidegger claims that it is the truth of truth.'[70] In this respect
Kafka's parable, which appears to Derrida as 'untouchable' ('*intangible*') and 'inaccessible', could be read as an allegory of Decon-
struction which confronts the reader with the paradoxical law that
he will never (fully) grasp its truth . . .

4 DERRIDA, DELEUZE AND THE CRITIQUE OF THE SUBJECT

What has been said in the previous section about *iterativity* and
iterability has far-reaching implications for the notions of *subject*,
subjectivity and *identity*. If one were asked to describe the link
between subjectivity and repetition in one sentence, one could say
that repetition in the sense of *iterativity* confirms and consolidates
the identity of the subject, while repetition in the sense of *iterability*
decomposes, deconstructs it.

The first philosopher to anticipate this deconstructive approach
to individual subjectivity was probably Nietzsche, and in this
respect, as in other respects dealt with above, Derrida's discourse
owes a lot to the German destroyer of metaphysics. What Nietzsche
writes in his posthumously published notes on the (Kantian,
Fichtean and Hegelian) concept of subject is reminiscent of Derrida's subversion of conceptual, textual and individual identity:
'"Subject" is the fiction insinuating that many *identical* states of
mind are the effect of *one* substratum: however, *we* have *created*
the "identity" of these states, to begin with . . . .'[71] For Nietzsche

this identity is an illusion comparable to that of a univocally defined concept: the latter merely hides the underlying linguistic diversity wilfully denied or glossed over by metaphysicians.

Derrida and Deleuze are Nietzscheans in so far as they develop this train of thought arguing that repetition which disrupts the presence of meaning – i.e. the identity of a sign or a text necessarily also subverts the identity of the individual subject, thus exposing the illusory character of the corresponding concept. Their two books, *L'Ecriture et la différence* (1967) and *Différence et répétition* (1968), published almost simultaneously, start from the assumption that 'Nietzschean repetition', as J. Hillis Miller says (cf. Chapter 4), leads to the disintegration of textual and individual identity.

Asserting that 'that which is written is never identical to itself',[72] Derrida denies both the presence of meaning in a text and of a text functioning in the communication process. Like Nietzsche he denies the possibility of identifying an inalterable concept or signified behind or under the polysemic signifiers. For him meaning merely *occurs* as an interminable *shift* from signifier to signifier: as *trace* or *différance*. In this permanent flux of meaning not only the identity of the text but also that of the subject founders. This is why Derrida argues – against Austin and Searle (cf. above) – that the subjective intention of a *speech act* cannot be made present: as soon as the speech act is received by my interlocutor it signifies in a new context and changes its meaning; as soon as it is repeated it is caught in the deconstructive process of iterability and *différance*.

What applies to signs in texts and texts themselves also applies to *events* in a person's life. This is one of the central arguments of Deleuze's *Différence et répétition*. Like Derrida's meaning, the event is never *present*, can never be made present, for it takes place between a past which is no more and a future which is not yet. Its presence is cancelled in the transition from past to future and endlessly differred. Its meaning is situated either in the past or in the future; it is never present, never there as the actual, original event. This is why in Deleuze's view – like in Derrida's – the repetition of events is always a repetition with difference, an 'iterability' which entails a disintegration of the individual subject.

Deleuze explains: 'That which is or returns has no prior consti-tuted identity: things are reduced to the difference which fragments them, and to all the differences which are implicated in it and through which they pass.'[73] Where the notion of identity (as presence of meaning) is radically challenged, the complementary notion of subjectivity also founders. For the individual subject can no longer be identified in relation to clearly definable events and meanings: it falls prey to the mechanisms of difference.[74]

In this context, Deleuze distinguishes two types of repetition: a Platonic and a Nietzschean one. Whereas Platonic repetition is geared towards the idea of an unalterable model or original which is re-presented in the repeated elements, the Nietzschean type of repetition excludes the idea of original or model, replacing it by the notion of *simulacrum*. The latter is irreducible to an original model; it is marked by constant disparity, by difference: 'The simulacrum seizes upon a constituent *disparity* in the thing from which it strips the rank of model.'[75] Where disparity and difference dominate, biographical events can no longer be identified as stable, 'present' meanings, and the individual subject dissolves in a process of repetition comparable to iterability.

Within this process the universal concept in the Platonic sense yields to the particular element or event in the Nietzschean sense: to the singular, the contingent, the arbitrary. These three phenomena contribute decisively to the disintegration of the individual subject as an homogeneous and identifiable entity. The singular which is not repeated without becoming the different, the divergent cannot be subsumed under a universally recognized concept and thus prevents the formation of subjectivity as a coherent whole. The contingent may obey its own stochastic laws and probabilities; but it emerges as a foreign body in the subject's biographical narrative based on the – possibly illusory – assumption that it constitutes meaning. If we adopt Deleuze's or Derrida's perspective, however, this biographical meaning falls to pieces, and the subject's *membra disiecta* appear to be an arbitrary conglomerate of events and facts.

The very idea of biography is tinged by the particular, the singular which resists universalization. In this respect Robert Smith quite rightly claims that from an Hegelian or logocentric point of view a philosophical text ought not to be *signed*. All references to a biographical context should be avoided: 'In principle, a philosophical text should not be signed. Its pretensions being toward universality any blot of specificity compromises it.'[76] This is a fundamental contradiction of Hegelian philosophy which pretends to coincide in a realistic manner[77] with the unfolding of History. It is a contradiction already pointed out by existentialist thinkers such as Kierkegaard and Sartre[78] and is due to the fact that Hegel's particular, contingent existence (his biography) prevents him from making universally valid statements about the history of humanity. Whatever he says *also* articulates his particular views, wishes and apprehensions.

In this respect the traditional, logocentric discourse of philosophy fails in its attempts to ban contingency and chance. The latter re-enters through the biographical backdoor marked by the philosopher's signature: 'But first, Hegel's signature. If reason sanitises itself and so achieves sanity by fictionalising and outlawing chance, this still will not have been enough.'[79] For it will never succeed in banning the particular, that which cannot be dissolved in or subsumed under universal reason.

Adopting Derrida's and Deleuze's perspective, one could therefore argue that particularity subverts philosophy's universalist pretensions on two levels: on the linguistic level, where the word as signifier thwarts conceptual universalization, and on the biographical level, where the contingency of the individual subject dooms all attempts to produce a universally valid discourse to failure. At the same time, Deconstructivist tendencies towards particularization make the notion of individual subjectivity appear doubtful: the individual subject can no longer identify with the grand design of historical reason and can no longer justify itself in a biographical discourse (a biographical narrative) geared towards conceptual coherence, towards meaningful totality.

In Deleuze's philosophy a neo-nominalist and neo-empiricist criticism of Hegelian totality leads to a deconstruction of the individual subject *as* totality, as coherence or unity. The French philosopher's early interest in David Hume's empiricism is not due to chance but to his anti-Hegelian critique of the category of totality and to his scepticism towards the principle of subjectivity. Two dicta coordinate the discourse of his *Empirisme et subjectivité* (a book on Hume): 'Totality is just a collection.'[80] And: 'The spirit is not a subject, it is subjected.' ('L'esprit n'est pas sujet, il est assujetti.')[81] The first dictum means that totality, far from being a coherent, meaningful whole in the Hegelian sense, is just a conglomerate of facts linked to each other by custom, illusion or ignorance.

No subjectivity can be based on this disparity or deduced from it. The subject thus appears as a product of socio-linguistic customs and illusions which can fairly easily be deconstructed by critical scrutiny. It is a product rather than a producer and discovers that it does not possess its language, but is possessed by it.

This discovery incites Deleuze 'to speak in *one's own language* like a foreigner' ('parler dans *sa langue à soi* comme un étranger').[82] The idea is: not to master a language in order to become subject in it, but to become conscious of one's subjection to the linguistic order and to escape from it by creative estrangement. Instead of imitating the child, the fool, the woman, the animal, the stutterer or the stranger, Deleuze argues, we should *become* all of these subjected creatures so as to be able to combat the dominant order with new forces and new arms.[83]

Derrida seems to resume this train of thought when he describes his strangeness within the French language in *Monolingualism of the Other*. This strangeness makes his subjectivity founder, for it makes him utter the very opposite of what he would like to say: 'The one who speaks, the subject of the enunciation, yourself, oh yes, the subject of the French language, is understood as doing the opposite of what he says.'[84] He sums up: 'The monolingual of whom I speak speaks a language of which he is deprived.'[85] This means – among other things and in conjunction with Deleuze's critique of the subject – that even native speakers do not possess or master their language, but are spoken of or deprived of their subjectivity by the latter. Jacques Lacan anticipates this idea when he points out (in 1955) that individuals are not 'at home' in 'their' language: 'L'homme n'est pas ici maître chez lui.'[86]

In spite of the differences between Derrida, Deleuze and Lacan (which are substantial) these thinkers share the conviction that the Cartesian, Kantian and Hegelian notions of the subject are idealist illusions: (a) because language is not a transparent conceptual system enabling autonomous subjects to utter their thoughts, but an open interplay of polysemic signifiers with shifting meanings; (b) because language, far from being the instrument of a sovereign subject, subjects the individual to its mechanisms; (c) because, in Lacan's case, the individual's discourse is partly determined by the unconscious. 'The subject discovered by Descartes is the very subject whom Lacan sees as being determined by the unconscious',[87] explains Alain Jurainville. In other words, Lacan's notion of the subject is the Cartesian *cogito* turned upside down. Similarly, Derrida's and Deleuze's linguistic and nominalist critique of the metaphysical notions of subjectivity can be considered as inversions of the Cartesian, Kantian and Hegelian concepts.

It may be asked, of course, whether such inversions are justified or whether they can only be made plausible by a one-sided discourse which thrives on the elimination of counter-arguments. One counter-argument was put forward in the previous section, where Derrida's *iterability* was confronted with Greimas's rationalist notion of *iterativity*. Even if one assumes that the rationalist idea of language as a transparent system of signs is an illusion, one will not wish to forget that on the whole people communicate successfully, that texts are translated in other languages without (always) becoming incomprehensible and that, on a biographical level, quite a few individuals succeed in 'making sense' of their lives. This 'making sense of one's life' is only possible, however, if concepts (*semes*, Greimas) and the corresponding semantic structures (*isotopies*, Greimas) can be relied on in speech, action and communication. In short: despite semantic shifts, misunderstandings and the openness of contexts (which may be conceded), meaning and coherence cannot be excluded.

The second counter-argument can be derived from this. If repetition is not *exclusively* considered as *iterability*, but *also* viewed as *iterativity* in the semiotic sense, then it should always be possible to understand subjectivity as a semantic-narrative process geared towards coherence. Naturally, this striving towards coherence can always be thwarted by those contradictions, semantic shifts and aporias highlighted by Deleuze and Deconstruction. But they can only exist where meaningful structures exist, where meaning is the rule. The very concept of contradiction presupposes logical coherence; the very concept of *iterability* or semantic shift presupposes the existence of *iterativity* and of semantic units which can be made to shift. If iterability reigned supreme, speech and communication would be impossible. In this light, subjectivity appears as a risky undertaking on a semantic, narrative and communicative level which is always threatened by contradiction and *iterability*. This dialectical approach which relates the extremes of *iterativity* and *iterability* to one another seems more realistic than a one-sided emphasis on *iterability* which prevents us from understanding the functioning of language and communication.

In his recent works, Derrida seems to have revised his radical Deconstructionist view of subjectivity. Simon Critchley mentions 'Derrida's willingness to accept the need for new discourses on subjectivity, for new names and new determinations of the "subject" that will supplement (in the full sense of the word) or succeed deconstruction'.[88] However, a viable notion of the subject need not be opposed to Deconstruction in a dualistic way; it may very well evolve from a dialogue between theories of iterativity and theories of iterability.

The third and last argument concerns the overdetermination of the individual subject by language and the unconscious. If one can assume that individuals are – at least partly – responsible for the constitution of meaning on a biographical level, then one also has to concede that they are not entirely overdetermined by linguistic and psychic structures, but are capable of reflecting and creatively transforming their social, linguistic and psychic situations. They may fail if *iterability* and contradiction prevail; however, this Deconstructionist scenario is only a possibility; it is not inevitable. In this respect, Deconstruction appears, once again, as an extreme philosophical position which ought to be dialogically related to its opposites (e.g. to Greimasian semiotics).

The following section will show that Derrida's critique of Jean-Pierre Richard's thematological interpretations may be justified in some respects (e.g. as an antidote to Hegelian hermeneutics), but that it is as one-sided as Deleuze's and Derrida's deconstruction of the subject.

5 *DISSÉMINATION* AND DIALECTICS OF TOTALITY: DERRIDA, JEAN-PIERRE RICHARD AND MALLARMÉ

The confrontation between Structuralism and Deconstruction in the previous section could be read as a theoretical introduction to Derrida's critique of Jean-Pierre Richard's thematic interpretation ('*analyse thématique*') of Mallarmé's poetry. Although Richard is no exponent of linguistic and semiotic Structuralism à la Greimas and Bremond, he systematically applies the concept of *semantic recurrence* (*itération*) in his voluminous study on Mallarmé and thus poses the 'Structuralist' question regarding the coherence of the text. He attempts to prove that the most important themes in Mallarmé's works form a *coherent whole*, basing his claim not merely on the semantic term *iterativity* (*itération*) but also on Hegel's concept of *totality*. Mallarmé's texts appear to him as a network of meanings whose elements mutually elucidate one another in their dialectical interdependence.

In this context, which, according to Dietmar Fricke, is dominated by the search for a 'unified vision',[89] Jean-Pierre Richard uses the term *dissémination* for the first time. It derives from Mallarmé's 'Préface à *Vathek*', where it acquires a clearly pejorative sense. Discussing the Anglicisms in William Beckford's 'Indian' novel *Vathek* (1778), Mallarmé criticizes the sentence that 'disseminates itself in shadow and vagueness' ('*se dissémine en l'ombre et le vague*') yet praises the 'sudden illumination of the words' ('*la mise en lumière des mots*').[90]

In *L'Univers imaginaire de Mallarmé* Richard refers to this evaluative comparison of shadow and light in Mallarmé and introduces the noun *dissémination* which Derrida eventually puts to fertile use in Deconstruction: 'Against the dissemination of sense the felicitous word will surround truth with a firm defensive wall' ('*Contre la dissémination du sens, le mot heureux campera donc la vérité d'un dur relief*').[91] Hence the disputed term appears for the first time in a logocentric, Platonic-Hegelian context whose unifying and totalizing tendencies provoke the wrath of the Deconstructionist. A chapter in Richard's book even bears the ominous (Hegelian) heading 'Towards a dialectic of totality' ('*Vers une dialectique de la totalité*'). But what exactly is meant by 'Richard's Hegelianism'?

It is first of all his attempts to interpret Mallarmé as a poet who defends meaning against the 'linguistic effects of chance' ('*invasions verbales du hasard*')[92] and aims at a coherent whole sustained by a subjectively imposed meaning. Richard explicitly refers to Hegel when he comments on Mallarmé's own reading ('Mallarmé seems to remember Véra's commentary on Hegel here'[93]) and when he emphasizes Mallarmé's synthesis of the sensual ('the sensual appearance of the idea', Hegel, see Chapter 1, section 1) and the 'abstract concept' in the 'idea', that which philosophers today call the 'concrete essence'.[94] He can only mean Hegelian philosophers.

In Richard's view Mallarmé's 'idea' turns into an Hegelian

synthesis. In his Indian fairy tale *Le Mort vivant*, for example, the poet is said to attempt a reconciliation of 'hostile opposites', such as day and night, life and death. In order to bring about this reconciliation he takes *metaphor*, a trope which appears to Richard as an instrument of dialectical *Aufhebung*: 'In Mallarmé the ideal balance emerges from the opposition of two elements. Thus metaphor is a union, and synthesis becomes a dialectical reduction of the twofold to the one.'[95]

The thematic analysis (*analyse thématique*) developed by Richard in his study of Mallarmé is reminiscent of the Genetic Structuralism practised by the Hegelian Marxist Lucien Goldmann, who attempts to understand the individual parts of a text in the context of the whole, and the whole in relation to its parts.[96] Richard seems to follow this hermeneutic movement when he insists on 'the dialectical confirmation of the whole by the part and the part by the whole'.[97] The guarantor of this coherent whole is Hegel's spirit, and Richard recognizes in Mallarmé's idea 'a supreme centre that is the spirit' ('*un centre suprême qui est l'ésprit*').[98]

On a semantic level 'the repetition of motifs' ('*l'itération des motifs*') is taken to guarantee 'the strictness of thematic development'.[99] Elsewhere Richard emphasizes the importance of *recurrence* for the constitution of the text.[100] Although it has a somewhat intuitive character, his thematic analysis relies on terms that are used in different ways in Greimas's structural semiotics. His way of looking at the semantic coherence of Mallarmé's text is reminiscent of Greimas's concept of *isotopy*: 'A flame, for example, is related to hair in order to stimulate in us the image of a fiery blossoming. The link between glacier and chastity conveys the essence of virginal coldness.'[101] We are faced here with analyses inspired by an Hegelian and 'Structuralist' aesthetics which aims to expose the conceptual structure or the *level of content* of a literary work.

It is therefore not surprising that Derrida feels provoked by Jean-Pierre Richard's book. In a long essay, first published in *Tel Quel* under the title 'La Double séance' (1970) and later reprinted in *Dissemination*, Derrida attempts to demonstrate how Mallarmé's poetry dissolves both Plato's and Hegel's concepts. Mallarmé, Derrida claims, does reiterate Plato's concept of mimesis, yet without taking over the Platonic definition of this term according to which 'somewhere the being of something that *is*, is being imitated'.[102]

According to Derrida there is mimesis or *imitatio* in Mallarmé, but not in the sense of an ideal essence postulated from Plato to Hegel: the *imitated Being* or the *transcendental signified*. From this Nietzschean and deconstructive position Mallarmé's textual experiment appears as an interplay of signifiers without truth, without conceptual anchoring.

'This is why Derrida insists that Deconstruction is a process of "displacement" endlessly at work in Mallarmé's text, rather than an act of critical intervention that would come, so to speak, *from outside* and simply apply the standard technique of reversing some "logocentric" order of priorities', writes Christopher Norris.[103] Deconstruction is therefore 'always already at work in the work', as Derrida puts it, and Mallarmé's poetry appears to him as a model of deconstructive practice.

In this context Derrida accuses the '*analyse thématique*' as practised by Jean-Pierre Richard of Platonic-Hegelian logocentrism and, in conjunction with Richard's book on Mallarmé, evokes 'an atmosphere of intimism, symbolism, and neo-Hegelianism'.[104] In a first move, he questions the possibility and *raison d'être* of thematic analysis. He reverses the core argument of this theory, according to which Mallarmé's aesthetic design strives towards a unification of the world in the book. At the same time he attacks Richard's complementary idea that Mallarmé attempted to contain or to master *dissemination* in order to bring about unity. Derrida is primarily concerned with liberating Mallarmé's verb '*disséminer*' from the Platonic-Hegelian yoke, to protect it from the grasp of a new metaphysics of totality in order to transform it into a (non-)concept of Deconstruction.

First he attempts, as might be expected, to demonstrate that there is no 'final signified' ('*signifié en dernière instance*') in Mallarmé, and no 'final referent'[105] ('*référent en dernière instance*') either. He cites as proof many ambivalent and polysemic passages from Mallarmé's work and shows to what extent an attentive reading transforms the thematic or structural *iterativity* asserted by Richard into *iterability*, into semantic plurality, that is into *dissemination* (as a consequence of iterability).

Thus Derrida dissects Richard's theme of the *fold* (*pli*), which plays an important part in several of Mallarmé's poems (for example in 'Hommage': '*Le silence déjà funèbre d'une moire/*

Dispose plus qu'un pli seul sur le mobilier') and which Richard turns into the element of a semantic totality held together by the concept of *intimité*. Derrida radically challenges this Hegelian construction by emphasizing all instances where 'the fold also marks dehiscence, dissemination, spacing, temporization, etc.'.[106] In the context outlined here the word 'also' is not without relevance: for Derrida does not deny the existence of the themes discussed by Richard (for instance *pli*, *blanc*, *azur*), but the possibility of bundling them into a conceptual totality that would have to be accepted as the 'truth' of Mallarmé's poetry.

In contrast to Richard's totalizing hermeneutics, the *dissemination* or *dispersal* introduced by Derrida excludes every form of conceptual fixing. It even makes the common distinction of 'actual' and 'metaphoric meaning' impossible. In a linguistic situation where truth as such dissolves into a 'mobile army of metaphors' (Nietzsche), every attempt to define metaphor conceptually is destined to fail from the start. There is only the figure of speech, and philosophy turns into rhetoric in the sense outlined by Nietzsche: 'The dissemination of the whites (not the dissemination of whiteness) produces a tropological structure that circulates infinitely around itself through the incessant supplement of an extra turn: there is *more* metaphor, *more* metonymy. Where everything is metaphoric there is no meaning as such and consequently also no longer a metaphor.'[107]

A term such as fold (*pli*) cannot be derived from the concept of metaphor; not only because the actual sense has vanished, but also because Mallarmé's signifier *pli* acquires contradictory meanings. According to Derrida it means *both* 'virginity' *and* that which destroys and violates it. At times, however, it means neither one nor the other, so that its meaning becomes undecidable or extremely ambivalent.

From what has been said so far it follows that Derrida's *dissemination* or *dispersal* is not identical with the semiotic concept of *polysemy* defined by Greimas and Courtés as pluri-isotopy: *as the interaction of two or more heterogeneous isotopies*.[108] For in the context of polysemy meaning is definable in so far as a word or sememe can be located on a particular isotopy. It therefore possesses no radically ambivalent character; it is not 'undecidable' (*'indécidable'*, Derrida). Hence Deconstruction distinguishes itself from

Greimas's rationalist semiotics by introducing into the debate Nietzsche's idea of extreme ambivalence which prevents an unequivocal definition of linguistic units. From this ambivalence derives the idea of aporia which plays a decisive role in the work of the American Deconstructionist Paul de Man.

Ambivalence in Derrida's sense leads to an attack on the institutionalized distinction between literature and philosophy. 'I will say', Derrida explains, 'that my texts belong neither to the "philosophical" register nor to the "literary" register.'[109] In a later interview published in *Points de suspension* he adopts once more an ambivalent attitude towards both philosophy and literature, declaring that he is neither a writer of literature nor a philosopher: 'No doubt I am neither one nor the other.'[110]

It is therefore dangerous to speak of aesthetics in conjunction with Deconstruction, since aesthetics is commonly regarded as an element of philosophy. Notwithstanding this difficulty Derrida's theory of literature and art can be conceived as a Nietzschean aesthetics of the signifier, the level of expression: as an aesthetics aiming to go beyond the limits of semiotic polysemy in order to describe the dispersal of sense, *dissemination*.

Despite his subtle critique of Jean-Pierre Richard, Derrida has not succeeded in demonstrating that all the key terms in Mallarmé's poetry are undecidable. One could counter that the texts of the French poet can indeed be read as heterogeneous, 'pluri-isotopic' units in the semiotic sense, whose significance changes from era to era and from society to society.[111]

Nonetheless, his critique of Richard is justified in so far as thematic analysis tends to privilege the monosemy of texts and to neglect the semantic heterogeneity of Mallarmé's poetry, as well as its potential to acquire new meanings in an open historical context. After all, some of the difficulties of structural semiotics show that the decision to locate a *sememe* such as *pli* on a particular isotopy or on several isotopies is sometimes (not always) arbitrary and that 'undecidable' words do exist in some extreme cases.[112] For this reason it seems necessary to intensify the dialogue between the two positions, between structural semiotics and Deconstruction.

6 DERRIDA AS A READER OF BAUDELAIRE:
LA FAUSSE MONNAIE

In his commentaries on Baudelaire's prose poem *La Fausse monnaie* (Counterfeit Money) (*Le Spleen de Paris*, XXVIII) Derrida reiterates some of the arguments of 'La Double séance' and illustrates his idea of *dispersal* or *dissemination* with the help of linguistic and anthropological examples. What is at stake is the application of this central (non-)concept which is located on the borderline of conceptuality and points beyond it to the notion of *don/gift* (*donner/to give*), suggesting that the meaning of the word is undecidable: in Marcel Mauss's *Essai sur le don* (1923/4), in Emile Benveniste's linguistics, and in Baudelaire's prose poem which now moves into the centre of the discussion. Its interpretation in Derrida's *Donner le temps 1. La Fausse monnaie* will provide a transition from French to American Deconstruction.

Baudelaire's text is marked by an unexpected turning point. On leaving a tobacco shop, the narrator observes how his friend starts to 'carefully separate' his money and looks particularly attentively at 'a silver coin of two Francs'.[113] The two companions encounter a beggar whose look fills the narrator with pity. They give him some coins. The narrator notices that his friend's donation is far more generous than his own and says 'Next to the pleasure of being surprised there is no greater one that creating a surprise for others'. 'It was the false coin', replies the other calmly, as if he wanted to justify his extravagance. What follows is a construction of diverse hypotheses by the narrator who attempts to explain such a course of action and to exculpate his friend who may only have attempted 'to create in the life of this poor devil an event'. This event can be positive as well as negative, and in the uncertainty that it harbours the ambivalence of the gift or present becomes visible. For the false coin can on the one hand 'multiply into real coins', but it can also get the poor man 'into jail' as a forger. The friend abruptly interrupts the narrator's daydreams by taking up his words: 'Yes, you are right; there is no sweeter pleasure than surprising someone by giving him more than he expects.' The narrator notices that his friend really means what he says and is upset because he realizes that the other wanted 'both to give a donation and to make a good deal'. He had nearly forgiven his bad intention but cannot accept an amalgam of evil and stupidity: 'One can never be excused when one is evil, but there is a certain merit in knowing that one is evil; and it is the worst of all incurable vices to commit evil out of stupidity.'

In his analysis of Baudelaire's *La Fausse monnaie* Derrida returns to his comments on Mauss's *Essai sur le don* and continues his attempts to prove the 'madness of the dissemination of the meaning "gift"' (*'la folie de la dissémination du sens "don"'*).[114] He refers to Mauss's anthropological investigation which confronts the reader with the many difficulties that emerge when one attempts to *distinguish* the gift from an economic exchange or a long-term debt. 'For there to be a gift', Derrida states, '*it is necessary [il faut]* that the donee does not give back, amortize, reimburse, acquit himself, enter into a contract, and that he never have contracted a debt.'[115] Now it is difficult to avoid reciprocity and indebtedness when donating an object, and the gift as such (if it exists at all, Derrida would add) is *temporalized (temporisé)* or *deferred (différé)* by the always implicit – and thus unavoidable – expectation of reciprocity or a counter gift.[116]

Consequently Derrida can claim that one can ultimately only 'give the time' (*'donner le temps'*) which makes this reciprocity possible. From his point of view, the gift resembles Heidegger's Being that should also manifest itself in time, yet whose presence in the realm of Existence is incessantly *deferred (différé)*. In other words, the gift can never really become a gift, since the always implicit demand for reciprocity or a counter gift never ceases. Thus the meaning of 'gift' falls victim to that *différance* which prevents the presence of meaning in general and leads to *dissemination*.

The gift that is defined by the forfeiting of a counter gift, yet implicitly excludes this forfeiting, is therefore ambivalent, and Derrida refers to the common etymological origin of the German and English terms *Gift* (donation in Old High German) and *gift* (donation, present in English) in order to demonstrate this ambivalence. It is confirmed in Benveniste's linguistic investigations where the Indo-European verb *do* appears as an ambivalent element: it can signify both giving and taking, and its meaning depends on the respective syntactic construction.

The basic ambivalence of the noun *gift (don)* and the verb *give (donner)* also appears in Baudelaire's prose poem, whose narrator speculates about the effect of a false coin on the life of the beggar: 'Might it not multiply into real coins? Could it not get him into prison?' Starting from this ambivalence of the gift whose 'actual', i.e. beneficial or evil, character is undecidable, Derrida attempts to describe the paradoxical, aporetic and ultimately undecidable structure of Baudelaire's prose poem.

In a note he mentions the ' "aporetics" of the gift' ('"*aporétique*" *du don*'[117]) and relates it to the term *différance*. The coin which the narrator's friend gives to the beggar can only be regarded as a gift in the positive sense of the term if it 'multiplies into real coins', thus bringing about the good fortune of the recipient. Yet even in this decisive phase the ultimate effect of the gift is uncertain, since the fortuitous moment could be followed by the discovery of the presumed forger and his arrest. In short, the false coin reveals the double character of the gift which can bring the recipient both fortune and misfortune, life as well as death – or both, if one takes into account its temporal dimension.

At this point, though, one might confront Derrida with the argument of analytic philosophy according to which each gift can lead to fortune and euphoria in the life of a human being at the time T_1, but to misfortune and dysphoria at the time T_2. A bottle of wine can make someone happy at first, but might simultaneously trigger his tendency towards alcoholism that only becomes evident later. A book by Derrida may transpose the recipient into a euphoric mood at first, when it gives him new insights; it can plunge him into deep depression at a later stage, since it destroys his belief in certain consoling truths. No one is therefore safe from the point in time $T_2 \ldots$

Yet this does not make it plausible to speak of the aporetic character of the gift, for one can only speak of an aporia when two mutually irreconcilable elements manifest themselves: for instance in a tragic situation in which the hero must perform two mutually exclusive feats. The false coin can bring fortune as well as misfortune to the beggar, but not both at the same time, only in a particular order, where the sequence *fortune-misfortune* is more likely than then the reverse. Thus Derrida's basic thesis that the false coin illustrates the aporetic character of each gift is not plausible.

One might merely claim that the false coin in Baudelaire's

narrative is ambivalent, since it has a particular value when it remains undetected, but is also – apart from all erroneous assumptions – worthless. Equally ambivalent in this case is the intention of the friend who could be characterized as an 'evil benefactor'. This ambivalence, however, generates no aporia, and by no means illustrates the 'aporia of the gift' in general, i.e. the aporetic structure of all gifts. For most gifts are accompanied by good intentions, are neither 'untrue' nor 'false', and therefore possess no aporetic, but at most a polyfunctional character: they can have positive or negative effects, and their effects depend on the inclination of the individual and the context.

Nonetheless, Derrida's thesis concerning the temporal ambivalence of the gift that is never clearly distinguishable from an economic transaction, since it forms a relation of exchange, remains plausible and stimulating. Moreover, Derrida rightly emphasizes the ambivalent and paradoxical character of the false coin, relating it to the paradoxical structure of Baudelaire's prose poem. He mentions the poet's plan to write a novella entitled *Le Paradoxe de l'aumône* (*The Paradox of Charity*) and reminds us 'that some of his editors consider this to be in fact the first title of *Counterfeit Money*'.[118]

He projects the problem of ambivalence and paradox onto the narrative plane when he adds that the friend's paradoxical gift 'requires and at the same time excludes the possibility of narrative' ('*requiert à la fois et exclut la possibilité du récit*').[119] For the double character of the false coin makes possible at least two competing stories which the narrator constructs as mutually exclusive hypotheses: the story of fortune and the story of misfortune. Here it becomes clear that the semantic ambivalence of the gift and the giver (the friend) leads to an *undecidability* on the narrative plane: Baudelaire's narrator can decide neither in favour of one nor the other story and never gets further than guesswork and hypotheses.[120]

In contrast to 'La Double séance' Derrida leaves the *semantic and narrative sphere* of the prose poem in his commentaries on *La Fausse monnaie* and continues his argument on a *pragmatic plane*: the level of reader response. He is quite right in distinguishing the author from his fictional first person narrator. With respect to the narrative in Baudelaire's prose poem he states: 'Truly fictive, but produced as *true narrative* by the fictive narrator in the fiction signed and forged by Baudelaire, here it goes and tells us the story of another fiction, of a fictive money.'[121] In the French original the word *'forgé'* (*'fiction signée et forgée par Baudelaire'*) is used instead of 'invented'/'inventé', and carries negative connotations. For it not only literally means 'forged' as by a blacksmith, 'imagined' or 'invented', but also 'forged' in the sense of 'imitated' with the intention to deceive (*'controuvé'*, *'faux'*; *Petit Robert*).

From these connotations Derrida derives the following hypothesis concerning the title *The False Coin*: 'It no longer says only: Here is a story of counterfeit money, but the story *as* literature is itself – perhaps – counterfeit money, a fiction about which one might say, at the limit and by looking for noon at two o'clock, everything that the narrator . . . could have said of the counterfeit money of his friend, of the intentions he attributes to his friend, of the calculation and all the exchanges that are thus provoked by the event that his friend has himself provoked with his counterfeit money.'[122]

Literature, however (despite Plato's claims), cannot be compared to a false coin, to false claims or any other falsehood. By starting from a false analogy between literary fiction and the forged coin Derrida ignores the crucial difference between aesthetic illusion and mere falsehood. This difference has been investigated by a large number of authors and has rightly become a commonplace of literary analysis.[123]

By neglecting all that distinguishes aesthetic illusion as *a construction of a second reality*, a *possible world* (Hintika, Eco) from false coins or statements, Derrida can likewise neglect the *semantic and narrative facts* in Baudelaire's text and engage in speculations on a pragmatic level. One could call these speculations with Eco 'overinterpretations', since they go beyond the limits of careful or responsible interpretation.

Regarding the narrator's friend, he inquires, for instance: 'What if he were an even greater counterfeiter than the narrator thinks? What if, with the simulacrum of a confession, he were passing off true money as false?'[124] But is it sensible to doubt the knowledge of the narrator when it is not doubted in the text itself (by competing discourses, for example)? Elsewhere Derrida claims 'The friend's response also *may be* counterfeit money.'[125] He seems to compete with Baudelaire's narrator when he sets out to speculate about the hidden intentions of the friend who, despite cheating the beggar, perhaps feels no guilt whatsoever, since 'One can also credit the friend with feeling innocent of having given a counterfeit coin – to the point that he does not hide it from the narrator – since, by means of this counterfeit coin, he withdrew from the cycle of the gift as violence toward the poor man.'[126] The ambivalence of the gift acquires a new dimension here: one donates a false coin in order to liberate the poor man from the constraints of a gift that might oblige him within the mechanism of exchange.

Adopting this stance, one could speculate about the honest or dishonest intentions of a character such as Madame de Bargeton in Balzac's *Illusions perdues*. The narrator tells us, among other things, that she has 'fallen in love with a gentleman, a simple sub-lieutenant' (*'s'éprit d'un gentilhomme, simple sous-lieutenant'*). When the same narrator evokes 'the remains of a heavenly Jerusalem, that is love without lover' (*'restes d'une Jérusalem céleste, enfin l'amour sans l'amant'*) with regard to Madame de Bargeton and confirms this verdict as true, saying *'c'était vrai'*, he creates an aesthetic illusion, or a possible world which *competes* with the world known to the reader by generating its own *facts* and *criteria of truth*.[127] The latter cannot be adapted to those of the readers.

Similar things could be said about Baudelaire's prose poem whose narrator states that his friend slips into his right trouser pocket 'a silver two Franc coin that he has subjected to a special examination'. We are faced with a fictional fact when we are told that the friend separates the two Franc coin from the rest of his money after careful examination. A further fact is given when the friend explains to the narrator: 'It was the false coin' (*'C'était la pièce fausse'*). In order to question this statement as a 'lie', 'trick' or 'joke' one would have to be able to quote certain elements of the text: for instance a remark by the narrator or the friend. Yet such elements are missing in the prose poem, and the interpretative strategy of Deconstruction turns in the void when Derrida – as if beyond the text – engages in guesswork about the acting figures in the poem as if they were living individuals.

This critique is not meant to discredit Deconstruction as a method of interpretation or to confirm wholesale rationalist condemnations of Derrida. For it has become clear that Deconstruction represents an important corrective within contemporary literary and linguistic analysis which continues to adopt the rationalist and Hegelian demand that texts be turned into monosemic structures.[128]

Derrida has shown that ambivalence and iterability not only feature in literature, but *can* also occur in philosophical texts, and that no semantic (Greimas) or dialectical (Hegelian) theory can eliminate all 'undecidable' text elements. Yet he tends to transform the difficulty of understanding a text *as a coherent or* (in some cases) *heterogeneous structure* into an impossibility. The term *pluri-isotopy* (coexistence of several heterogeneous isotopies) coined by Greimas shows, however, that structural semiotics is not wedded to the postulate of coherence for better or worse and that contradiction and incoherence are no foreign terms within Structuralism. In his commentaries on various Structuralist theories Derrida has never dealt with this fact. Ultimately, he cannot be spared the reproach that he does not distinguish clearly between textual structures and his own reading experience (as in his analysis of *La Fausse monnaie*). We shall see that these two tendencies are reinforced in the works of the American Deconstructionists who aim to bridge the gap between literature and theory rhetorically.

7 BABEL OR THE IMPOSSIBLE TRANSLATION: FROM BENJAMIN TO DERRIDA AND DE MAN

Walter Benjamin and Jacques Derrida share the view that, as Benjamin puts it, language 'is not an agreed system of signs'[129] and that signifiers cannot function as conventional markers of general concepts in the sense outlined by Saussure. Benjamin's theory of language and translation rests on the idea that the mimetic principle is responsible for the particularities of languages and that the 'onomatopoeic explanation' is most relevant for linguistic theory.[130]

His conception of language, like that of the Romantics, emphasizes the particularity and non-exchangeability of the individual word and is diametrically opposed to rationalist and Hegelian semiotics. Hegel appears as the antipode of Benjamin and Derrida when, discussing poetry, he states in his *Lectures on Aesthetics*: 'Thus the spirit becomes objective to itself on its own ground and it has speech only as a means of communication or as an external reality out of which, as out of a mere sign, it has withdrawn into itself from the very start. Consequently in the case of poetry proper it is a matter of indifference whether we read it or hear it read; it can even be translated into other languages without essential detriment to its value, and turned from poetry into prose, and in these cases it is related to quite different sounds from those of the original.'[131]

This long quotation is important because it leads to a contrastive exposition of Benjamin's and Derrida's theories of translation. Benjamin implicitly refers to Hegel's 'logocentric' and bluntly simplifying exposition when he criticizes Humboldt: 'Humboldt ignores of course the magical aspect of language at every point. . . . He is only concerned with spiritual objectivity in Hegel's sense.'[132] The strong emphasis on this 'spiritual objectivity' projects the entire problematic of translation onto the *level of content* (Hjelmslev), the plane of the signifieds. It is based on the assumption that even a poem by Hölderlin or Mallarmé can, 'without essential detriment to its value', be translated into other languages. Benjamin as well as Derrida would reverse this argument and claim that a poem by Mallarmé is simply untranslatable, because there are no *equivalents* for its polysemic signifiers in the target language. Derrida would add that the meaning of these signifiers (for instance *pli*; see Chapter 2, section 4) is undecidable and that the task of the translator therefore becomes aporetic.

The extent to which Benjamin emphasizes the level of expression of language and considers the level of content secondary is demonstrated in his well-known essay 'The Task of the Translator', where he asks at the outset: 'Whatever a poem contains apart from the message – and even the worst translator admits that this is the essential part – is it not generally held to be the ungraspable, mysterious, "poetic"? Something that the translator can only reproduce when he also writes poetry.'[133] He adds: 'Translating is a form. To perceive it as such means going back to the original.'[134]

At this point a second crucial aspect of Benjamin's theory of translation becomes evident: like the Romantics (see Chapter 1), he not only reveals the dark sides of language which foil the conceptual transparency postulated by rationalists, but also looks towards the original text and its context. In this respect he also departs from the rationalist theories of the Enlightenment that foregrounded the elegant and reader-friendly translation,[135] and continues the argument of the Romantic Schleiermacher who advocates faithfulness to the original.[136]

This orientation towards the original and the mimetic conception of language explains why Benjamin radicalizes the Romantic approach, so hostile towards reception and communication, and remarks by way of introduction: 'For no poem is meant for the reader, no picture for the viewer, no symphony for the assembled listeners.'[137] For this reason it is inconceivable that the translation of the foreign text be adjusted to the demands of the target language and the expectations of the new audience. What matters is the mimetic reformulation of the expression, of the 'how' of the original in the target language.

Benjamin calls this 'how' the 'way in which something is meant' and distinguishes it carefully from the content, from 'that which is meant'. ' "Bread" and the French word "*pain*", may mean the same thing, but the "ways of meaning" are different. The way of meaning is responsible for the fact that the two words mean something different to an Englishman and a Frenchman, that they are not exchangeable, indeed even tend to claim exclusive validity. What is meant, however, indicates that, taken as absolutes, they are identical and the same.'[138] Benjamin imagines a translator who attempts to reproduce the 'way of meaning' of this foreign text in his own language in order to 'redeem this pure language that has been exiled into the foreign one in his own language' in a kind of dialogue of languages.[139] The 'pure language', however, means neither a rationalist or Hegelian conceptualization nor 'a language that would be entirely freed from the illusion of meaning', as de Man interprets it.[140] Rather is it a theologically conceived idea of the general within the particular expression.

At this point Derrida joins in when in 'Des Tours de Babel' (1985), a detailed commentary on Benjamin's essay, he reveals the basic contradiction of translation, the contradiction between the 'way of meaning' and 'that which is meant' as an aporia. Starting from an interpretation of the myth of Babel according to which the God of the Old Testament (YHWH = Yahweh) descended to Earth in order to prevent the development of a universal language and to create linguistic confusion, Derrida remarks: 'He *simultaneously* demands and forbids translation.'[141] By exposing His untranslatable name, He not only destroys all hopes of a universal language and a universal reason, but he also undercuts the imperial demands inherent in such a language: 'He smashes the transparency of reason, but simultaneously dissolves colonial violence or linguistic imperialism. He condemns them [the Semites] to translation and subjects them to the law of a necessary and impossible translation; because of His translatable-untranslatable proper name he makes possible a universal reason (it is no longer subject to one single nation); at the same time he limits its universality: transparency is forbidden, absence of ambiguity impossible.'[142]

Here it becomes clear that Derrida, like Benjamin, is an heir of the Romantics in terms of philosophy (the religious components of his thinking cannot be examined in this context). The translator cannot ignore the level of expression as the plane of mere signifiers and pretend that there is a one-to-one relationship between signifier and signified that leads to equivalence between various linguistic systems. Herder's observation concerning the heterogeneity of linguistic forms, which had a lasting impact on Romantic theories of language, becomes relevant here: 'But words themselves, meaning, soul of language – what an infinite field of diversity!'[143] This diversity impedes the transparency and universality desired by all rationalists since the Enlightenment. It prevents – like the God of Babel – that process of translation that nonetheless remains necessary if communication between peoples is not meant to cease.

Considering the typological similarity between Derrida's and Benjamin's conceptions of language it is not surprising that the French philosopher, and after him Paul de Man, pay particular attention to the essay 'The Task of the Translator'. They endorse Benjamin's insight into the untranslatability of Mallarmé's poetry and confirm his claim that the translator neither writes for the recipient nor reproduces content, but should attempt to find an analogy for the particularity and singularity of the original in his own language.

Paraphrasing Benjamin, Derrida writes: 'Translation does not pretend to say this or that, to transpose this or that sense or communicate a definite meaning, but wants to *point out* the affinity between languages ('remarquer *l'affinité entre les langages*') and to uncover its own possibility.'[144] What is at stake is to re-establish the 'transient' ('*fugitif*') 'points of contact of meaning' which connect languages with one another, despite the distance that separates the different 'ways of meaning' from one another.

In his commentary Derrida seems to agree with Benjamin to a large extent when he finally remarks: 'That which is forever intact, ungraspable, untouchable is what fascinates the translator and determines his way of working' ('*Le toujours intact, l'intangible, l'intouchable* [unberührbar], *c'est ce qui fascine et oriente le travail du traducteur*').[145]

This 'ungraspable remainder' is at the centre of Paul de Man's commentary on Benjamin's famous essay. Thus de Man interprets the term 'task' ('Aufgabe') in 'The Task of the Translator' as 'forfeiting', as 'capitulation' in the face of the untranslatable which emerges from an aporia. It is generated by the irresolvable contradiction between the demands of faithfulness to the original and a free translation faithful to the demands of the target language. In this context de Man speaks of an 'aporia between freedom and faithfulness to the text'.[146]

According to de Man, the core of this aporia is formed by the insight that the original harbours no meaning (as a *signified*) that could be translated and transposed. As Eve Tavor Bannet remarks, this insight of the translator implies the death of the original, for it appears that it has 'nothing to say': 'Hence literary criticism and translation kill the original in order to step in its place . . . .'[147] In other words, they treat the original rhetorically as an interplay of multivalent signifiers to be continued by the translator.

These interpretations of Benjamin's article, whose plausibility cannot be further commented on here, show that de Man and Derrida notice above all the resistances encountered by the translator. Hence it is the untranslatable remainder (the 'unintelligibility' as Friedrich Schlegel would say) that fascinates both Benjamin and the Deconstructionists and plays an important part in contemporary translation theories.

The crucial difference between these theories and those of Benjamin and Derrida lies in the strong theological tendencies that the latter display when they turn 'the magical side of language' into a quasi-religious enchantment, while translation theorists tend to believe with Greimas that 'there are no secrets in language'. They are not entirely wrong, for it would be irrational to turn the ungraspable and untouchable into the main topics of scientific debate. Nonetheless, Benjamin's and Derrida's musings might contribute to the development of contemporary translation theories that have hitherto not paid sufficient attention to the limits of translation itself.

When Basil Hatim and Ian Mason question the concept of equivalence ('usually intended in a relative sense') in *Discourse and the Translator* and rightly claim that there is no complete semantic equivalence between words in different languages,[148] they touch upon a crucial theorem of Deconstruction (and Benjamin) without really debating it. For a solution (if there is one at all) is not reached, as the two authors seem to believe, by proposing the more modest term 'adequacy' as an alternative: 'But the concept of "adequacy" in translation is perhaps a more useful one.'[149] The 'stricter' linguist could counter that this is a non-concept, since the term 'adequacy' has neither been defined on a phonetic nor on a syntactic and semantic level. Philosophers like Benjamin and Derrida would merely be provoked into a sceptical smile by the suggested alternative.

A solution is no nearer when Roger T. Bell admits that the transition from one language into another brings with it changes of form and that something is always 'lost': 'Something is always "lost" (or, might one suggest, "gained"?) in the process . . . .'[150] For the question is precisely *when* and *why* the translator is confronted with the problem of untranslatability and *what* exactly is lost in the solving or overcoming of this problem or gained through original creativity. Contemporary theorists of translation have so far not concerned themselves very systematically with these questions, which apply particularly to literary texts. Therefore a more thorough engagement with Benjamin's and Derrida's linguistic theories of the 'untranslatable remainder' would be desirable. Derrida's and de Man's global assessment of translation as aporia, however, appears as a Deconstructionist extremism which contributes to a better understanding of their own concepts of language and text, but not to an advance in translation studies.

In the context of his practice of interpretation (Mallarmé, Baudelaire, Kafka), Derrida's thesis concerning the aporetic character of translation can only be regarded as a consequent development of his aesthetics of contradiction crucial to almost all of his critical works on literature. Commenting on Maurice Blanchot's *La Folie du jour*, for example, he discovers the 'narrative of an impossible narrative' ('*C'est le récit d'un récit impossible . . .*').[151]

In the following chapters it will become clear that in the American types of Deconstruction – particularly in Paul de Man's and J. Hillis Miller's – the concept of aporia moves to centre-stage, supplanting notions such as *différance* or *dissémination*.

NOTES

1. T. Eagleton, *Literary Theory: An Introduction* (1983), chapter 4: 'Post-Structuralism'.
2. See, for instance, Anon. 'Derrida Derided', *The Economist* (16 May 1992).
3. J. Derrida, *Positions* (1981), p. 9.
4. Ibid., p. 10.
5. J. Derrida, *Geschlecht (Heidegger): Sexuelle Differenz, ontologische Differenz, Heideggers Hand* (1988), p. 78.
6. Derrida, *Positions*, p. 10.
7. J. Derrida, *Dissemination* (1981), p. 70.
8. Ibid., p. 103.
9. Ibid., p. 76.
10. J. Derrida, *Of Grammatology* (1974), pp. 271–2.
11. Ibid., p. 60.
12. Ibid., p. 316.
13. J. Derrida, *The Archaeology of the Frivolous: Reading Condillac* (1987), p. 126.
14. E. Husserl, 'Philosophy as Rigorous Science', in *Phenomenology and the Crisis of Philosophy* (1965), p. 96.
15. Ibid., p. 118.
16. J. Derrida, *La Voix et le phénomène* (1967), p. 15.
17. Ibid., p. 84.
18. Ibid., p. 83.
19. Husserl, 'Philosophy as Rigorous Science', p. 98.
20. Derrida, *La Voix*, p. 116.
21. Derrida, *Dissemination*, p. 130.
22. M. Heidegger, *Identity and Difference* (1969), p. 71.
23. J. Derrida, *Margins of Philosophy* (1982), p. 38.
24. Derrida, *Of Grammatology*, p. 24.
25. Ibid., p. 26.
26. G. W. F. Hegel, *Science of Logic* (1969), p. 43.
27. Derrida, *Glas*, p. 26.
28. Ibid., p. 8.
29. J. Derrida, *Memoirs – For Paul de Man* (1986), p. 137.
30. J. Derrida, *Writing and Difference* (1978), p. 280.

31. J. Derrida, *Spurs: Nietzsche's Styles* (1978), p. 97.
32. Ibid., p. 99.
33. J. Derrida, *The Ear of the Other: Otobiography, Transference, Translation* (1985), p. 31.
34. Ibid., p. 29.
35. Derrida, *Points . . .* , p. 281.
36. Derrida, *Of Grammatology*, p. 19.
37. S. Kofman, *Lectures de Derrida* (1984), p. 65.
38. Derrida, *Margins of Philosophy*, p. 219. Compare also Derrida's reflections in *Psyché: Inventions de l'autre* (1987), p. 65: 'What happens *with* the metaphor? Well, everything; nothing exists that does not happen with the metaphor and through metaphor. Everything that is uttered as a subject, whichever it may be, comprises the metaphor, and is *not ever* produced *without* metaphor.' It therefore seems impossible to talk or think without or outside metaphor.
39. M. Haar, 'Le Jeu de Nietzsche dans Derrida', *Revue philosophique*, 2 ('Derrida') (1990), p. 215.
40. R. Rorty, 'Deconstruction and Circumvention', *Critical Inquiry*, 11 (September 1984), 11.
41. F. de Saussure, *Course in General Linguistics* (1960), p. 116.
42. J. Derrida, 'La Différance', in: *Théorie d'ensemble* (1968), p. 53.
43. Ibid., p. 51.
44. Derrida, *Positions*, pp. 40–41.
45. Heidegger, *Identity and Difference*, p. 65.
46. Derrida, *Writing and Difference*, p. 25.
47. Derrida, *Margins of Philosophy*, p. 318.
48. M. Frank, 'Die Grenzen der Beherrschbarkeit der Sprache', in *Text und Interpretation* (ed. P. Forget) (1994), p. 207.
49. J. Culler, *On Deconstruction: Theory and Criticism after Structuralism* (1982), p. 128.
50. Derrida, *Memoirs – For Paul de Man*, p. 115.
51. Derrida, *Margins of Philosophy*, p. 327.
52. The Russian philosopher and literary theorist Mikhail M. Bakhtin (1895–1975) developed a dialogical theory of language and literature based on the idea that especially the polyphony of the novel (from Rabelais to Dostoevsky) can be related to the critical and rebellious and polyphonic carnival celebrations of the late medieval period and the renaissance. See, for example, M. M. Bakhtin, *Problems of Dostoevsky's Poetics* (1984).
53. Culler, *On Deconstruction*, p. 112.
54. Derrida, *Margins of Philosophy*, p. 322.
55. J. R. Searle, 'Reiterating the Differences: A Reply to Derrida', *Glyph*, 1 (1977), p. 202.
56. Ibid., p. 208.
57. J. Derrida, *Limited Inc.* (1988), p. 62.

58. Ibid., p. 53.
59. Ibid., p. 119.
60. Ibid., p. 118.
61. M. Masterman, 'The Nature of the Paradigm', in *Criticism and the Growth of Knowledge* (eds I. Lakatos and A. Musgrave) (1970), pp. 61–5.
62. On the impossibility of defining or delineating concepts that presuppose the definition of the 'limit', see G. Bennington, 'La Frontière infrachissable', in *Le Passage des frontières: Autour du travail de Jacques Derrida* (1994), p. 7: 'The definition of the concept of the concept can never be complete, since it depends on a definition of the limit that delineates it . . . .'
63. A. J. Greimas and J. Courtés, *Semiotics and Language: An Analytical Dictionary* (1982), p. 163.
64. A. J. Greimas, *Structural semantics* (1983), p. 65.
65. Derrida, *Memoirs – For Paul de Man*, p. 73.
66. Derrida, *Limited Inc.*, p. 41: 'How was he capable of replying an Austin so unrecognizable as to bear *almost* no relation to the original, i.e. an Austin who is never *quite* himself?'.
67. B. Malmberg, 'Derrida et la sémiologie: quelques notes marginales', in *Semiotica*, 11, 2 (1974), p. 196.
68. J. Derrida, 'Préjugés', in *Spiegel und Gleichnis: Festschrift für Jacob Taubes*, ed. N. W. Bolz and W. Hübener (1983), p. 350.
69. Derrida, 'Préjugés', p. 356.
70. Ibid.
71. F. Nietzsche, *Aus dem Nachlaß der Achtzigerjahre*, in F. Nietzsche, *Werke*, vol. VI (1980), p. 627.
72. Derrida, *Writing and Difference*, p. 25.
73. G. Deleuze, *Difference and Repetition* (1994), p. 67.
74. Cf. F. Zourabichvili, *Deleuze. Une philosophie de l'événement* (1994), pp. 92–3.
75. Deleuze, *Difference and Repetition*, p. 67.
76. R. Smith, *Derrida and Autobiography* (1995), p. 35.
77. As far as Hegel's 'realism' is concerned cf. J. E. Smith, 'Hegel's Critique of Kant', in *Hegel and the History of Philosophy. Proceedings of the 1972 Hegel Society of America* (ed. J. J. O'Malley, K. W. Algozin, F. G. Weiss) (1974), p. 118: 'Hegel was, in this regard, a thorough going realist: what we know is the things themselves, their properties, unities and relations.'
78. Cf. J.-P. Sartre, 'L'Universel singulier', in *Kierkegaard vivant. Colloque organisé par l'Unesco à Paris du 21 au 23 avril 1964* (1966), pp. 39–40.
79. R. Smith, *Derrida and Autobiography*, p. 34.
80. Ibid.
81. G. Deleuze, *Empirisme et subjectivité. Essai sur la nature humaine* (1993, 5th ed.), p. 21.

82. Deleuze, *Empirisme et subjectivité*, p. 15.
83. G. Deleuze, C. Parnet, *Dialogues* (1977), p. 11.
84. Ibid.
85. J. Derrida, *Monolingualism of the Other, or, The Prosthesis of Origin* (1998), p. 3.
86. J. Lacan, *Le Séminaire, livre II. Le Moi dans la théorie de Freud et dans la technique de la psychanalyse* (1978), p. 354.
87. A. Juranville, *Lacan et la philosophie* (1966, 2nd ed.), p. 112.
88. S. Critchley, 'Prolegomena to Any Post-Deconstructive Subjectivity', in *Deconstructive Subjectivities* (eds S. Critchley and P. Dews) (1996), p. 39.
89. D. Fricke, 'Jean-Pierre Richard', in *Französische Literaturkritik in Einzeldarstellungen*, ed. W.-D. Lange (1975), p. 187.
90. S. Mallarmé, 'Préface à Vathek', in *Oeuvres complètes* (1945), p. 568.
91. J.-P. Richard, *L'Univers imaginaire de Mallarmé* (1961), p. 380.
92. Ibid.
93. Ibid., p. 422.
94. Ibid., p. 412.
95. Ibid., p. 424.
96. See L. Goldmann, *The Hidden God* (1970), Chapter 1; and L. Goldmann, *Towards a Sociology of the Novel* (1975), Chapter 5: 'The Genetic-Structuralist Method in the History of Literature'.
97. Richard, *L'Univers imaginaire de Mallarmé*, p. 432.
98. Ibid., p. 419.
99. Ibid., p. 22.
100. Ibid., p. 24.
101. Ibid., p. 412.
102. Derrida, *Dissemination*, p. 206.
103. C. Norris, *Derrida* (1987), p. 56.
104. Derrida, *Dissemination*, p. 271.
105. Ibid., p. 207.
106. Ibid., p. 271.
107. Ibid., p. 258.
108. Greimas and Courtés, *Semiotics and Language*, p. 236.
109. Derrida, *Positions*, p. 71.
110. Derrida, *Points . . .* , p. 189.
111. In this context, Derrida might have taken F. Rastier's structural analysis 'Systématique des isotopies' in *Essais de sémiotique poétique* (1972) into account. Rastier describes the metaphorical collaboration of three semantic isotopies in Mallarmé's poem 'Salut'.
112. See my chapter 'Algirdas J. Greimas' Ästhetik der Inhaltsebene', in *Literarische Ästhetik: Methoden und Modelle der Literaturwissenschaft*, 2nd. ed. (1995), p. 331.
113. All quotations are translated from C. Baudelaire, *Oeuvres complètes* (1975), vol. I, pp. 323–4.

114. J. Derrida, *Given Time: I. Counterfeit Money* (1992), p. 55. [*Donner le temps 1. La Fausse monnaie* (1991), p. 77.]

115. Ibid., p. 13 (*Donner le temps*, p. 163).

116. On the problem of temporality and the reciprocity of the gift in Derrida and Sartre, see D. Giovannangeli, 'Mauss entre Sartre et Derrida', in *Le Passage des frontières* (ed. G. Bennington) (1994), pp. 65–8.

117. Ibid., p. 127.

118. Ibid.

119. Ibid., p. 102. (*Donner le temps*, p. 133).

120. The relation between ambivalence and the dissolution of narrative structure is of particular interest and has been outlined in detail by myself in connection with Proust's, Musil's, and Kafka's novels in *L'Ambivalence romanesque: Proust, Kafka, Musil*, 2nd ed. (1988).

121. Derrida, *Given Time*, p. 94.

122. Ibid., p. 86.

123. See F. Burwick and W. Pape (eds), *Aesthetic Illusion: Theoretical and Historical Approaches* (1990).

124. Derrida, *Given Time*, p. 96. See also Derrida's speculative remark on p. 150: 'It is to the narrator that he would have passed on counterfeit money by letting him *believe* that he had chosen the counterfeit coin.'

125. Ibid., p. 149.

126. Ibid., p. 149–50.

127. A. J. Greimas examines the role of criteria of truth in fictional and non-fictional discourses in 'Le Contrat de véridiction', in *Du Sens II: Essais sémiotiques* (1983).

128. See my essay 'Der Mythos des Monosemie', in *Einführung in Theorie, Geschichte und Funktion der DDR-Literatur* (ed. H.-J. Schmitt) (1975), pp. 86–98.

129. W. Benjamin, 'Über das mimetische Vermögen', in *Gesammelte Schriften*, vol. 2, 1 (1977), p. 212.

130. Ibid.

131. Hegel, *Aesthetics*, p. 949.

132. W. Benjamin, 'Zur Sprachphilosophie und Erkenntniskritik', in *Gesammelte Schriften*, vol. 6, p. 26.

133. W. Benjamin, 'Die Aufgabe des Übersetzers', in *Gesammelte Schriften*, vol. 4, 1, p. 9.

134. Ibid.

135. See, for instance, J. C. Gottsched, '*Von den Übersetzungen*', in *Ausgewählte Werke*, vol. 7, 2 (1975), p. 7.

136. See F. Schleiermacher, 'Über die verschiedenen Methoden des Übersetzens', in *Das Problem des Übersetzens*, ed. H. J. Störig (1973), p. 69.

137. Benjamin, 'Die Aufgabe des Übersetzers', p. 9.

138. Ibid., p. 14.

139. Ibid., p. 19.

140. P. de Man, *The Resistance to Theory* (1986), p. 84.

141. Derrida, 'Des Tours de Babel', in *Psyché*, p. 220.
142. Ibid., p. 210.
143. J. G. Herder, *Über den Ursprung der Sprache*, quoted in F. Apel, *Sprachbewegung: Eine historisch-poetologische Untersuchung zum Problem des Übersetzens* (1982), p. 87.
144. Derrida, 'Des Tours de Babel', p. 220.
145. Ibid., p. 224.
146. de Man, *Resistance to Theory*, p. 91.
147. E. T. Bennet, 'The Scene of Translation: After Jakobson, Benjamin, de Man, and Derrida', *New Literary History*, 24 (1993), p. 583.
148. B. Hatim and I. Mason, *Discourse and the Translator* (1990), p. 8.
149. Ibid.
150. R. T. Bell, *Translation and Translating* (1991), p. 6.
151. J. Derrida, *Parages* (1986), p. 267.

3

PAUL DE MAN

RHETORIC AND APORIA

Deconstruction in the United States of America should not be discussed separately from the institutionalization of literary studies, or literary criticism, at American universities. While in the 1950s and 1960s the methods of New Criticism which did not go beyond the literary work dominated the academic scene, in the late 1970s the breakthrough of Deconstruction took place, and the hegemony of the New Critics – John Crowe Ransom (*The New Criticism*, 1941), Cleanth Brooks, Robert Penn Warren, *et al.* – was gradually replaced by that of the Deconstructionists. Their influence, which – despite all polemical attacks and criticism – has lost little of its force, originated at Yale University, where the most important exponents of this approach (Paul de Man (1919–83), J. Hillis Miller and Geoffrey Hartman) taught.

David Lehman remarks on the dominant position of the Deconstructionists in philosophical and literary studies in the early 1990s: 'The deconstructors of "hegemony" are observed to be working toward their own hegemony, scorning their rivals as retrograde, reactionary, or even anti-intellectual.'[1] This evaluation, reminiscent of the disputes between Formalists and Marxists in the post-Revolutionary Soviet Union and of the conflicts between *critique universitaire* and *nouvelle critique* in France in the 1960s, is complemented elsewhere by Lehman's remarks that Paul de Man is 'generally considered to be the guiding light of literary Deconstruction'.[2]

This provides one of the reasons for assessing de Man's theoretical approach before those of the other Deconstructionists. The second and more important reason is his explicit interest in philosophical questions, questions that relate him to Derrida, whose critique of Kant, Hegel and Rousseau, de Man continues and occasionally noticeably modifies.

Yet an engagement with de Man is meaningful only after the question concerning the institutional and methodological relationship between Deconstruction and New Criticism is answered, to which the Belgian-American theorist refers continually. For, as Lehman writes, it is no coincidence that the dominance of the New Critics was replaced by an hegemony of the Deconstructionists. Like New Criticism, American Deconstruction is a predominantly immanent, text-oriented theory that in many ways continues the tradition of close reading (comparable to the German *textimmanente Interpretation* and French *explication du texte*). Yet in contrast to the New Critics of the 1950s and 1960s, the American followers of Derrida do not aim to expose the semantic or syntactic coherence of the text, but focus on its ambivalences, contradictions and aporias.

To them, their search for incoherence and contradiction, or 'unreadability' in Paul de Man's terminology, appears ethically motivated, a form of duty. The lucid reader, the 'good reader', as J. Hillis Miller claims, realizes the 'unreadability' of the text and sternly rejects any attempt to disguise it by Hegel's category of totality or any other such hermeneutic postulate of coherence.

For both Hillis Miller and de Man, the 'ethics of reading' therefore consist in recognizing the contradictory and unreadable character of the text and in openly admitting the failure of reading. The reader refrains from subjecting the object of his analysis to the conceptual discourse of his own theory. In this perspective reading appears as 'an allegory of unreadability', as Werner Hamacher aptly remarks.[3] At the same time, a basic scepticism towards theory and its concepts becomes noticeable in Paul de Man, J. Hillis Miller and Geoffrey H. Hartman.

In spite of his proximity to Nietzsche, Miller seems to rely on the denial of concepts in Kant's aesthetics when he remarks on the relationship of literature and theory in *Theory Now and Then* that '[g]ood reading is more likely to lead to a disconfirmation or severe modification of a theory than to offer any firm support for it'.[4] Similar statements are frequently encountered in Paul de Man.

The second ethical aspect of American Deconstruction is closely related to the 'truthful reading' to which de Man and Miller repeatedly refer. It is based on the idea of an authentic dialogue with the text and its alterity. This alterity is only given its due weight when the reader lets him- or herself be guided by the non-conceptual character of Kantian aesthetics, instead of succumbing to an Hegelian *tour de force* which culminates in the subjection of the object to a subjective will. In this vein, Simon Critchley questions the cognitive value of Hegel's logocentrism in *The Ethics of Deconstruction*: 'Philosophy, particularly in its Hegelian moment, has always insisted on thinking of its other (art, religion, nature, and so forth) as its *proper* other, thereby appropriating it and losing sight of its otherness'[5] (see Chapter 1). Critchley rightly emphasizes the importance of Emmanuel Levinas's work for Derrida's philosophy and shows how much the two writers reject all philosophical attempts to incorporate the Other (the alterity of the object) into the same, the Hegelian subject. The exponents of American Deconstruction confirm this refusal when they advocate a 'truthful reading' that refrains from idealistically eliminating the contradictions inherent in the object.

The question concerning the ethics of reading raised by Derrida, de Man, and Hillis Miller also has a cognitive aspect. How can one assert that a particular way of reading – Deconstructive or otherwise – is the correct one, and that the contradictions revealed by de Man or another Deconstructionist are 'contained' in the object?

Thus, de Man seems to commit the very Hegelian error he criticizes when he declares that 'a deconstruction always has for its target to reveal the existence of hidden articulations and fragmentations within assumed monadic totalities'.[6] Like the 'realist' Hegel who assumed that the categories of dialectical thought corresponded to the reality identified with the philosophical subject, de Man clings to the idea that Deconstruction simply needs to detect the illogicalities contained in the text, in the object.

He thereby overlooks the problem of the meta-language which is responsible for the theoretical construction of the object in all cases. For the theoretical object is never represented or mirrored photographically, but is always (re-)constructed by the ever contingent discourse of a theory. This aspect of theory formation has so far been neglected by the Deconstructionists – and by most of their Structuralist, Hegelian or Marxist opponents, who tend to identify texts with certain semantic structures they have contrived and then projected into their objects without paying attention to the process of construction.

It will become clear in what follows that the neglect of object constructions on a metalinguistic level is a decisive weakness of the discourses of Deconstruction. It accounts for the fact that theorists such as de Man and Miller continually overlook the social and historical components of texts and of their own discourses.

1 PAUL DE MAN BETWEEN HEGEL, NIETZSCHE AND HEIDEGGER

A certain continuity between Paul de Man's Deconstruction and Anglo-American New Criticism has already been observed in the preface. De Man returns to the positions of the New Critics when he makes a variant of close reading his own and refuses, in the same way as Ransom, Brooks or Wimsatt, to reduce the literary text to a concept in the scientific sense. Like the Kantian Ransom, Paul de Man might say: 'It is my feeling that we have in poetry a revolutionary departure from the conventions of logical discourse . . . .'[7]

Like Kant, de Man assumes the position of the reader or viewer and rejects all attempts of Hegelian aesthetics of production to explain works of art within the framework of conceptual systems. He seems to confirm Ransom's rejection of science when he asserts in *Blindness and Insight*: 'The semantics of interpretation have no epistemological consistency and can therefore not be scientific.'[8]

Yet he goes far beyond Ransom's Kantianism and the theoretical scepticism of the New Critics when he attempts to prove with Nietzsche that the rhetorical dimension of the theoretical discourse governs its logical and grammatical components. In *The Resistance to Theory* he explains: 'Difficulties only occur when it is no longer possible to ignore the epistemological thrust of the rhetorical dimension of discourse, that is, when it is no longer possible to keep it in its place as a mere adjunct, a mere ornament within the semantic function.'[9] The rhetorical element discussed in detail by Nietzsche

is what, according to de Man, condemns systematic conceptualization to failure and explains at the same time why each theory of
literature encounters insurmountable obstacles. For the literary text
as literariness 'foregrounds the rhetorical over the grammatical and
the logical function'.[10]

Even conceptual theory cannot do without this rhetorical function, and de Man questions the premises of a Rationalist and
Structuralist like Greimas who tacitly assumes that the grammatical
and the logical functions of language are co-extensive and that
grammar forms an 'isotope of logic'. This isotope dissolves, however, as soon as the rhetorical interferences *within* grammar
are noticed, since rhetoric can be reduced neither to grammar nor
logic. For '[t]here are elements in all texts that are by no means
ungrammatical, but whose semantic function is not grammatically
definable, neither in themselves nor in context'.[11]

In so far as de Man claims complete validity for his rhetorical
approach, not only in the literary but also in the rhetorical realm,
his argument leads to an extreme particularization of the concept of
theory. As rhetoric, as a figurative discourse governed by tropes,
theory resists its own formations of concepts and systematizations:
'Nothing can overcome the resistance to theory since theory *is* itself
this resistance.'[12] Paradox and Romantic irony resound in this
statement which announces the aporias in de Man's Deconstruction.

With Nietzsche and in opposition to Hegel, who insists on the
conceptual character of the dead and automatized metaphor (for
instance *field of study, isotopy, tangent*), reducing metaphor to its
'abstract meaning',[13] de Man attempts to let the rhetorical, figurative origin of theoretical key terms come to the fore. Like Derrida,
who reminds us of the metaphorical character of the concept of
metaphor, de Man doubts the possibility of taming the rhetorical
elements of language by a terminology which is itself of rhetorical
origin. Should this claim be confirmed by a scientific practice (which
is by no means certain), then one would also have to accept the
complementary thesis proposed by Jonathan Culler, another spokes-
man for American Deconstruction: 'There is, for example, no
question of escaping from the pitfalls of rhetoric by becoming aware
of the rhetorical nature of discourse.'[14]

As pertinent as de Man's and Culler's claims may appear at first
glance, they by no means lack counter-arguments. Mathematics and

formal logic, whose strategies of deduction are not troubled by rhetorical interferences and not exposed to the uncertainties of *iterability*, *can* play an important role in theoretical discourses – from linguistics all the way to aesthetics.[15] Moreover, a semiotician like Greimas demonstrates at crucial points that it is indeed possible to explain metaphor by concepts such as *seme* and *sememe*.[16]

Faced with such – always debatable – conceptual definitions, the claims of the Deconstructionists appear as Nietzschean exaggerations which locate the rhetorical figure in the centre of the scene, thus neglecting the *role of formal logic in each theoretical argument*. The aim is not to side with Greimas or de Man, but to understand that both conceptions of theory ought to be regarded merely as contingent constructions which should be placed in a dialectical and dialogical relationship to each other.

De Man's Nietzschean exaggerations have a long history beginning with the Young Hegelian critique of Hegel (see Chapter 1, section 3). Like the Young Hegelians, de Man attacks Hegel's systematic dialectic by emphasizing the insurmountable ambivalence and the unity of opposites without synthesis. In *The Resistance to Theory* he claims: 'Binaries, to the extent that they allow and invite synthesis, are therefore the most misleading of differential structures.'[17]

This critique of Hegelian *Aufhebung* or synthesis leads de Man, like the Young Hegelians in their time and much later Benjamin and Adorno, to a re-evaluation of the particular, the singular, and to a radical critique of the universal, the general concept. This re-evaluation of the particular, which led to an anarchistic apotheosis of the individual will in Stirner, to a materialist praise of the senses in Feuerbach, to a new aesthetics of autonomy in Vischer, and to an individualist interiorization of Hegel's history in Kierkegaard, leads to an overemphasis on rhetoric, on tropes, in de Man.

His response to a critique by Raymond Geuss in *Critical Inquiry* shows how much he views his own thought in the context of this anti-Hegelian particularization originating in the intellectual revolt of the Young Hegelians: 'If truth is the appropriation in thought and, hence, in language, of the world by the I, then truth, which by definition is the absolutely general, also contains a constitutive element of particularization that is not compatible with its universality. This question always surfaces, in Hegel, when language surfaces.'[18] In the linguistic sphere this process of particularization brings about *a re-evaluation of the level of expression* and of rhetoric in Nietzsche's sense. Yet it begins with the staging of existential contradictions within the individual, as it did in the Young Hegelians and Kierkegaard. For this reason it seems reasonable to insist with Christopher Norris on the affinity between de Man and the Danish philosopher, who was perhaps the first to doubt the normative relations between language, truth and subjectivity.[19]

In this context, it is hardly surprising that de Man regards literary and philosophical problems from an existentialist perspective in his early writings (from the 1950s and 1960s) and seeks orientation in Heidegger's ontology of Being. Ortwin de Graef, who has commented in detail on these texts, distinguishes two modes of reading in early de Man: an *existential* and a *rhetorical* mode. He describes a 'conflict between modes of reading that are founded upon "existential categories" and modes of reading that are based on "rhetorical categories"'.[20] While the first mode of reading strives towards a unity of the text guaranteed by an existential design, the second mode is guided by the idea that any reading aiming at unity and fulfilment of meaning is ultimately subverted by the rhetorical elements of language. In an essay on Wordsworth and Keats from 1962 de Man writes about 'two distinct readings' which derive from 'altogether divergent uses of imagery'.[21] Still, Ortwin de Graef may be right when he concludes that a rigid separation of the two modes of reading is impossible, since they interact in heterogeneous and hybrid textual analyses which evolve both on an existential and on a rhetorical level.

The common denominator of the 'existential' and the 'rhetorical' reading, however, is the tendency towards particularization, and Ortwin de Graef's investigations seem to confirm the view that most modern critiques of the Hegelian system lead to an enhancement of the particular. In this view the two modes of reading outlined in early de Man by de Graef appear to be complementary, since the existential (Young Hegelian and Nietzschean) particularization adds to the rhetorical (Nietzschean) one.

It is therefore hardly surprising that, on the one hand, de Man refers to Heidegger, in order to find a base for his analyses of the unity of Being, and that, on the other hand, he attempts to expose the rhetorical contradictions of different literary works. If one reads his essay 'Keats and Hölderlin' (1956) as an endeavour to start from the Hegelian and existentialist tension between subject and object, subject and world, and to view Hölderlin's work as an attempt 'to recover the unity of being, lost at the start',[22] one discovers that it relates in a complementary manner to his 'pre-rhetorical' critique of Sartre's *Les Mots*. In this critique de Man declares that *Les Mots* might be read as an autobiography in the sense outlined by Rousseau, but in fact contains a thesis that has very little in common with the autobiographical genre: *Les Mots* 'is thus not the kind of book it pretends to be'.[23] We shall see that this search for an historically grounded and irreconcilable (i.e. non-Hegelian and non-dialectical) contradiction will be intensified in de Man's late work.

2 CRITIQUE OF AESTHETIC IDEOLOGY

The anti-Hegelian tendency towards existential and rhetorical particularization forms the philosophical basis of what de Man calls the *ideology of the aesthetic*. A concise definition of this term – its meaning varies in de Man – can be found in Lindsay Waters's introduction to de Man's *Critical Writings*: 'It is an ideology that requires that literature be dominated by the knowing subject who ascribes meaning and a moral to the text. It is an ideology that monumentalizes literature by setting it up as a symbol of civilization.'[24] One could add that it is an ideology which has evolved within Hegelian logocentrism which identifies art and literature with certain historical meanings.

In an essay from the late 1980s where he addresses the function of the symbol in Hegel, de Man regards Hegel's entire aesthetic as an aesthetic of the symbol. He ignores Hegel's critique of the symbol and of symbolic art[25] and claims bluntly: 'Hegel, then, is a theoretician of the symbol.'[26]

De Man's critique of the symbol cannot be separated from his anti-Hegelian stance, since the symbol appears in his writings as a unifying principle which allows Hegel and the Hegelians (for instance Lukács or Lucien Goldmann) to understand works of art as meaningful totalities expressing political, moral or religious ideas in sensuous terms. This is why the concept of the symbol in de

Man's discourse – most prominently in his commentaries on Hegel – is fraught with negative connotations.

De Man suggests *allegory* as a critical counter-concept and redefines it in the tradition of Rousseau and the Romantics (F. Schlegel): 'Whereas the symbol postulates the possibility of an identity or identification, allegory designates primarily a distance in relation to its own origin, and, renouncing the nostalgia and the desire to coincide, it establishes its language in the void of this temporal difference. In so doing, it prevents the self from an illusory identification with the non-self . . . .'[27] Allegory appears to de Man as the non-Hegelian or even anti-Hegelian category *par excellence*: it negates the unity of subject and object and challenges the Hegelian idea that thought and reality are reconciled. At the same time it dissolves the Romantic aesthetic illusion of a unified work of art conceived as a sensory manifestation of the idea. It will become clear that the concept of irony derived from the German Romanticism of F. Schlegel and E. T. A. Hoffmann assumes a similar function to allegory in de Man's work (see Chapter 3, section 5).

Michael Cebulla remarks on the role of allegory in de Man: 'In contrast to the symbol it is, on the one hand, a form of authentic speech, since it resists the illusion of embodiment and reconciliation; it is capable, on the other hand, of designating the very impossibility of embodiment, the distance in relation to its own origin, the non-phenomenal experience of failure.'[28] Since allegory avoids the – often forced – reconciliation of subject and object that characterizes Hegel's philosophy, it also negates the appearance of aesthetic ideology: the idea that beauty, knowledge, moral and political action form a whole.

According to Christopher Norris, Hegel's definition of art as 'the sensory manifestation of the Idea' appears to a critic like de Man as 'a considerable slackening of philosophic rigour when compared with Kant's more complex, and endlessly self-qualifying treatment of cognate themes'.[29] In Schiller's work, de Man claims to notice a weakening of the Kantian argument due to the poet's questionable attempt to adapt the Kantian ethic to the demands of a unifying aesthetic. By conceiving the beautiful as a sensuous manifestation of the good, he lays the foundation of an aesthetic ideology dominated by the illusion of unity. De Man points out that this logocentric, unifying and potentially repressive ideology was later simplified, vulgarized and abused for political aims by the Nazis.

The following quotation from *Lectures on Aesthetics* shows that aesthetic ideology in its classical shape already appeared in Hegel's work, and that it was influenced by Schiller's writings: 'It is *Schiller* [1759–1805] who must be given great credit for breaking through the Kantian subjectivity and abstraction of thinking and for venturing on an attempt to get beyond this by intellectually grasping the unity and reconciliation as the truth and by actualizing them in artistic production.'[30] It is precisely this 'unity and reconciliation' which de Man considers ideologically and politically fatal.

It is very likely that he would also have remarked a dangerous tendency towards aesthetic ideology in an Hegelian Marxist such as Lucien Goldmann who seeks to overcome Kantian dualism, regards works of art as 'meaningful totalities' and views history as moving towards the *telos* of 'human community'. Does de Man not accuse Georg Lukács of being unable to make do without totality and 'organic continuity'?[31] In this respect his critique of (Hegelian) aesthetic ideology is reminiscent of Adorno's critique of ideology which culminates in the correct conclusion that 'the philosophy of the absolute, the total subject [is] a particularising one'.[32] Like de Man, who comments on the contradictions and aporias of literature as 'allegories of unreadability', Adorno attempts to preserve the negativity of art from affirmative thinking and ideological encroachment. At the end of this analysis and in Chapter 7 it will become clear, however, that this affinity is merely apparent, for the negativity of Critical Theory (of the Frankfurt School) has little in common with de Man's.

For the starting point of the Deconstructionist is not a Critical Theory of society which considers the decline of individual autonomy as one of its main topics, but rhetoric in a Nietzschean sense. In this respect Christopher Norris is right when he claims that de Man fights aesthetic ideology with the weapons of rhetoric and close reading: 'For de Man, then, the ethics of reading is closely bound up with a *political* critique of the powers vested in aesthetic ideology.'[33] What matters is exposing the inaccuracies and contradictions which aesthetic ideology conceals by its notion of harmony, by overemphasizing the semantic pattern of interpretation. In this respect, one can indeed speak of a critical dimension in de

Man's literary analyses. For this critique is meant to prevent an 'aesthetization of politics, which seeks the fusion of form and idea'.[34]

It is quite possible that Marxist critics of Deconstruction such as Terry Eagleton have overlooked this critical dimension in de Man's thinking. It is also possible that the Marxists would have escaped some one-sidedness and reductionism if they had dealt more thoroughly with de Man's critique of the symbol and his concept of allegory.[35] Norris, however, goes decidedly too far when he compares Deconstructive critique of ideology with that of Adorno in his defence of de Man.[36] For Adorno's theory, concerned as it is with the truth content of the text, has nothing in common with a Nietzschean or rhetorical destruction of truth (see Chapter 3, section 3, and Chapter 7).

Although de Man – like Benjamin and Adorno – rejects the genetic concept of history, founded upon the commonplace notion that each new fact derives from previous phenomena, thus ensuring a coherent continuum, one should not overlook the differences. That de Man regards the historical sciences as textual disciplines on the one hand,[37] and defines their hermeneutics as analogous to literary criticism in its search for aporias on the other, becomes evident in *Blindness and Insight* and *The Resistance to Theory*.

From a rhetorical perspective not only the literary or philosophical text, but also the historic one appears as aporetic, and history as presented in de Man's essay 'Literary History and Literary Modernity' dissolves into competing aporias. From this follows, for example, that Nietzsche as a modern thinker breaks with historical consciousness, but simultaneously fails to disentangle himself from this form of consciousness. A similar aporia occurs in the sphere of literature between Mallarmé and Baudelaire: on the one hand Mallarmé breaks with the 'sensual' poetry of his predecessor; on the other hand his late works show clearly how much he is still enthralled with his model.[38] If, however, the history of literature as 'literary history' is governed by aporia, the suspicion arises that even the historical sciences in a general sense become 'self-contradictory' and fall victim to aporia.[39] At least they fall victim to rhetoric, of which de Man claims that its 'linguistic factors threaten to interfere with the synthesizing power of the historical model'.[40]

Such a view of history, however, does not match that of Adorno or other members of the Frankfurt School. Their theories distance themselves from the genetic and immanent conceptions of the Hegelians and Marxists, but do not give up the critical idea that, despite all negativity and despite the always present possibility of catastrophe, the absolute Other, whose realization is also latent in the historical process, remains visible. The ambivalence that already features in Benjamin's 'theses on the philosophy of history' does not lead to aporia, to an impossibility of knowledge and action, but retains the idea of utopia (see Chapter 7).

3 PAUL DE MAN AS A NIETZSCHEAN: RHETORIC AND APORIA

Nietzsche's philosophy is important for de Man since it emphasizes the rhetorical aspects of language while radically challenging the metaphysical concepts of truth upheld by the Rationalists, Kantians and Hegelians. It is no coincidence that the Deconstructionist stresses the importance of 'Nietzsche the philologist',[41] for he is fascinated by Nietzsche's project of deconstructing the philosophers' discourses through the rhetorical strategies of literature: 'The critical deconstruction that leads to the discovery of the literary, rhetorical nature of the philosophical claim of truth is genuine enough and cannot be refuted: literature turns out to be the main topic of philosophy and the model for the kind of truth to which it aspires. . . . Philosophy turns out to be an endless reflection on its own destruction at the hands of literature.'[42]

It is worth examining this claim in detail, for its decisive moments are, as is always the case, its selections and definitions. The process of *selection* leads towards a confrontation of philosophy and litera- ture and is responsible for the *definition* of philosophy as literature. Eventually it is claimed that literature is the central object of philosophy which is ultimately deconstructed by this very object. The question whether de Man renders Nietzsche's ideas correctly (is not the 'will to power' the central theme of this philosophy?[43]) is not crucial here. It is more to the point that de Man makes the daring claim that philosophy is deconstructed by its own object on the basis of rather arbitrary selections and definitions. The fact that this claim is as arbitrary as the selections on which it rests is demonstrated by the philosophies of Hobbes and Leibniz, Hegel,

Marx and Popper, whose main object is by no means literature. Marx, for example, who as a philosopher is interested primarily in the economy of society, would have regarded the shift of emphasis towards literature with great scepticism and commented on it with a sharp critique of ideology. Popper, in turn, would have held the – very plausible – view that in contemporary society it is not literature but the development of the sciences which ought to be the object of philosophy.

What then justifies de Man's selections and definitions? It is a possible, though by no means inevitable, Nietzschean interpretation according to which the 'trans-valuation of all values' topples the established hierarchies and leads to a drastic reassessment of art and literature. This interpretation is also relied on by Barbara Johnson, an exponent of American Deconstruction, when she remarks 'yet Nietzsche's deconstruction of the value of values leads precisely to the discovery that philosophy *is* always already literature'.[44] Following Derrida, de Man refuses to acknowledge the border-lines between the institutionalized genres and tends to dissolve philosophy in literature.

Like Derrida he claims that logic, grammar and rhetoric are not merely different aspects of language, but enter into conflict with one another, thus producing *undecidabilities* or *aporias*. These are responsible for the *unreadability* of texts. The ambivalences de Man highlights in almost all philosophical and literary works result from an extreme (Nietzschean) ambivalence and are symptoms – as they were in Derrida – of a 'dialectic without synthesis' which Culler also mentions with respect to de Man.[45] To what extent ambivalence, aporia and rhetoric are related in de Man is amply illustrated by the following statement from *Allegories of Reading*: 'Tropes are neither true nor false and are both at once.'[46] This claim, which refers to Nietzsche's meditation 'On Truth and Falsehood in an Extra-Moral Sense' (see Chapter 1), provokes the suspicion that de Man's ambivalence, as aporia, tends towards indifference, i.e. the exchangeability of values.

His undecidability, which also implies exchangeability and indifference, is not the equivalent of semiotic polysemy inherent in historical reception as a change of meaning. It is rather an *aporia inherent in the text* and independent of the historical reader. This aporia of the Deconstructionist also differs qualitatively from the ambiguity of a New Critic like Empson. Michael Cebulla remarks: 'Empson thus remains within the horizon of New Criticism, since he does not question the organic unity of the work.'[47] In contrast to Empson, de Man challenges the work radically as an aesthetic unity and a meaningful totality. In his own way, however, he also remains within the argumentative framework of New Criticism, since he neither moves beyond an immanent view of the work nor analyses the historical shifts of meaning in the reception process. He shows no interest in the social origins of aporias.

In this respect his arguments resemble those of some American architects who work with Deconstruction: 'A deconstructivist architect', remarks Mark Wigley, 'is therefore not an architect who demolishes buildings, but an architect who locates the inherent dilemmas within buildings.'[48] Yet who defines something as a *dilemma* or *aporia*, and from which point of view? Could it not be that something appears as a dilemma or aporia to me that someone else perceives quite differently – for example as part of a greater harmony I fail to perceive?[49]

In Wigley's statement the terms *locates* and *inherent* have particular salience. They show that the exponents of Deconstruction – philosophers, literary scholars and architects – ascribe certain characteristics to the object without concerning themselves with the origins of their object constructions in certain architectural projects or philosophical and philological metalanguages. They naïvely assume that aporias and dilemmas are inherent in the object – in a building or text – itself. Therefore one could call their discourses ideological. 'The view of a material reality is ideological', explains the semiologist Prieto, 'when the subject regards the limits and the identity of the object which this reality has become for it as located within reality itself, i.e. when the subject identifies reality with the *idea* that it has deduced from it.'[50] In many (indeed most) discourses of Deconstruction this is the case, and in the next chapter it will appear that J. Hillis Miller overlooks the problems of metalanguage and the process of construction in the same way as de Man.

Some examples deriving from literature and philosophy will illustrate de Man's text-immanent approach. It will become apparent that the aporia de Man encounters in all works he comments on is by no means inherent in the works, but rather a contingent construction which ought to be exposed to critique and dialogue.

In his analysis of Yeats's poem 'Among School Children' he considers the text as an allegory of its own unreadability and emphasizes the undecidable character of the last verses:

> O body swayed to music, O brightening glance,
> How can we know the dancer from the dance?

In his commentary de Man claims, among other things, that the question asked at the end of the poem can be read rhetorically ('it is impossible to distinguish') as well as literally ('it is important to distinguish'). He locates the undecidable or unreadable character of the poem in this feature. The text can be read simultaneously as the icon of an organic unity – between the erotic body and the music, for example – and as an attempt at differentiation: 'For it turns out that the entire scheme set up by the first reading can be undermined, or deconstructed, in terms of the second, in which the final line is read literally as meaning that, since the dancer and the dance are not the same, it might be useful, perhaps even desperately necessary – for the question can be given a ring of urgency, "Please tell me, how *can* I know the dancer from the dance?" – to tell them apart.'[51]

Faced with these arguments, the temptation is strong to follow (a generally conservative) common sense and to object with D. Lehman that it is of course a rhetorical lyrical question which – at least in the traditional reader – asks for no response, since it merely points towards that which is self-evident and requires no clarification: the unbreakable unity of dancer and dance. 'Yeats's question is sublimely unanswerable; you can't distinguish the dancer from the dance . . . .'[52]

Common sense, however, should not become a substitute for theoretical reflection. For in the present case it is perfectly possible to counter de Man's undecidability with what Greimas writes about the often cited *infinite openness* of texts, namely that it 'is often produced by partial readings', i.e. by an incomplete analysis that does not pay tribute to the global interplay of structures.[53] For de Man focuses in his 'rhetorical' commentary on the closing verses of the poem and is therefore far from a semiotic or linguistic analysis which would correlate the phonetic, semantic and syntactic structures of the poem.

The problem of undecidability, however, should not be addressed within a single text, but ought to be dealt with in the context of Yeats's complete works and that of the literary evolution in the Anglo-Irish sphere. The fact that de Man is tempted to make apodictic statements without analysing the complete text and without paying attention to the extratextual components does not speak in favour of his deconstructionist approach.

Finally one should add that the final line of Yeats's poem does contain a genuinely undecidable element which de Man does not even notice: the gender of the dancer. Is it concerned with a male dancer or with a female dancer, as the French translator believes when he writes '*Comment distinguer la danseuse et la danse?*' This undecidability may not affect the entire text and it may not constitute an aporia; yet it cannot be overcome. However, it can be confirmed by semiotic as well as translation theories. Theory focuses both on the whole and the detail – rhetoric apparently does not.

In his commentaries on Rilke's poems de Man is also primarily concerned with demonstrating that two crucial elements of this poetry are irreconcilable and mutually exclusive. At stake is the relationship between truth and figuration (the rhetorical figure of speech). In formal terms de Man's argument matches his comments on Yeats's 'Among School Children'. Starting from a general 'ambivalence of poetic language',[54] de Man refers to a paradigm which, in his view, forms the basis of both the *Duino Elegies*, *Sonnets to Orpheus* and the *New Poems*: 'In conformity with a paradox that is inherent in all literature, the poetry gains a maximum of convincing power at the very moment that it abdicates any claim to truth. The *Elegies* and the *Sonnets* have been the main source of evidence in trying to prove the adequacy of Rilke's rhetoric to the truth of his affirmations, yet his notion of figural language eliminates all truth-claims from his discourse.'[55]

In this passage two aspects are striking: the generalization ('inherent in all literature') and the artificial character of the ambivalence or paradox. For it is by no means certain that all poetry possesses a paradoxical or ambivalent structure, and the ambivalence which de Man discovers in Rilke's works depends largely on how one defines the 'truth' of Rilke's claims and his 'truth-claims'. Who speaks, and which discourse is responsible for the definition, classifications and constructions? This question, which concerns the self-reflexivity of the discursive subject, is not raised by de Man, and consequently his interpretations have an air of arbitrariness. For it is quite conceivable that in a different discourse (e.g. that of structural semiotics) the irreconcilability constructed by de Man dissolves and Rilke's rhetoric does match his 'truth-claims'.[56]

Equally arbitrary seems to be the contradiction construed by de Man between Proust's theory of metaphor and his use of metonymy. In his commentaries on a long passage from Proust's *Du côté de chez Swann*[57] de Man makes the claim that Proust's texts contain a 'metafigural theory' concerning the 'aesthetic superiority of metaphor over metonymy'.[58] This theory, however, is supposed to be betrayed, indeed deconstructed by Proust's metonymical practice: 'Yet, it takes little perspicacity to show that the text does not practice what it preaches. A rhetorical reading of the passage reveals that the figural praxis and the metafigural theory do not converge and that the assertion of the mastery of metaphor over metonymy owes its persuasive power to the use of metonymic structures.'[59]

This statement will once again provoke readers who pay attention to the coherence and plausibility of an argument. In general, literary texts do not make claims ('The *Poet*, he never affirmeth', as Sir Philip Sidney stated long ago), and the passage from *Du côté de chez Swann* certainly contains no claim concerning the 'superiority of metaphor'.[60] In this context, de Man might have done better to refer to Proust's famous essay 'A propos du "style" de Flaubert', where the claim is made that the metaphor 'alone is capable of giving a kind of eternity to style' ('*seule peut donner une sorte d'éternité au style*').[61] However, this passage also refrains from positing an hierarchical relation between metaphor and metonymy, for metonymy can have certain advantages (for example as a syntactic and narrative figure of contiguity) that metaphor lacks.

Moreover, the relationship between metaphor and metonymy can hardly be conceived as an opposition that produces aporias and deconstructs the text. Gérard Genette rightly claims, in his well-known essay 'Métonymie chez Proust', also quoted by de Man, that '[f]ar from being antagonistic and irreconcilable, metaphor and metonymy are mutually dependent on and function with each other . . . .'[62] While Genette describes the specific interaction of metaphor and metonymy in Proust, the semioticians Greimas and Courtés define the general relationship of the two figures as 'a substitution phenomenon . . . produced on the basis of a semantic equivalence'.[63] The opposition between metaphor and metonymy postulated by de Man can be made plausible neither in the context of Genette's narratology nor in that of Greimas's semiotics. Hence the questions arise whether de Man's constructions are not merely arbitrary and whether his approach does not monologically prevent a dialogue with other theories. More will be said on this question at the close of this chapter.

It should be made clear at this stage that the Deconstructionist not merely considers all literary texts he analyses aporetic, but also perceives irreconcilable contradictions within philosophical works. Thus he attempts to describe Kant's theory of the sublime as an aporetic construction in his essay 'Phenomenality and Materiality in Kant'. One of the core arguments of this complex and in parts rather obscure text is that in Kant two irreconcilable definitions of the sublime clash: on the one hand, he postulates a purely aesthetic vision of nature which evades every attempt to integrate it into teleological and pragmatic thought and possesses a purely 'material' character (de Man speaks of a 'formal materialism'[64]); on the other hand, he postulates a natural sublime which can be represented ideally and has a moral effect.

'The vision of heaven and world entirely devoid of teleological interference, held up here as a purely sublime and aesthetic vision, stands in direct contradiction to all preceding definitions and analyses of the sublime given in section 24 on until this point in section 29. Still in the condensed definition that appears in the same chapter the stress falls on the sublime as a concrete representation of ideas (*Darstellung von Ideen*).'[65] Here a rupture is postulated between the culturally and morally 'useful' sublime of nature and a purely 'material' sublime we cannot fully grasp because of its magnitude and strangeness. De Man speaks elsewhere of a Kantian materialism, 'a materialism that Kant's posterity has not yet begun to face up to'.[66]

To this interpretation many Kantians might object that in Kant a 'purely material sublime' beyond all human uses and objectives cannot exist, since in Kant's teaching all categories are related to the subject (see Chapter 1). They might refer to Kant's explanations in section 26: 'That makes it evident that true sublimity must be sought only in the mind of the judging subject, and not in the object of nature that occasions this attitude by the estimate formed of it.'[67]

We are not concerned here with resolving the problem of the sublime in favour or against de Man, but with the insight that nearly all of his arguments – both in the literary and in the philosophical sphere – are teleologically geared towards aporia. The discovery of aporia, however, can contain no critique whatsoever, since it excludes all forms of truth content and merely demonstrates to the reader with merciless monotony the dissolution of meaning.

At this point the distance from Adorno, with whom de Man is occasionally compared (for example by Christopher Norris), becomes visible. In contrast to de Man, whose aporia destroys the concepts of meaning and truth by extreme ambivalence, Adorno conceives ambivalence dialectically as the *unity* of opposites, and not as a loss of meaning. He demonstrates, for instance, how in Stefan George's poetry, ideology and the critique of ideology contradict one another, yet also rely on each other and interact. George's critique originates in his aristocratic and élitist frame of mind that constantly jeopardizes the critical effect of his texts. His 'aristocratic outlook' is both the nourishing soil and the grave of his critique. It makes possible the refusal of a language degraded by commerce, yet simultaneously ties George's language to social domination. Hence Adorno can claim: 'It is the poems that appear inauthentic, without social context, that are authentic.'[68]

In Adorno's case, ideology and the critique of ideology are not simply contradictory elements which mechanically produce the dissolution of meaning, but two complementary aspects of George's poetry we need to distinguish carefully on the level of language, in order to save its truth content from the grasp of ideology. Not contradiction as such, but the moment of truth that subverts ideology is the *telos* of Adorno's argument. Thus the apparent proximity of the two post-Hegelians Adorno and de Man becomes, on closer inspection, extreme difference. For the search for truth and aporia as dissolution of meaning or undecidability are mutually exclusive.

4 DE MAN, DERRIDA AND ROUSSEAU: WAS ROUSSEAU A DECONSTRUCTIONIST?

De Man's commentaries on Derrida's critique of Rousseau are particularly characteristic of his rhetorically oriented interpretation of texts. The first example which springs to mind is *Of Grammatology* (see Chapter 2, section 1), where Derrida criticizes Rousseau's attempts to explain writing (*écriture*) as derived from *parole* and therefore as *supplement*. Rousseau, Derrida claims, contradicts this explanation every time he emphasizes the importance of literary writing. In *Blindness and Insight*, de Man confirms some of Derrida's arguments, yet claims at the same time that Derrida's *insights* are accompanied by *blindness*.

De Man holds the view that Rousseau is always aware of the rhetorical and literary character of his own discourse, one 'that puts the truth or falsehood of its own statement in question'.[69] According to de Man, one of Derrida's mistakes consists in overlooking the radically deconstructive character of Rousseau's text, thus confirming the prophecy inherent in it: 'The text knows that it is misunderstood and says so. It tells the story, the allegory of its misunderstanding . . . .'[70] Derrida's attempt to deconstruct Rousseau's text as part of an interpretation which demonstrates that the rhetorical or literary moment considered to be a derivative or supplement by the philosophers is really a cornerstone of his philosophical system, has an air of naïvety, since Rousseau is well aware of the crucial role of rhetoric in his work. In other words, 'Rousseau knows at any time what he is doing and as such there is no need to deconstruct Rousseau.'[71]

The critical reader, unwilling to throw formal logic overboard completely, is troubled by some questions at this point: why does Rousseau uphold the primacy of the spoken word and the derivative character of writing if he is completely aware of the 'writerly', i.e. rhetorical and literary character of his writing? How can one *explain* that an eighteenth-century philosopher possesses such an advanced understanding that he can not only pre-empt the discoveries of Deconstruction, but prophetically go beyond the *insights* of Derrida's critique? Is the concept of genius to be reiterated once again in the late twentieth century, despite the objections of Marxist critique, sociology and semiotics? How else can one explain the assumption that Rousseau outlines a Deconstruction *avant la lettre* in contrast to authors such as Kant, Hegel, Proust and Rilke, and hence need not be deconstructed? De Man does not address these last two questions.

He attempts to answer the first one and to prove that Rousseau by no means postulates the primacy of the spoken word, the presence of meaning and of the *sens propre* (the literal sense). In *Blindness and Insight* he quotes from Rousseau's *Essai sur l'origine des langues*, where it is claimed '*que le premier langage dût être figuré*' ('that the first language must have had figurative character'), and adds: 'In the narrative rhetoric of Rousseau's text, this is what is meant by the chronological fiction that the "first" language had to be poetic language. Derrida, who sees Rousseau as a representational writer, has to show instead that his theory of metaphor is founded on the priority of the literal over the metaphorical meaning, of the "sens propre" over the "sens figuré". And since Rousseau explicitly says the opposite, Derrida has to interpret the chapter on metaphor as a moment of blindness in which Rousseau says the opposite of what he means to say.'[72]

A strange textual hermeneutic: when the philosopher states something that does not fit the concept of the critic, then he must have meant the opposite ... Here the suspicion is confirmed that the Deconstructionists who accuse Hegel of integrating ruptures and contradictions into meaningful totalities have no scruples about committing similar acts of arbitrariness when the postulates of their own discourse are at stake. Derrida need not have interpreted the chapter on metaphor as an *oversight* (*blindness*); he could simply have stated that Rousseau contradicts himself.

Not only is Derrida's interpretation of Rousseau dubious; de Man's could also be questioned. The author of the *Essai* may claim 'that the first language must have had figurative character', yet this does not prevent him from speculating in a logocentric manner on the primacy of thought over speech in *Discourse on the Origin of Inequality*: 'for if men stood in need of speech to learn to think, they must have stood in even greater need of the art of thinking to invent that of speaking . . . .'[73] The development and specialization of language Rousseau imagines as follows: 'When the ideas of men began to extend and multiply, and a closer communication began to take place among them, they labored to devise more numerous signs, and a more extensive language.'[74] These arguments do not seem to bear out de Man's claim concerning the primacy of figurative speech and the dependence of thought on the figure of speech in Rousseau. They rather agree with Derrida who places Rousseau in the logocentric tradition and accuses him of making contradictory statements.

De Man's claim that, in Rousseau, 'the "first" language must have been a poetic one' is also not confirmed in *Discours*. There 'the first language of man' is identified with the 'cry of nature'.[75] Even someone who does not place as great an emphasis on the language of the poets as does de Man (reader of Mallarmé) will hesitate to liken it to the cry of nature. The suspicion arises that de Man (similarly to Lucien Goldmann who claims to have found in Goethe a precursor of dialectical thinking) searches for precedents in order to establish a Deconstructive tradition.

For how does de Man know that Rousseau puts a rhetorical Deconstruction *avant la lettre* into practice? Does his own commentary not suffer from an hermeneutic and semiotic 'oversight', when it projects a deconstructionist model of the late twentieth century into a text of the eighteenth? Does he not project the aporias of his own discourse into Rousseau's text when he analyses the aporias of *The Social Contract*, speaking of 'two distinct rhetorical models' in conjunction with this book?[76]

His commentaries on *The Social Contract* moreover reveal a contradiction within de Man's own discourse. If it is correct that Rousseau's political study merges two heterogeneous rhetorical models, thus producing an aporia which makes it susceptible to Deconstruction, then de Man's claim that it is not necessary 'to deconstruct Rousseau' is questionable. The only way out would be to claim that the narrating subject of *The Social Contract* deliberately deconstructs its own discourse in the same way as the subject of *Discourse on the Origin of Inequality*.

De Man himself asks in this context whether one must therefore conclude that *The Social Contract* is a deconstructive narrative like the second *Discourse*. He adds that even this is untrue, for the *Contract* is obviously productive and generative as well as deconstructive, in a manner that the second *Discourse* is not.[77] What is the significance of the terms 'productive' and 'generative' in contrast to 'deconstructive' here? Do they signal that a purely 'productive' text cannot become deconstructive? Do Rousseau's *Discourses* contain no 'productive' or 'generative' elements? Why not? De Man leaves these questions open. He merely attempts to show that *The*

Social Contract is an aporetic text, since it is split by the discrepancy between a rhetoric geared towards the individual and a rhetoric geared towards the state (the *volonté générale*).[78] Ultimately, an old topos of Rousseau scholarship is rhetorically reiterated here: the fact that the philosopher fails to bridge the gap between the '*volonté individuelle*' and the '*volonté générale*'. Yet this might have more to do with the concept of democracy in the eighteenth century or with Rousseau's political theory than with the 'rhetorical models' which de Man discusses and which are, at best, symptoms of a political malaise.

5 A CONCLUDING VIEW:
A RHETORIC OF ROMANTICISM

In conclusion this section will review briefly all the advantages and disadvantages of de Man's Deconstruction and relate them to the problems of Romanticism. After what has been said so far no one will be surprised to hear that the disadvantages seem to dominate. This is partly due to de Man's problematic constructions outlined above, whose weaknesses emerge in the light of a Critical Theory that does not deny historical, social and linguistic contingency, but indeed emphasizes them. The possibility of reading de Man's works differently is amply demonstrated by Christopher Norris.[79]

An achievement of de Man's approach is certainly the insight that literary and philosophical texts are not in all cases homogeneous structures, but may contain irreconcilable ambivalences, contradictions and aporias. This insight ought to become part of the methodological repertory of contemporary philosophy and literary criticism as a justified critique of Hegelianism, some variants of Structuralism and New Criticism. Thus de Man quite rightly deconstructs the claim of the New Critics regarding the unity of the work by pointing out that these critics did not succeed in discovering a 'single meaning', but only ambiguity and discontinuity: 'This unitarian criticism finally becomes a criticism of ambiguity, an ironic reflection on the absence of the unity it has postulated.'[80] The terms *unity* (New Criticism), *totality* (Hegel, Lukács, Goldmann) or *depth structure* (Greimas) ought therefore to be confronted by dialectically opposed concepts such as *ambivalence, contradiction* and *aporia*. This is also confirmed by Adorno's commentaries on

Stefan George's poetry. They should be dialectically *complemented* and not *replaced*. This is crucial, since it was shown that de Man – like Derrida – raises contradiction, undecidability and aporia to all-pervading principles without asking whether the 'coherence of the text' might not also be a viable hypothesis and whether coherence and contradiction could not coexist. A text may contain contradictions and aporias and still display a certain structural coherence on the semantic plane that de Man does not acknowledge.

When de Man moves aporia into the centre of his discourse in almost all of his later writings and regards all philosophical and literary texts as aporetic structures, he forgets the historicity of literature and philosophy. This does not mean that he ignores historical and historiographical problems; yet he believes that he can solve them within the framework of his rhetorical approach where history itself appears as an ensemble of aporetic texts, i.e. texts that can be deconstructed.[81] The historicity of texts, however, cannot be reduced to 'aporia' and 'Deconstruction'. It rather manifests itself in a *textual diversity* caused by social, cultural and ideological factors. It contains irreconcilable contradiction as well as strict coherence, classical soundness and avant-garde destruction of the work of art. Rousseau may be contradictory; yet for social reasons his contradictions cannot be compared to those of Rilke and Proust.

Since de Man ignores this socio-historical context, he denies his own discourse the possibility of reflecting on itself as an historical construct and of opening up dialogue. In this situation he develops an often obscure monologue which tends to isolate itself from other discourses with a variety of apodictical statements and ambivalent rhetorical figures. The extreme particularity of this monologue is closely related to the 'anti-universalist implications of the term rhetoric' that Michael Cebulla discusses,[82] and, more globally, to the particularistic tendencies of post- and Young Hegelianism mentioned at the beginning of this section.

It therefore sounds absurd when de Man refers in his essay on Bakhtin to 'dogmatic principles' 'that make the dialogic ideology so attractive and so diverse'.[83] Bakhtin's writings are certainly not free from ideology, but a crucial element of ideological discourse is the monologue which implicitly or explicitly excludes the arguments of other discourses and identifies itself in an Hegelian manner with the object (of reality).[84] De Man does exactly this whenever he defines a text dogmatically as an aporetic structure, eliminating its ambivalence between coherence and incoherence, thus implicitly excluding other possible interpretations. He thereby violates his own ethics which demand an acknowledgement of the alterity of the object.

His rhetorical monologue, which plausibly opposes some forms of rationalism and Hegelianism, not only derives from a Nietzschean but also from a Romantic origin. It was pointed out that the transparency of language was already drastically questioned by Friedrich Schlegel, who thereby weakened its conceptuality and universality (see Chapter 1, section 2). Like the Romantics, de Man emphasizes the opaque character of the word – for example in his essay 'Shelley Disfigured' – and the separation of the level of expression from that of content: 'the relative independence of the signifier and its free play in relation to its signifying function.'[85]

It is not surprising when he considers Romanticism as 'a process that now includes us within its horizon' at the beginning of this essay.[86] For besides the concept of allegory which he borrows from the Romantics and develops further in his critique of the symbol (see Chapter 3, section 2),[87] his concept of irony is further proof of the Romantic bias of his type of Deconstruction. Like allegory, irony resists all unifying tendencies: 'at the very moment when irony is thought of as a knowledge able to order and to cure the world, the source of its invention immediately runs dry.'[88]

In contrast to Jean Starobinski, who thinks to have discovered in irony 'a preliminary movement towards a recovered unity, . . . a reconciliation of the self with the world by means of art',[89] de Man regards irony as a Deconstructive factor which blocks the process of unification. He reads Stendhal's La Chartreuse de Parme as characterized by such an irony, a novel telling the fate of two lovers who are not granted unrestricted union: 'When they can see each other they are separated by an unbreachable distance; when they can touch, it has to be in a darkness . . . .'[90] One could also read de Man's work ironically: a theory which claims to present texts as they truly are – namely aporetic – continually confronts the reader with the insight that truth does not exist.

De Man's definition of the concept of irony (in the same way as his concepts of aporia and allegory) is tainted by a negativity which is simultaneously of Nietzschean and Romantic origin. It also appears in the works of the other Deconstructionists – especially in Hillis Miller's. Despite its metamorphoses in different theories, this linguistic and aesthetic negativity is the common denominator of the Deconstructive approaches analysed here.

NOTES

1. D. Lehman, *Signs of the Times: Deconstruction and the Fall of Paul de Man* (1991), p. 79. Cf. also F. Lentricchia, *Criticism and Social Change* (1983), p. 39.
2. Ibid., p. 24.
3. W. Hamacher, 'Unlesbarkeit', in P. de Man, *Allegorien des Lesens* (1988), p. 17.
4. J. H. Miller, *Theory Now and Then* (1991), p. 339.
5. S. Critchley, *The Ethics of Deconstruction: Derrida and Levinas* (1992), p. 28.
6. P. de Man, *Allegories of Reading* (1988), p. 249.
7. J. Ransom, *The New Criticism* (1941), p. 280.
8. P. de Man, *Blindness and Insight* (1983), p. 109.
9. P. de Man, *The Resistance to Theory* (1986), p. 14.
10. Ibid.
11. Ibid., pp. 15–16.
12. Ibid., p. 19.
13. G. W. F. Hegel, *Aesthetics* (1975), p. 404: 'But gradually the metaphorical element in the use of such a word disappears and by custom the word changes from the metaphorical to a literal expression.'
14. J. Culler, *Framing the Sign: Criticism and its Institutions* (1988), p. 122.
15. See, for example, the design for a 'numerical aesthetics' in M. Bense, *Aesthetica* (1965).
16. See A. J. Greimas and J. Courtés, *Sémiotique: Dictionnaire raisonné de la théorie du langage* (1979), pp. 226–8: 'Métaphore'.
17. de Man, *The Resistance to Theory*, p. 109.
18. P. de Man, 'Reply to Raymond Geuss', *Critical Inquiry*, 10 (December 1983), p. 388.
19. C. Norris, *The Deconstructive Turn* (1984), p. 88.
20. O. de Graef, *Serenity in Crisis: A Preface to Paul de Man, 1939–1960* (1993), p. 61.
21. P. de Man, *The Rhetoric of Romanticism* (1984), p. 143.
22. P. de Man, *Critical Writings 1953–1978* (1989), p. 50.
23. Ibid., p. 117.
24. L. Waters, in de Man, *Critical Writings*, p. lviii.
25. G. W. F. Hegel, *Aesthetics* (1975), p. 382: 'But the kinds indicated belong to the *praeambula* or the symbolic form of art because they are generally imperfect and therefore a mere search for true art.'

26. P. de Man, 'Sign and Symbol in Hegel's *Aesthetics*', *Critical Inquiry*, 8 (1982), p. 765.
27. de Man, 'The Rhetoric of Temporality', in *Blindness and Insight*, p. 207.
28. M. Cebulla, *Wahrheit und Authentizität: Zur Entwicklung der Literaturtheorie Paul de Mans* (1992), p. 124.
29. C. Norris, *Paul de Man: Deconstruction and the Critique of Aesthetic Ideology* (1988), pp. 59–60.
30. Hegel, *Aesthetics*, p. 61.
31. de Man, *Blindness and Insight*, p. 58.
32. T. W. Adorno, *Negative Dialectics* (1973), p. 92.
33. Norris, *Paul de Man*, p. 118.
34. Culler, *Framing the Sign*, p. 131.
35. See T. Eagleton, *The Function of Criticism: 'The Spectator' to Post-Structuralism* (1984), ch. 5.
36. Norris, *Paul de Man*, p. 61: 'And if one wanted to find a parallel for de Man's hermeneutics of suspicion, his thoroughgoing principled mistrust of all aesthetic ideologies, then Adorno provides the most striking instance.' A little below he talks about a 'kinship with Adorno'.
37. See de Man, *Blindness and Insight*, p. 165: 'The bases for historical knowledge are not empirical facts but written texts . . . .' Do objects, archeological discoveries, and pictorial representations (such as photographs) have no role to play? Not all of them can be reduced to 'texts', subsumed under a textual concept.
38. Ibid., p. 184.
39. Ibid., p. 162.
40. de Man, *The Resistance to Theory*, p. 63.
41. Ibid., p. 24.
42. de Man, *The Rhetoric of Romanticism*, p. 115.
43. The interplay of various leitmotifs in Nietzsche's philosophy is discussed in T. Meyer, *Nietzsche und die Kunst* (1993), pp. 1–2.
44. B. Johnson, 'Rigorous Unreliability', *Critical Inquiry*, 11 (1984), p. 281.
45. Culler, *Framing the Sign*, pp. 112–13.
46. de Man, *The Rhetoric of Romanticism*, p. 242.
47. Cebulla, *Wahrheit und Authentizität*, p. 61.
48. M. Wigley, in P. Johnson and M. Wigley, *Deconstructivist Architecture* (1988), p. 13.
49. Mark Currie demonstrates how de Man identifies the literary or philosophical text with his own reading and changes points of view constantly in 'The Voices of Paul de Man', *Language and Literature*, 3 (1993), p. 186: 'Through the interplay of these voices de Man can disguise the extent of his own intervention and, like the ventriloquist, put words in Rousseau's mouth.'
50. L. J. Prieto, 'Entwurf einer allgemeinen Semiotik', *Zeitschrift für Semiotik*, 1 (1979), p. 263.

51. de Man, *The Rhetoric of Romanticism*, pp. 11–12.
52. Lehman, *Signs of the Times*, p. 129.
53. Greimas and Courtés, *Semiotics and Language*, p. 255.
54. de Man, *The Rhetoric of Romanticism*, p. 49.
55. Ibid., pp. 50–1.
56. Compare W. Falk, *Leid und Verwandlung: Rilke, Kafka, Trakl und der Epochenstil des Impressionismus und Expressionismus* (1961), pp. 39–98.
57. 'The dark coolness of my room related to the full sunlight of the street as the shadow related to the ray of light, that is to say it was just as luminous and it gave my imagination the total spectacle of the summer, whereas my senses, if I had been on a walk, could only have enjoyed it by fragments; it matched my repose which (thanks to the adventures told by my book and stirring my tranquility) supported, like the quiet of a motionless hand in the middle of a running brook the shock and the motion of a torrent of activity'; trans. from the Pléiade edition (1951), p. 83; de Man, *The Rhetoric of Romanticism*, pp. 13–14.
58. Ibid., pp. 14–15.
59. Ibid., p. 15.
60. See my critique of de Man's reading of Proust in *Literarische Ästhetik*, pp. 352–5. M. Currie questions de Man's approach to Proust in even greater detail in 'The Voices of Paul de Man', where he states on p. 190: 'De Man's progress towards the aporia of hidden and manifest content in Proust is nothing more than the elaboration of his initial imperfect translation.'
61. M. Proust, 'A propos du "style" de Flaubert', *Contre Sainte-Beuve* (1971), p. 586.
62. G. Genette, 'Métonymie chez Proust', *Figures III* (1972), p. 42.
63. Greimas and Courtés, *Semiotics and Language*, p. 193.
64. P. de Man, 'Phenomenality and Materiality in Kant', *Hermeneutics: Questions and Prospects* (1984), p. 136.
65. Ibid., p. 137.
66. Ibid., p. 143.
67. I. Kant, *The Critique of Pure Reason, The Critique of Practical Reason, The Critique of Judgement* (1952), p. 501.
68. T. W. Adorno, 'George', *Notes to Literature IV*, vol. 2 (1992), p. 182.
69. de Man, *The Rhetoric of Romanticism*, p. 226.
70. P. de Man, 'The Rhetoric of Blindness', *Blindness and Insight* (1989), p. 136.
71. de Man, *The Resistance to Theory*, p. 118.
72. de Man, 'The Rhetoric of Blindness', p. 133.
73. J.-J. Rousseau, *The Social Contract and Discourse on the Origin of Inequality* (1967), p. 194.
74. Ibid., pp. 194–5.
75. Ibid., p. 194.
76. de Man, *The Rhetoric of Romanticism*, p. 265.

77. Ibid., p. 275.
78. Ibid.
79. See Norris, *Paul de Man*, ch. 2.
80. de Man, *Blindness and Insight*, p. 28.
81. Ibid., p. 165.
82. Cebulla, *Wahrheit und Authentizität*, p. 139.
83. De Man, *The Resistance to Theory*, p. 111.
84. On the discursive demarcations between ideology and Critical Theory, see my *Ideologie und Theorie* (1989), ch. 12.
85. de Man, *The Rhetoric of Romanticism*, p. 114.
86. Ibid., p. 94.
87. See M.-G. Choi, 'Frühromantische Dekonstruktion und dekonstruktive Frühromantik: Paul de Man und Friedrich Schlegel', in *Ästhetik und Rhetorik: Lektüren zu Paul de Man* (1993), p. 192: 'In contrast to Szondi and Starobinski, who both think to have discovered in irony an historical and philosophical synthesis of the real and the ideal, art and life, self and world, de Man regards irony as the negation of synthesis, as a permanently discontinuous process.' In the same way as aporia and allegory, irony features here as an anti-Hegelian concept.
88. de Man, 'The Rhetoric of Temporality', *Blindness and Insight*, p. 218.
89. Ibid., p. 219.
90. Ibid., p. 228.

4

J. HILLIS MILLER, OR
CRITICISM AS ETHICS

In contrast to Paul de Man, who started from Heidegger's existential ontology and attempted to apply Nietzsche's concept of rhetorics to literary criticism, J. Hillis Miller was a disciple of Georges Poulet (who taught in the United States) and began to work in the literary and philosophical tradition of the so-called Geneva School of Jean-Pierre Richard, Marcel Raymond, Albert Béguin and Georges Poulet. The two versions of his thesis on *Charles Dickens: The World of His Novels* (1959), his monographs *The Disappearance of God* and *Poets of Reality* as well as various articles from the 1960s (some of which were reprinted in *Theory Now and Then*) all bear the imprint of Geneva methodology.

The influence of Poulet, Raymond and Béguin is particularly pronounced in Miller's thematic and phenomenological analyses, all of which aim at the unification of the world in view of an individual consciousness (see Chapter 2, section 4; Jean-Pierre Richard). '[T]he work of the Geneva critics took possession of my imagination', Miller explains in *Victorian Subjects*.[1] In his deconstructive phase he turns away from this tradition of thought which focuses on coherence and even attempts to deconstruct Poulet's phenomenological approach.[2]

He nonetheless continues to use some key concepts of the Geneva School and also remains faithful to the close reading of New Criticism, turning it into a subtle instrument of Deconstruction by over-refining its semantic grid. Howard Felperin shows that this subversive 'refunctionalization' of close reading is a strategy common to all Yale theorists: 'What the Yale Deconstructionists, institutional heirs apparent to new criticism, did, was to reveal the formal project of their predecessors as having barely scratched the surface of the rhetorical multiplicity it had set out to explore.'[3]

In this theoretical scenario critics like de Man and Miller have no choice but to analyse the cognitive theoretical premises of New Criticism and to show that the structures of meaning defined by the New Critics for example are nothing but metaphysical fantasy creations. 'Unlike the New Critics', Miller remarks, 'Deconstructionists argue that you can't take it for granted that a good work of literature is going to be organically unified.'[4]

His aim to deconstruct Poulet's unifying project which, in Miller's view, undercuts its own fundamental assumptions,[5] corresponds to his critique of the coherence postulate in New Criticism. Poulet's problems, the Yale scholar argues, confirm Derrida's view that the presence of meaning is a logocentric chimera and that each metaphysical project eventually founders in *différance* (see Chapter 2, section 3).

Nonetheless, Miller remains faithful to a crucial aspect of New Criticism when he rejects the demand for a scientific literary theory. He claims, for example, that '[t]he study of literature cannot be justified in the same way as scientific research can'.[6] His rejection of a scientific criticism in the sense of semiotics (Bense, Greimas), Marxism (Althusser) or phenomenology (Husserl) leads to an assault on the boundaries between criticism and literature – similar to Derrida's and Hartman's. 'Literary criticism is literature at a second degree', we read in *Theory Now and Then*.[7] In this respect the Deconstructionist appears as an heir of the Romantics, who also regarded the literary critic as an extended author (see Chapter 5).

The Romantic orientation of theory towards literature and the rhetorical figure is coupled in the later Miller with an orientation towards Derrida's and de Man's Deconstruction. 'By deconstruction', he explains his own project, 'I mean reading as it is practiced by Jacques Derrida, Paul de Man and myself, along with an increasing number of others in this country and abroad.'[8]

1 CRITICISM AS ETHICS

In the United States this form of reading assumes an ethical character which, as G. Douglas Atkins claims, serves Deconstruction as a
kind of insurance policy against relativism from which it can only
disentangle itself with difficulty.[9] An ethical moment is certainly
inherent in Deconstructive close reading, since readers are expected
to refrain from inventing anything and to focus on the textual
structure which they find in the literary work. This, however, is an
impossible task, for each reading is made up of theoretical and
ideological decisions. In other words: the ethics of reading are
inseparable from the politics of reading.

A definition of ethical reading is to be found in Miller's *Victorian
Subjects*, a study of nineteenth-century English Literature: 'The
ethics of reading is the power of the words over the mind and
words of the reader.'[10] What is primarily at stake is what Simon
Critchley calls the 'alterity of the text' (see Chapter 3). This aspect
is the starting point of every 'good reading' and can be considered
the basis of Deconstruction of which Miller claims in *The Ethics of
Reading*: 'Deconstruction is neither more nor less than good reading
as such.'[11]

Like the proponents of close reading or the French *explication de
texte* Miller refers to 'adequate interpretation'[12] and claims that the
unreadability diagnosed by the American Deconstructionists in
every possible context is inherent in the text itself: 'The "unreadability" is not located in the reader but in the text itself . . . .'[13] This
idea is not new, for it is to a large extent compatible with the New
Critics' text-oriented approach which is based on the assumption
that readers have to discover the objective structure of the work in
question.

It contradicts the insights of modern hermeneutics and aesthetics
of reception, both of which claim that the meanings of texts emerge
in a complex interaction of text and reader and can therefore differ
from audience to audience.[14] In other words: this ethical or Deconstructionist conception of the text ignores the creative contribution
of the reading subjects and simultaneously obliterates the complementary problems of *meta-language* and the *object construction*
within meta-language.

Those literary scholars and philosophers who are primarily con-

cerned with these problems (especially the semioticians and herme-
neuticians) would undoubtedly claim that Miller has fallen victim
to a common-sense assumption when he states that *unreadability*
must exclusively be sought in the text itself. There is no doubt
that unreadable, contradictory and aporetic texts exist; yet the
(re-)construction of the contradictions and aporias partly depends
on the recipient's meta-language, which can have a theoretical,
moral or political character.

Considering the heterogeneity of theoretical meta-languages it is
not surprising that the metaphysical and aesthetic contradictions
described by a Marxist, like Lucien Goldmann, or an exponent of
Critical Theory, like Theodor W. Adorno, strongly differ from
aporias described or constructed by Derrida, de Man and Miller.
Hence it is futile to claim at this stage that a Marxist or Deconstructionist theory is 'wrong'. For a critical debate between heterogeneous positions seems sensible only when the question of
meta-language is raised, the very question that de Man and Miller
neglect. The commendable respect for the alterity of the object
should encourage us to recognize the role of meta-language in the
construction of objects (the reconstruction of texts) and to take self-
critical reflection on a meta-linguistic level seriously. After all, the
alterity of objects is only recognizable when the theoretical subject
is aware of the particularity of its own discourse and of its
constructions.

It will become clear that their neglect of the crucial question
concerning the construction of objects in the context of a meta-
language prevents the Deconstructionists from recognizing the historical character of literature and from reflecting on the historicity
and contingency of their own discourses. For both de Man and
Miller tend to assume that *all* texts of *all* ages are aporetic,
undecidable and unreadable and, in the last instance, deconstruct
themselves.

Yet at this stage it is the ethical aspect of Miller's Deconstruction
and not the problem of historicity that deserves closer scrutiny. For
one suspects that Miller's respect for the alterity of the text leads to
an hidden dogmatization of his own reading. The overall validity of
his theory which Miller postulates, availing himself of Kant's
universalism, is hardly a fact that one must simply acknowledge.

It is quite unlikely, for example, that the majority of Kantians would agree with Miller when he remarks about Kant's ethics: 'What the good reader confronts in the end is not the moral law brought into the open at last in a clear example, but the unreadability of the text.'[15] Even if one considers Miller's reading of Kant productive, or at least stimulating, one would hesitate to accept it as generally applicable or simply 'true'. As a matter of fact, the majority of readers and critics of Kant do not consider his *Foundations of a Metaphysics of Morals* unreadable. The 'unreadability' Derrida and de Man located in the *Critique of Judgement* and Miller in Kant's writings on ethics cannot simply be traced back to philosophical or logical incompetence, but it is nonetheless linked to the particularities of a Deconstructive discourse motivated by the search for contradictions and aporias.

One might have similar reservations concerning Miller's commentaries on literature, whose claim of general applicability should stun every scholar of literature trained in dialectics and semiotics. Thus Miller claims, for instance, pondering on his interpretation of Yeats's poem 'Nineteen Hundred and Nineteen': 'I would say that my reading of Yeats's poem is right, that all right-thinking people will come, given enough time, to my reading.'[16]

It is worthwhile dissecting this sentence critically in terms of its ideology, paying particular attention to two questions: who defines the ideas of the 'right-thinking people'? And how much time should these people be granted? It seems that this thinking is defined by Miller himself in the context of his own discourse where 'right-thinking people' become a mythical actant[17] comparable with the actant 'God' in the sermon of a priest, the actant 'the people' in a politician's speech or the actant 'proletariat' in many Marxist-Leninist discourses: 'God expects you to ... The German, French, Russian people demand that ... The proletariat (the working classes) will not accept that ...' Expected and demanded is what the orator and his group expect, demand and hope for. Mythical actants such as 'God', 'the people' and 'the proletariat' serve as their rhetorical points of reference with whose aid they attempt to convince their listeners or readers. The 'right-thinking people' also become such a mythical and rhetorical reference point whose ideological value consists in the fact that it cannot make any claims itself, but provides a semblance of consensus all the same. In order to ensure that the mythical actant does not suddenly spring to life and raise his voice (as a critical reader), Miller advises that he be 'given enough time'.

In other words: we are faced here with a classical immunization strategy along the lines of Critical Rationalism.[18] In this context one should also read Miller's generalization in *Hawthorne and History*: 'I'm prepared to say that all good readers are deconstructionists . . . .'[19] From this follows that those who are not Deconstructionists are bad readers. There ought to be an ethics of discourse as well, not only one of reading.

Finally, Miller himself questions the universal applicability of his mode of reading when he remarks in a particularistic manner: 'Each act of reading is unique.'[20] If one takes this argument seriously, it becomes difficult to imagine any form of reading that can be generally applied and be self-evident to all 'right-thinking' people. This shows how much the striving for universality inherent in all theory clashes with a Nietzschean and rhetorical particularism in Miller – as it does in de Man.[21]

2 AMBIVALENCE AND DIALECTICS: NIETZSCHE'S LEGACY

Like Derrida and Paul de Man, Miller also argues from within a Young Hegelian and Nietzschean context when he rejects Hegel's concept of *Aufhebung*, thereby putting the entire Hegelian dialectic into question. Commenting on the logocentrism and nihilism that, in his opinion, interact in Shelley's poem 'The Triumph of Life', he points out that they 'are related to one another in a way which is not antithesis and which may not be synthesized in any dialectical *Aufhebung*'.[22] Here Miller once more confirms the idea that the Deconstructive contradiction must be understood in a Nietzschean context as an extreme ambivalence which excludes the unity of opposites as 'synthesis in a higher sphere' (Hegel) or as 'truth content' (Adorno).

The unity of opposites envisaged by Miller or de Man and anticipated by Nietzsche in his critique of metaphysics functions deconstructively and aporetically. It does not generate a dialectical synthesis or a new concept of truth. The mechanisms of dialectics are rendered dysfunctional by Derrida's *différance* to which Miller refers in *Theory Now and Then*, where he questions opposites as such: 'In the place of the notion of opposites . . . Nietzsche would put the idea of degrees of difference, differentiated forces which are not opposites, but points on the same scale, distinctions of the same energy, as reason is nature deferred or separated from itself.'[23] In other words: the opposition cannot be resolved, since it does not really exist, since it is projected into infinity as part of a gradual differentiation, of *différance*.

Miller seems to read Hegel against the grain when he claims in *The Linguistic Moment* that it is impossible to find a synthesis of consciousness and nature in Wordsworth's poetic works and that a systematic comparison of his poems does not produce a meaningful totality, but 'an unfixable sequence of deferred readings'.[24] At this point one will recall Marxist and psychoanalytic interpretations in which the systematic textual hermeneutic serves to determine the 'structure of meaning' (Goldmann) or the 'personal myth' (Mauron) and to prove that in every textual part a meaningful totality is at work. Miller does follow this dialectic strain of thought, but turns it in a Deconstructive way against the postulate of coherence, thus dismantling what dialecticians and psychoanalysts have joined meticulously.

Especially in his commentaries on William Wordsworth's poems, he tries to prove that the contradictions and oppositions of this poetry cannot be resolved in an all-embracing structure of meaning. He rejects all attempts of traditional philologists to view the development of Wordsworth's work within the framework of a three-phase Hegelian scheme, at the end of which stands a reconciliation with nature. It seems important to retrace Miller's argument in detail, for it reveals how much contemporary literary criticism (aesthetics and philosophy) still struggles against Hegelian dialectics and its postulates of coherence. It shows, moreover, that Miller – in a similar way as the other Deconstructionists – continues the Young Hegelian and Nietzschean rebellion against Hegel's system with new means.

Miller regards the contradictions which pervade Wordsworth's work as irreconcilable: 'Conflict there may be in Wordsworth, but this conflict has been seen by many critics as a middle stage in a three-stage dialectic leading from an early harmony with nature to an antithetical period of self-consciousness and alienation. This second stage is the discovery of the dangerous autonomy of the imagination. The final stage is the rejection of that detachment and a consequent return at a higher level to a calm reconciliation with nature, for "Nature never did betray/The heart that loved her".' Miller comments on this view with the throwaway remark: 'Wordsworth's thought in fact is not dialectical.'[25] For the early phases of his literary experience (for example the alienation from nature) are not overcome even in the climaxes of his poems. They continually outbalance one another and cannot be contained in an unambiguous formula.

Miller's commentaries on Wordsworth's so-called *Lucy* poems can be read as variations of this argument. In his theoretically and methodically rather heterogeneous interpretation of the poem 'A Slumber did My Spirit Seal' he attempts among other things to demonstrate that the protagonist appears as a *thing* in two different ways: as a 'young thing' on an anthropomorphic plane and (after her death) as a lifeless body on the physical and natural plane, i.e. as a 'thing' in the literal sense. Between these two meanings of the term 'thing' no mediation is possible, Miller claims, when he insists on 'the unbridgeable gap between one meaning of the word "thing" and the other'.[26]

It is understandable that not only Miller, but every other reader finds it hard to mediate between the 'young thing' full of life and Lucy's lifeless body as a 'thing'. Yet a semantic analysis (even a non-Hegelian one) need not stop at the opposition between life and death. The text shows that the two stanzas have semantic elements in common which may also make the postulate of coherence appear plausible:

> A slumber did my spirit seal;
> I had no human fears:
> She seemed a thing that could not feel
> The touch of earthly years.
>
> No motion has she now, no force;
> She neither hears nor sees;
> Rolled round in earth's diurnal course,
> With rocks, and stones, and trees.

We are neither concerned with Miller's overall interpretation of the poem (which also displays psychoanalystic aspects) nor with the poem as a whole, but with the word *thing* and the 'thing-likeness' of the female protagonist which is linked to the concept of *life* in the first stanza, to that of *death* in the second. At closer inspection it becomes clear that this 'thing-likeness' is defined both in the first and the second stanza beyond the opposition *life/death* as *privative*: as lacking consciousness ('could not feel'; 'neither hears nor sees') and *non-human* ('no human fears'; 'with rocks, and stones, and trees'). Could it not be that these common elements bridge the gap between life and death postulated by Miller, thus creating the fascinating paradox of the poem that Lucy remains 'the same' despite her transition from life to death? This question in itself, which is of course not intended as an alternative to Miller's global interpretation, makes one suspect that his poetics is perhaps just as one-sided as that of the Hegelians, semioticians or other Deconstructionists.[27]

It is a Nietzschean poetics. For Nietzsche was the first to reject Hegel's synthesizing dialectic without searching, like the thinkers of Critical Theory, for a truth content in the unity of opposites. Harold Schweizer comments on Miller's Nietzscheanism: 'Miller's philosophical position, which is in part grounded on Nietzsche's, a work without ground, is thus, like Nietzsche's work, post-philosophic.'[28]

Its post-philosophical character is not only confirmed by its rejection of Hegelian dialectics, but also by Miller's Nietzschean critique of the concept of subject. The Deconstructionist continues the destruction of metaphysics when he mentions approvingly Nietzsche's 'attempt to deconstruct the idea of the unity of the "thinking I"'.[29] In *Ariadne's Thread*, a more recent work, he continues his critique of the concept of subject and continually refers to Nietzsche: 'Nietzsche's dismantling of the notion of the substantial self culminates in the idea that a single body may be inhabited by multiple selves.'[30]

This plurality of the individual self is matched by the heterogeneity of the literary and philosophical text, for as an anti-Hegelian and Nietzschean Miller claims: 'After the disappearance of the gods the poet finds himself in a place where opposites are simultaneously true.'[31] At this stage it becomes obvious that even Miller's quite heterogeneous work displays a continuing thread which links his early texts (for example *The Disappearance of God* of 1963) with his Deconstructionist analyses: the death of God and the resulting impossibility of conceptualizing the history of mankind as a meaningful unity.

3 UNDECIDABILITY AND CONTRADICTION

The Nietzschean claim that 'opposites are simultaneously true' which Miller repeats in connection with the American poet Wallace Stevens appears in a variety of forms in almost all of his critical comments on literature. It is reminiscent of the aporias discovered by Paul de Man and regularly referred to by Miller. Both in Shelley's 'The Triumph of Life' and in George Eliot's *Adam Bede*, (see Chapter 4, section 4), in Joseph Conrad's *Lord Jim* and in Goethe's *Die Wahlverwandtschaften*, Miller claims to encounter two incompatible structures of meaning which make the text appear as an aporetic construct and confront the conscientious reader with the dilemma of *undecidability*.

Miller's commentary on Conrad's *Lord Jim* is particularly characteristic of the Nietzschean problematic of ambivalence. At the very beginning of his analysis the Deconstructionist questions the Hegelian and Structuralist idea of the work's unity: 'The concept of the organic unity of the work of art cannot be detached from its theological basis.'[32]

This basis has to be deconstructed, and Miller attempts to show that the protagonist Jim in particular remains an enigmatic figure which cannot be defined at any point and whose ambivalence is confirmed at the end of the novel: 'The ending is a tissue of unanswered questions in which Marlow affirms once more not that Jim is a hero or that Jim is a coward, but that he remains an indecipherable mystery.'[33]

This enigma is partly created by the novel's main protagonist's ambivalent construction which at one point makes him appear as a 'light that illuminates the darkness', at another as 'blackness that stands out against a blinding light'.[34] Confronted with such contradictions the reader is unable to define protagonist or plot unambiguously and to draw clear conclusions.[35]

In accordance with his theses on the ethics of reading, Miller assumes that contradictions and ambiguities are to be sought in the text itself and that it would be a mistake to locate the heterogeneity and *indeterminacy* of the novel outside it – for instance in the consciousness of the reader: 'The indeterminacy lies in the multiplicity of incompatible explanations which the novel offers and in the lack of evidence justifying a choice of one over the others.'[36] In other words, undecidability is a feature of the text and closely related to the extreme ambivalence of protagonists and actions.

Yet the indeterminacy of Conrad's novel not only results from ambivalence and the contradictions emerging from it, but also from the fact that in this novel repetitions are only seemingly repetitions, since the recurring elements of the text are in fact heterogeneous, incommensurable and fail to explain one another. They merely increase the reader's confusion. Hence Miller emphasizes the fact of 'each example being as enigmatic as all the others'[37] and throwing no light on the total context.

Miller's commentary on Emily Brontë's *Wuthering Heights* shows what this kind of deconstructive repetition looks like in close-up. In this novel not so much incompatibility or ambivalence, but the incommensurability of textual elements appears to be crucial. In *Fiction and Repetition* Miller sums up his basic thesis concerning *Wuthering Heights*: 'My argument is that the best readings will be the ones which best account for the heterogeneity of the text, its presentation of a definite group of possible meanings which are systematically interconnected, determined by the text, but logically incompatible.'[38]

Irreconcilable or incommensurable? This question comes to mind when Miller compares three longer passages from Emily Brontë's novel and discovers that they may be similar as realist descriptions, but ultimately remain incommensurable. 'This uniqueness', he explains, 'makes each incommensurate with any of the others.'[39] First of all one needs to ask how three texts can be 'similar' on the one hand, yet unique and incommensurable on the other. Does not the similarity of two or more elements imply that they are comparable and therefore commensurable? Moreover, according to which semantic or syntactic criteria has Miller selected and classified the three passages when he considers them incommensurable? The attentive reader would also like to know how the irreconcilability postulated by Miller at the outset relates to incommensurability.

Miller does not deal with the relationship of these terms. He merely attempts to clarify the relationship between uniqueness and similarity when he states: 'These three texts are similar, but its similarity is, in part at least, the fact that each is unique in the structural modes it presents the reader.'[40]

He appears to advocate a kind of *iterability* or *dissemination* in a Derridean sense when he claims that the three texts are only similar because of their uniqueness, i.e. their incomparability. This paradox is tempered by the remark that each of the quoted passages is 'realist', since it describes certain natural and man-made objects. The three texts thus seem to possess a common denominator, namely 'realism'.

'Yes and no', would be Miller's reply, reminding us of a crucial argument of his interpretation: the 'fact' observed or constructed by him that all similarities in *Wuthering Heights* are seeming similarities only which lead both the main narrator Lockwood and the readers astray. They believe they are witnessing a repetition of similar or comparable elements forming a coherent whole, and thus overlook the irreducible heterogeneity of these elements. This explains why the novel lacks a centre (Miller mentions a 'missing centre'[41]) and forms no semantic unity.

Repetition as a deconstructive principle will be dealt with in more detail in the next section. Here we are primarily concerned with Miller's concept of undecidability based on the idea that literary texts contain irreconcilable elements, so that the reader cannot decide which meaning is the correct one. Miller's commentary on *Wuthering Heights* shows, however, that terms such as irreconcilability and incommensurability are not clearly distinguished, so that the argument loses focus.

Another aspect of Miller's Deconstruction related to extreme ambivalence is the contradiction or self-contradiction inherent in the text. It is brought about by the author's and narrator's conscious betrayal and destruction of their aesthetic or stylistic ideal. Miller's commentaries on Goethe's *Die Wahlverwandtschaften* and George Eliot's *Adam Bede* can serve as illustrations of this thesis, reminiscent of Paul de Man's claim that Proust praises the metaphor, yet, despite himself, heavily relies on metonymy.

Goethe himself, Miller claims, interprets *Die Wahlverwandtschaften* on an 'aesthetic-metaphysical' plane and points out that the novel is founded on a 'totalizing ontology'.[42] He admits that many elements of the novel appear to confirm such an ontology, since they encourage the reader to regard individuals as 'indestructible preexisting substances securely grounded in some transhuman being'.[43]

This metaphysical harmony sanctioned by superficial readings is, however, challenged by the figure of Mittler. For it is Mittler, in whom many recognize Goethe's stand-in within the novel, who destroys the metaphysical-aesthetic harmony he attempts to preserve by all means. Whenever he interferes in a mediating way [*Mittler* in German means 'mediator' (translator's note)] in order to save a human relationship in accordance with God's word, he destroys it and even brings about the death of two protagonists. At the same time Goethe undermines his plan to convince the readers of the sacred character of marriage. This contradiction is summed up by Miller in *Ariadne's Thread*: 'Far from being a conservative work defending the sanctity of marriage, as Goethe himself sometimes wanted to think it was, *Die Wahlverwandtschaften* is, on one side of its sustained ironic double meaning, a radical questioning of the marriage bond.'[44]

In order to make such general claims, Miller ought to have engaged in a thorough analysis of the semantic and narrative structures of *Die Wahlverwandtschaften*. His highly selective and limited strategies that are also characteristic of his interpretations of *Wuthering Heights* and *Lord Jim* by no means justify such claims, and one could object with Greimas that the text appears contradictory, ambivalent or open because it has not been analysed systematically. This objection, however, should not be confused with the claim that all texts are homogenous structures which can be reduced to a single meaning.

Miller's reading of *Die Wahlverwandtschaften* amply illustrates his own definition of Deconstruction: 'An antimetaphysical or "deconstructive" form of literary study attempts to show that in a given work of literature, in a different way in each case, metaphysical assumptions are both present and at the same time undermined by the text itself.'[45]

His comments on George Eliot's novel *Adam Bede* are also based on brilliant *aperçus* rather than on semantic or narrative analysis. They start from the assumption that the doctrine of realism which the novelist explains in the famous seventeenth chapter of her novel ('In Which the Story Pauses a Little') is systematically undermined by her own narrative. On the one hand Eliot derives her own realist aesthetics from a truthful style that renounces the fantastic and abandons a rhetoric of exaggeration; on the other hand her text continually reveals its dependence on tropes such as metaphor, metonymy and catachresis and on rhetorics in general. The seventeenth chapter as such owes its persuasive force to a rhetoric of tropes: 'Realist narration must depend, as this chapter of *Adam Bede* conspicuously does, on figurative language.'[46] In *Victorian Subjects* Miller sums up his critique of Eliot's realism: 'The text warns against the argument by tropes on which the text itself depends.'[47]

Miller calls this contradiction between the aesthetics or stylistics of authors and their narrative the linguistic moment: 'By "linguistic moment" I mean the moment in a work of literature when its own medium is put in question.'[48] At this point the deconstructive search for contradictions becomes a rhetorical critique meant to demonstrate the dependence of all texts on the trope, the figure of speech.

It remains questionable, however, whether George Eliot actually claims that realism and the rhetorical figure are irreconcilable. An attentive reading of *Adam Bede* merely shows that the author rejects exaggeration and a Classicist idealization of the protagonists. She turns against writers 'who pant after the ideal', and explains: 'I aspire to give no more than a faithful account of men and things as they have mirrored themselves in my mind.'[49] Her theses on realism are directed against an abstract idealization of reality, not against the use of the mirror metaphor, the metonymy or any other figure of speech. Hence the contradiction between realism and figurative speech in Eliot is an abstract construction comparable to de Man's improbable opposition between metaphor and metonymy in Proust. It is quite unlikely that such a *tour de force* is compatible with an ethics of reading in Miller's sense.

4 REPETITION AND RHETORICS

In the preceding section it became clear that Miller considers the repetition of textual elements a deconstructive principle in the manner of *iterability*. Although he does not explicitly refer to Derrida's *iterability* in *Fiction and Repetition*, he argues along similar lines as the author of 'La Double séance' and 'Signature, Event, Context' when he distinguishes two kinds of repetition: a Platonic and a Nietzschean one.

Following Gilles Deleuze, he defines Platonic repetition as a process 'that rests on a solid archetypal model that remains unaffected by the repetition'. He adds 'All other examples are copies of this model'.[50] In other words: that which is repeated is a copy of the original model, the pure form or idea in Plato's sense, and repetition can only be understood as a re-occurrence of that which is identical with itself.

Repetition assumes a completely different character in a Nietzschean context: 'The other, Nietzschean mode of repetition posits a world based on difference. Each thing, this other theory would assume, is unique, intrinsically different from every other thing. Similarity arises against the background of this "*disparité du fond*". It is not a world of copies but of what Deleuze calls "simulacra" or "phantasms".'[51]

At this point one is reminded not only of Miller's commentaries on *Wuthering Heights* based on the idea that the similarities in the novel are only apparent similarities lacking coherence, but also of the tendency towards extreme particularization which marks the entire Nietzschean inheritance of Deconstruction. One need only recall Nietzsche's polemic against conceptualization: 'Each concept evolves from the equation of the unequal . . . Overlooking the individual and real gives us the concept . . . .'[52] The Deconstructionist argues with Nietzsche in favour of this individual and unique quality and against conceptual generalization or *iterativity* (see Chapter 2, section 3).

In several, sometimes very stimulating essays, published in *Fiction and Repetition* and *Tropes, Parables, Performatives*, Miller demonstrates how the two contrary forms of repetition interact and how much they resist a reading geared towards coherence. In his analyses of Gerard Manley Hopkins's poem *The Wreck of the Deutschland* he attempts to show that in this long poem the two forms of repetition coexist engendering an irreconcilable contradiction. This contradiction is due to the fact that Hopkins's theological framework ('overthought') articulates the first, Platonic form of repetition, while in his linguistic theory ('underthought') the second form of repetition predominates and dissolves the metaphysical frame. 'His overthought', concludes Miller, 'is an example of the first theory of repetition, his underthought of the second.'[53]

Miller applies this model of analysis to *Wuthering Heights* and other nineteenth-century novels. His reading of Thomas Hardy's *Tess of the d'Urbervilles* demonstrates in great detail the coincidence of the two modes of repetition. It will therefore be briefly summarized here. As in his analyses of *Wuthering Heights*, Miller starts from the assumption that the second, deconstructive kind of repetition is 'generated out of difference', 'out of a chain of events, characters or gestures which are always different from one another'.[54]

In a first step he chooses a theme of the novel which appears particularly important: the rape of Tess associated with other elements of violence and with writing as 'inscription', 'imprint' and 'graft': 'The word "graft" comes from a word meaning carving, cutting, or inscribing.'[55] All of these elements have the colour red in common, a symbol of sexuality and the 'masculine sun'.

In this context a concatenation of red things becomes visible which accompanies the novel's plot: the red ribbon in Tess's hair, the strawberry she is forced to eat by Alex, who has raped her; the rose Alex offers to her which hurts her chin, etc. The recurrence of 'red' continually evokes 'sexual union', 'physical violence' and 'writing'.

Some readers might get the impression that Miller is engaged in a rather conventional thematic analysis – for example along the lines of Jean-Pierre Richard (see Chapter 2, section 4) – an analysis primarily concerned with presenting the coherence of the text on a thematic level. They are also reminded of Greimas's structural semiotics according to which the iterativity of certain *semes* (*classemes*) leads to coherence. Yet Miller outlines this Platonic recurrence so thoroughly only in order to subvert it: in order to show how *iterativity* (Greimas) turns into *iterability* (Derrida).

In a first step, Miller discovers that the text consists of a number of meanings among which the sequence of 'red things' assumes an important, though not dominant, part. Metaphoric expressions for writing, themes such as sexuality or murder, theoretical or quasi-mythological elements (for example the association of Tess with harvest) fulfil equally important functions, although none of these functions is clearly dominant. The various elements of the novel keep one another in check and cannot be combined in one structure of meaning or depth structure in a Structuralist sense.

The 'red things', for example, form no *isotopy* in Greimas's sense, since, 'The relation among the links in a chain of meaning in *Tess of the d'Urbervilles* is always repetition with a difference, and the difference is as important as the repetition.'[56] Disparity reigns between the individual strands of meaning, and not homogeneity, so that Miller can speak of 'multiple incompatible explanations of what happens to Tess'. He adds: 'They cannot all be true, and yet they are all there in the words of the novel.'[57] The second, Nietzschean kind of repetition therefore leads to contradiction and aporia.

The fact that Miller's notion of a Nietzschean or Deconstructive repetition is questionable was already mentioned in the preceding section. Every Structuralist, every theoretician indebted to dialectics would agree with him that in a literary or philosophical text difference is just as important as repetition. After all, redundancy entails differentiation in the same way as didactic examples which illustrate a problem elucidate various aspects of this problem and thus follow the principle of differentiation. Yet Miller, like Derrida, starts from the one-sided assumption that repetition (as *iterability*) must have disparity and heterogeneity as its consequence. That this need not be the case is demonstrated by the Platonic or metaphysical principle of repetition which does create coherence. One would have to relate the two forms of repetition dialectically instead of opposing them in an aporia. For iterativity and redundancy *need* not lead to contradiction and the destruction of meaning, especially since every text deriving from formal logic or mathematics demonstrates that signs can be repeated without losing their identity.

The idea that Miller's scepticism leads to a radical agnosticism is borne out by his study *Hawthorne and History*, which focuses on Hawthorne's short story *The Minister's Black Veil*. This text is also important because it connects crucial components of Miller's premises: the repetition which dissolves coherence (this time in the process of reading), semantic undecidability and the rhetorics of tropes.

The theme and plot of the short story can be rendered in a few words: Reverend Hooper, who is in charge of a religious congregation in New England, one day appears before the assembled believers with his head covered by a black veil. Even the pleas of his fiancée Elizabeth fail to make him take off the veil or explain his behaviour, and Hooper wears the veil until he dies.

Miller attempts to show, among other things, that the story is an allegory of its own unreadability and that the veil acts as a metaphor of this unreadability: 'The veil is the type and symbol of the fact that all signs are potentially unreadable or that the reading of them is potentially unverifiable. If the reader has no access to what lies behind a sign but another sign, then all reading of signs cannot be sure whether or not it is in error. Reading would then be a perpetual wandering or displacement that can never be checked against anything except another sign.'[58] In this context, Miller refers once again to the 'linguistic turn' which implies that as readers we are only ever faced with signs that cannot be referred back to concepts or 'ideas' in Plato's sense, but merely hide further signs. The 'linguistic turn', Miller adds, emphasizes 'the role of figurative language in the "constitution of meanings" '.[59] In *The Minister's Black Veil*, the veil functions as symbol and metaphor of this 'linguistic turn' and of unreadability in general. The short story which carries the subtitle *A Parable* becomes a parable of its own inscrutability and makes the reader face yet another veil behind the one he is supposed to lift. The human face itself appears as an opaque ensemble of signs not dissimilar to the veil: 'I look around me, and, lo! On every visage a Black Veil', exclaims Reverend Hooper at the close of the story.

Since there is no true face, no truth or concept that can be pinned down behind any of the many veils evoked by the metaphors and metonymies of the text, the reader cannot decide in favour of any one meaning, and Miller opts for undecidability: 'The veil and the story are undecidable in meaning.'[60]

It is quite impossible to decide in favour of an ideological or psychoanalytic reading, whose proponents would like to lift the veil once and for all in order to discover the 'repressive character of Puritanism' or 'repressed sexuality'. In Hawthorne's story sexuality and repression certainly play an important part, Miller admits, yet they only form one of the chains of meaning and not a conceptual basis to which the literary system of signs could be reduced. Miller calls the idea that such a conceptual basis exists the 'ideology of unveiling'[61] that is itself in need of being deconstructed. His commentary on Hawthorne's story is meant to be a contribution to this kind of Deconstruction.

Since Miller asserts the 'impossibility of expressing anything verifiable'[62] in the context of this story, one must assume that his Deconstruction of ideology aims at *nothing*. For why do we criticize ideologies – and Miller claims to criticize also the 'theoretical ideology' (whatever that may be) along with the 'ideology of unveiling' – if the truth remains inaccessible even as a provisional or partial one? The concept of ideology itself loses its meaning when its antonyms such as truth, science and theory are rhetorically deconstructed or simply abandoned.

5 DECONSTRUCTING HISTORY: CRITIQUE AND OUTLOOK

In *Hawthorne and History* Miller suggests that not only the literary text and the human face are opaque constellations of signs that cannot be made transparent by concepts, but that history itself is a complex ensemble of signs lacking a fixed meaning. Hawthorne's short story, read by Miller as a 'parable of history',[63] leads to the assumption 'that an historical event cannot be fully incorporated into concepts of exteriority, material fact, "experience", the body, power, force, social or economic "realities"'.[64] History itself, Miller claims, can only be understood as a system of signs in a wider sense and must therefore be *read*. Even the term 'reading' assumes a general meaning: 'It means not just reading literary works, but reading historical documents, works of art, material artefacts, cultural signs of all sorts.'[65] If these signs are read in a manner analogous to *The Minister's Black Veil*, it appears that they, too, cannot be grasped by concepts. This leads to a process of 'unveiling' or *différance*, in which signs endlessly refer to other signs.

In this context period labels such as 'Baroque' or 'Renaissance' are not considered as concepts that somehow correspond to their object, but as ambivalent and flexible figures that can themselves become objects of a rhetorical or 'tropological' analysis: 'One way to see the complexities of what might be meant by calling period names fictions is to observe that they are all figures of speech. They are therefore are open to tropological analysis.'[66]

Such an analysis reveals, among other things, the proximity of period concepts to nature: 'Both "the baroque" and "the Renaissance" imply an assimilation of the period to nature.'[67] 'Baroque' (Portuguese *barroco* = imperfectly rounded) appears as a rough, irregular pearl, the Renaissance as a rebirth. This rhetorical (metaphorical) aspect of period labels emphasized by Miller foregrounds their particular character, making their generalizing potential as conceptual instruments of classification retreat into the background. As always, the deconstructive analysis leads to an extreme particularization in the Nietzschean sense.

Particularity and contingency are closely related, and it is therefore hardly surprising that Miller tends to regard period labels as purely contingent inventions whose arbitrariness is revealed by their failure to form a coherent whole. Thus he points out that the label 'modern English literature' refers to all works since Shakespeare at Zurich University, while Modernism begins around 1890 at Yale University. His comparison, however, is – like many of his arguments – quite arbitrary. For the Zurich philologists obviously refer to the modern period in history, while their colleagues in Yale refer to literary and artistic Modernism, which many Europeans also locate between 1850 and 1900. This Modernism corresponds by and large to that of Malcolm Bradbury, Hispano-American *Modernismo* or to Benjamin's and Adorno's *Moderne* (since 1850). It appears once again that the discrepancy 'discovered' by Miller has in fact been constructed within the framework of a Deconstructionist discourse marked by an aversion towards concepts.

The dialectical response to this discourse cannot be a logical positivist plea for rigorous terminology, but should concentrate on the permanent interaction of concept and absence of concept. It may be true that Modernism as a period cannot be defined once and for all in the sense of a universally acceptable 'presence of meaning'. However, this does not mean that period labels have no conceptual character or that they cannot be used as concepts. As long as we remain aware of the fact that they are theoretical constructs which never completely overcome their particular and contingent character, we shall be able to demonstrate their potential for dialogue and consensus, i.e. their pragmatic usefulness. This approach is confirmed by the capacity of these heuristic constructs to describe and explain aesthetic problems, styles, stylistic variants and textual structures (for example that of modernity).[68]

Miller's – like de Man's – negation of historicity and periodization ultimately makes him accept circularity and Nietzsche's 'eternal return'. This becomes clear in *Victorian Subjects*, where he conceives the interaction between culture and counter-culture in just these terms: 'The counter-culture has no instruments with which to attack the official culture but those drawn from the twenty-five-hundred year old official culture. For this reason, the counter-culture turns out regularly and inevitably, in spite of itself, to be another version of what it attempts to destroy.'[69] This reductionist circularity of his own thinking does not prevent Miller from identifying Western European and North American democracy as a new form of government which has emerged from a century-old struggle led by counter-cultures. It could never have materialized if those counter-cultures had merely reproduced in a circular manner the forms of dominant cultures. That these forms *also* reproduce themselves cannot be denied. Yet it is this dialectical and historical *also* which Deconstruction deletes.

This explains why its notion of text – as has been pointed out before – is ahistorical. For Miller, like de Man, is fond of the idea that all texts are contradictory, aporetic and unreadable regardless of their origin and their reception: 'Each reading culminates in an experience of the unreadability of the text at hand. The text hovers between two or more logically incompatible things.'[70] It hovers in particular above society and history, for a poem by Mallarmé is not unreadable and aporetic in the same way as a propaganda poem of the Russian Revolution. The discourses of Deconstruction have also come about in a particular linguistic and historical situation. They are socially contingent. The Deconstructionists, however, who despite their Nietzschean leanings towards the particular believe their own analyses to be of general validity, fail to notice this fact. For they have not considered the origins of their own discourses in a particular historical, social and linguistic situation.

NOTES

1. J. H. Miller, *Victorian Subjects* (1990), p. 215.
2. See J. H. Miller, 'Geneva or Paris: George Poulet's "Criticism of Identification"', in *Theory Now and Then* (1991), pp. 31–61.
3. H. Felperin, *Beyond Deconstruction* (1985), pp. 107–8.
4. Miller, *Theory Now and Then*, p. 193.

5. Ibid., p. 54.

6. Ibid., p. 69.

7. Ibid., p. 14.

8. Ibid., p. 231.

9. See G. D. Atkins, *Reading Deconstruction, Deconstructive Reading* (1983), p. 27. Atkins points out that in Miller's opinion not all interpretations are equally valid: 'According to Abrams, deconstructive criticism places even the most arbitrary reading on an equal footing with the most rigorous, for there appears no way of determining right from wrong readings. But Miller, for one, explicitly denies that all "readings are equally valid or of equal value".' This argument is convincing in so far as Miller repeatedly speaks of a 'good reader' and 'good reading'. As a consequence, not all readings can be equally good. Yet one wonders whether the good or deconstructive way of reading is not characterized by wilfulness.

10. Miller, *Victorian Subjects*, p. 255.

11. J. H. Miller, *The Ethics of Reading* (1987), p. 10.

12. J. H. Miller, *Fiction and Repetition: Seven English Novels* (1982), p. xviii.

13. Miller, *Theory Now and Then*, p. 345.

14. See, for example, R. Warning, ed., *Rezeptionsästhetik* (1975), especially the contributions by F. V. Vodicka, H. G. Gadamer, and H. R. Jauß.

15. Miller, *The Ethics of Reading*, p. 33.

16. Miller, *Theory Now and Then*, p. 196.

17. For a definition of the 'mythical actant', see my *Ideologie und Theorie: Eine Diskurskritik* (1989), ch. 8, 2, c–d.

18. For a definition of 'immunization' in critical discourses, see, for instance, H. Albert, *Treatise on Critical Reason* (1985), pp. 92–146.

19. J. H. Miller, *Hawthorne and History: Defacing It* (1991), p. 158.

20. Ibid., p. 135.

21. This particularism is also addressed by M. Cebulla when he remarks on the self-subversion of the deconstructionist truth claim: 'Yet when all theoretical approaches are equally subject to the process of deconstruction, it becomes impossible to understand what the advantage of de Man's theory could be.' Cebulla, *Wahrheit und Authentizität*, p. 183.

22. Miller, *Theory Now and Then*, p. 151.

23. Ibid., p. 92.

24. J. H. Miller, *The Linguistic Moment: From Wordsworth to Stevens* (1985), p. 48.

25. Ibid., pp. 43–4.

26. Miller, *Theory Now and Then*, p. 181.

27. Cf. Paul de Man's remarks concerning this Lucy poem in 'The Rhetoric of Temporality', in *Blindness and Insight* (1983), p. 224: 'It could be said that, read within the perspective of the entire poem, these two lines are ironic . . . .'

28. H. Schweizer, 'Introduction', in Miller, *Hawthorne and History* (1991), p. 34.

29. Miller, *Theory Now and Then*, p. 85.
30. J. H. Miller, *Ariadne's Thread* (1992), p. 50.
31. J. H. Miller, *Tropes, Parables, Performatives: Essays in Twentieth-Century Literature* (1990), p. 36.
32. J. H. Miller, *Fiction and Repetition*, p. 24.
33. Ibid., p. 30.
34. Ibid., p. 38.
35. Ibid., p. 39.
36. Ibid., p. 40.
37. Ibid., p. 34.
38. Ibid., p. 51.
39. Ibid., p. 55.
40. Ibid.
41. Ibid., p. 67
42. Miller, *Ariadne's Thread*, pp. 174–5.
43. Ibid., p. 175.
44. Ibid., p. 177.
45. Miller, *Theory Now and Then*, p. 175.
46. Miller, *Ethics of Reading*, p. 73.
47. Miller, *Victorian Subjects*, p. 292.
48. Miller, *Theory Now and Then*, p. 168.
49. G. Eliot, *Adam Bede* (1980).
50. Miller, *Fiction and Repetition*, p. 6.
51. Ibid.
52. F. Nietzsche, *Werke* (1980), vol. 5, p. 313.
53. Miller, *Fiction and Repetition*, p. 16.
54. Miller, *Tropes, Parables, Performatives*, p. 131.
55. Miller, *Fiction and Repetition*, p. 122.
56. Ibid., p. 128.
57. Ibid.
58. Miller, *Hawthorne and History*, p. 97.
59. Ibid., p. 108.
60. Ibid., p. 114.
61. Ibid., p. 89.
62. Ibid., p. 97.
63. Ibid., p. 117.
64. Ibid., p. 113.
65. Ibid., p. 127.
66. Miller, *Theory Now and Then*, p. 210.
67. Ibid., p. 211.
68. For a definition of the concept of period as a construct in the sense of semiotics and Radical Constructivism, cf. my *Komparatistik: Einführung in die Vergleichende Literaturwissenschaft* (1992), chap. VII, 1.
69. Miller, *Victorian Subjects*, p. 287.
70. Miller, *Ariadne's Thread*, p. 224.

5

GEOFFREY HARTMAN

ROMANTIC AND NIETZSCHEAN

Like the other theoretical approaches within American Deconstruction, Geoffrey Hartman's literary analysis is rooted in Anglo-American New Criticism. In agreement with some New Critics such as Ransom, Brooks or Wimsatt, Hartman categorically rejects an approximation of the discourse of literary analysis to that of the social or natural sciences. In *Criticism in the Wilderness* he argues against all kinds of submission to these sciences, which, in his view, have created 'the model of a *mechanism* that fascinates by its anonymous, compulsive, impersonal character'.[1] In this point he agrees with the New Critics who have time and again stressed the non-scientific character of their approach and thus anticipated the Deconstructionist critique of scientism. G. Douglas Atkins speaks of a symbiosis of Deconstruction and New Criticism.[2]

Yet in contrast to the New Critics, who tended to view the totality of the text from a classical position, Hartman relies on English and German Romanticism, where he rediscovers the fragment, the essay and the aphorism. Against the classical tendencies of Matthew Arnold, Northrop Frye and the New Critics, he defends a *creative criticism* whose borders with poetry are permeable: 'All these strands now come together into a new view of the relation between poetry and criticism, which is a challenge to the "objective" style that has dominated from Arnold to Frye.'[3]

This idea of literary criticism is of Romantic origin and was developed with great subtlety by the Schlegel brothers (see Chapter 1, section 2). Hartman frequently refers to German Romanticism, especially to Friedrich Schlegel, of whom he claims that he envisaged a *synthesizing criticism* 'that would combine art and philosophy'.[4]

In Hartman, this criticism, poised between literary analysis, literary essay and literature itself, continues and expands fictional writing. Concomitantly, the reader turns into an enhanced author in Friedrich Schlegel's sense – just as in the commentaries of the Romantics. Hartman himself states this clearly: 'In *Criticism in the Wilderness* and *Saving the Text* I try to define the symbiosis or tangled relations of literature and literary commentary.'[5] In this respect his idea of criticism coincides to a large extent with that of J. Hillis Miller, for Hillis Miller writes about the interaction of literature and criticism: 'It is this shared linguistic predicament, not some vague right to be "poetic" or "creative", that is meant, or should be meant, when it is said that criticism is a form of literarture.'[6] Miller thus maintains that literary criticism cannot claim to reproduce the meaning of the literary text scientifically, conceptually or literally.

Hartman shares the view that there is no scientific meta-language qualitatively different from literary writing. Literature and literary criticism have a common 'linguistic predicament' which cannot be bracketed off, overcome or simply negated. Hence criticism appears to be literature about literature. Yet Hartman does not want critical writings to be understood as 'secondary literature'. For him they are a (literary) genre *sui generis* that, even on an institutional level, should not be separated from fiction. Thus criticism becomes a form of *creative writing*. At the same time he envisages the critic as a writer of the second degree, whose word responds to the literary word like an echo.

1 HARTMAN'S ROMANTICISM

In the conflict of Classicism and Romanticism, period labels he views sceptically, Hartman clearly sides with the consciousness of the Romantics. In his early study *Beyond Formalism* (1970) which can hardly be considered Deconstructionist, he defended Romanticism against Malraux's claim that the Classical element in modern art implies a 'lucid horror of seduction'. 'Today it is clear', Hartman responds, 'that Romantic art shared that lucidity. Romanticism at its most profound reveals the depth of the enchantment in which we live.'[7]

Hartman's idea of a symbiosis between literature and literary criticism pervades his commentaries on William Wordsworth's poems, which he would like to enhance and multiply in the same way as an echo multiplies the human voice. In doing so he turns the reader-critic into an author and imagines the author as a reader. Wordsworth's poetry, Hartman claims, suggests that we must read the poet as reader.[8] This neo-Romantic view of the text involves a change of roles: the poet becomes a reader, and the reader an extended author.

G. Douglas Atkins remarks on the 'symbiotic' link between Wordsworth and Hartman that the American critic is not content with a detailed analysis of the former's poetry, but develops it further: into a 'work he not only elaborates but also extends'.[9] He might have added that this view of literature derives from the German Romantics, especially from Friedrich Schlegel, to whom Hartman refers in *Criticism in the Wilderness*.

His commentary on Wordsworth's *Lucy* poem 'A Slumber Did My Spirit Seal' illustrates what 'creative literary criticism' or 'criticism as literature' means in this context. At the same time it demonstrates how much Hartman's views of Deconstruction depart from Paul de Man's and J. Hillis Miller's, who analyse the same Lucy poem (see Chapter 4, section 2), quoted again for convenience:

> A slumber did my spirit seal;
> I had no human fears:
> She seemed a thing that could not feel
> The touch of earthly years.
>
> No motion has she now, no force;
> She neither hears nor sees;
> Rolled round in earth's diurnal course,
> With rocks, and stones, and trees.

In his commentary, which also relies on Freud's dream interpretation, Hartman is concerned primarily with certain phonetic and semantic associations or anagrams (words that are created by the reversal of letters of other words, e.g. *amor-Roma*) that pervade the Romantic poem. It attempts to show how Wordsworth uses certain euphemisms to evoke words like *die* or *grave*. What is crucial is Freud's idea that elements of dreams, associations of words and names can give rise to ambivalent combinations which link greatness and triviality, the sacred and the profane. Hartman reminds us of Freud's reference to Herder's satirical game with Goethe's name: 'Thou who art the descendant of Gods or Goths or dung [*Kote* in German (translator's note)].'[10] He explains: 'Freud has realized, in short, the profaning power of dreams; yet not of dreams only, but of language as it allows that chiming to mock and madden anything sacred.'[11]

Which associations and anagrams are at stake in Wordsworth's poem? They are certain puns that evoke in particular motifs of dying and death: 'So "diurnal" (line 7) divides into "die" and "urn", and "course" may recall the older pronunciation of "corpse".'[12] Of the second stanza, Hartman claims that its expressivity ought to be sought in particular 'in the euphemistic replacement of the word "grave" by an image of gravitation ("Rolled round in earth's diurnal course").' He adds: 'And though there is no agreement on the tone of this stanza, it is clear that a subvocal word is uttered without being written down. It is a word that rhymes with "fears" and "years" and "hears", but which is closed off by the very last syllable of the poem: "trees". Read "tears", and the animating, cosmic metaphor comes alive, the poet's lament echoes through nature as in pastoral elegy. "Tears", however, must give way to what is written, to a dull yet definitive sound, the anagram "trees".'[13]

This is the crucial argument of an interpretation that is not so much geared towards Hillis Miller's aporia but is closer to Derrida's *différance*: to a postponement of meaning based on the idea that the text cannot be interpreted in purely random ways, yet that its anagrams, associations and connotations allow for many different meanings, or actually encourage them. Hartman seems to be unimpressed by the fact that the meanings suggested by him have a rather subjective character and cannot always be confirmed by other readers.

Readers schooled in semiotic and linguistic analysis will resist a straightforward splitting of the adjective diurnal into *die* and *urn*.

This lacks any etymological and semantic foundation. Moreover, the association of *trees* and *tears* will hardly convince them, since the discourse of the lyrical subject lacks elements of mourning. Hartman himself remarks that the poet neither expresses mourning nor sadness: 'The poet does not exclaim or cry out.' He adds that the events of the poem 'are described without surprise or shock'.[14] Faced with such – quite plausible – statements, it becomes difficult to associate trees with tears, unless purely subjective associations of an individual reader are to be given credit. But how can such an endeavour be reconciled with Hillis Miller's *ethics of reading*, an ethics asking the reader to remain close to the text and to respect its alterity?

A possible answer is that Hartman's deconstructive or anagrammatical reading cannot be subsumed under Hillis Miller's deconstructive approach and its 'ethics'. It is more closely related to Roland Barthes's idea of the 'writerly' text according to which some – especially avant-garde – texts can be 'rewritten' because of their openness.[15] On Barthes, Hartman writes: 'As he puts it, literature "disseminates" (a fertility metaphor) rather than establishes truth.'[16] Both Hartman and Barthes are primarily concerned with the associative and semantic potential of texts and with refuting the thesis that a poem or a narrative can be defined as a semantic or syntactic structure, i.e. reduced to what Barthes calls with abhorrence the '*dernier Signifié*', the ultimate signified.[17]

Once again the question arises (see Chapter 4, section 3), whether the openness or 'writerliness' of the text is not accounted for by Hartman's essayistic and fragmentary discourse which ignores syntactic and semantic structures completely and does not even refer to the word 'thing' that is so crucial for J. Hillis Miller and Paul de Man (see Chapter 4, section 2). The systematic analysis abhorred by the Deconstructionists would probably reveal the syntactic and semantic functions of the word *thing* in the text and explain the meaning of the negations also mentioned by Hartman (*no motion ... no force ... neither hears nor sees*). In an essayistic commentary, however, it seems quite impossible to elucidate such intricacies.

This kind of commentary is not only post-structuralist (ill-disposed critics would call it pre-structuralist), but also Romantic. For Hartman is not concerned with a scientifically based or systematic investigation, but with a creative enhancement, a 'multiplication' of Wordsworth's poem. This type of criticism is commented on by the young Walter Benjamin in his doctoral thesis *The Concept of Art Criticism in German Romanticism* (1920): 'Criticism is therefore, very much in contrast to today's idea of its essence, in its central intention not judgement, but on the one hand completion, addition, systematization of the work, on the other hand its dissolution in the absolute.'[18] Although there is no mention of 'systematization' or 'dissolution in the absolute' in Hartman, his interpretation aims at completion (without conclusion) and enhancement. It is intended to be literature about literature.

In some respects Hartman's literary criticism is a conscious return to the controversies between Hegel and the Romantics. Hartman does not hesitate to side with the Romantics, with whose concept of literature and history he has concerned himself repeatedly,[19] since he shares their scepticism towards rationalism and the Hegelian system. This scepticism reappears in much modernist and postmodern thinking which tends to replace the Classicist notion of an harmonious and rounded work of art by an aesthetics of heterogeneity and polyphony.

His *parti pris* in favour of Romanticism also includes language, whose opacity he considers indispensable for the survival of imagination. 'In fact, to deny imagination its darker food, . . . is to wish imagination away', he writes in *The Unremarkable Wordsworth*. One is struck by the spiritual kinship with Friedrich Schlegel's treatise 'On Incomprehensibility'. It is undoubtedly one of the main achievements of Deconstruction to have pointed out the opaque aspects of language that Enlightenment thinkers and rationalists decided to ignore in an irrational manner. Unfortunately, however, Deconstruction as a whole tends to reduce the problem of language to these aspects and to increase the irrational dimensions of Romanticism in a new context.

2 FROM NIETZSCHE TO DERRIDA

Every attempt to define Hartman as a renewer of Romanticism or as a neo-Romantic would be an unfair simplification. For his reworking of Romantic themes and theorems is globally mediated by the influence of Nietzsche, whom Hartman justly considers Hegel's antipode and a central reference point of Deconstruction.

The Yale critic owes his art of bridging the institutionalized rift between literary and critical-theoretical discourse to Nietzsche's re-evaluation of rhetoric as figurative speech and 'tropology'. By adopting Nietzsche's linguistic criticism and his rhetorical approach, he can regard the new type of literary critic as an author *sui generis* and bid farewell to the traditional idea of criticism as a secondary or derivative genre.

Like the other exponents of Deconstruction Hartman feels haunted by Hegel's shadow and locates the central problem of Deconstruction in the tension between Hegel and Nietzsche, i.e. in the Young Hegelian context outlined in Chapter 1. His remarks on Derrida's philosophy, which he considers as oscillating between the past and the future, can be read as reflecting his own 'Young Hegelian' position. Hartman believes that he can identify two main strands in Derrida's thinking: 'One is the past, starting with Hegel who is still with us; the other is the future, starting with Nietzsche who is once again with us, having been rediscovered by recent French thought.'[20]

The 'recent French thought' which also includes writers such as Foucault and Baudrillard, is identified in a somewhat naïve manner with Deconstruction and especially with Derrida's *Glas* (see Chapter 1, section 3), an experimental text and an attempt to overcome the logocentric opposition between literature and philosophy in a large-scale collage. In *Saving the Text* Hartman deals in detail with *Glas*, and it is worth discussing his commentaries thoroughly, especially since their author explains in an interview with Imre Salusinszky: 'I probably did not engage fully with Derrida until *Glas* came out.'[21]

In the first chapter of Hartman's book, *Glas* appears as a 'Young Hegelian' and avant-garde polemic which relates Feuerbach's, Stirner's, B. Bauer's and F. Th. Vischer's ideas to Marx's radical critique and Nietzsche's subversion of the Hegelian system. Derrida's parallel reading of Hegel's idealist texts and Genet's materialist-anarchist ones can be interpreted as a confrontation between Hegel's idealism and an avant-garde materialism (Feuerbach-Genet), between systematic thought and anarchism (Stirner-Genet), between metaphysics and a critique of religion (Bauer-Genet, Marx-Genet). Hartman's commentaries are situated in this philosophical context and are geared towards Nietzsche's synthesis of various Young Hegelian themes.

Among these are the Dionysian vision and the dream, whose mechanisms of association underline Derrida's textual collage. Discussing the arrangement of *Glas*, Hartman speaks of 'Nietzsche's shuttle-play between Dionysus and Apollo'.[22] He points out that Derrida combines in a playful experiment the linguistic conventions of philosophy, science and the dream, interlinking – like Freud and Lacan – 'metaphoricity with scientific model-making'. Writing becomes a 'fantastic machine' which Hartman reconstructs, adapting it to the needs of literary criticism.[23] His own commentary on *Glas* is a rhetorical game with signs, associations, connotations and puns that transcends all genre boundaries announcing new models outside established literature and literary theory. 'For Hartman', Christopher Norris remarks, 'the only way out is for the critic to throw off his "inferiority complex" and enter wholeheartedly – with a Nietzschean swagger – into the dance of meaning.'[24]

Hartman, who in *Criticism in the Wilderness* describes *Glas* as a 'work of *philosophic* art',[25] develops a playful essayism inspired by Nietzsche's anti-systematic and fragmented style. In *Beyond Formalism* he presents his own style as a 'playful poetics' governed by the rhetorical figure and by literary techniques.[26] The overall idea is to turn literary criticism into a gay science in Nietzsche's sense, combining it with the Romantic serenity mentioned by Hartman in *Saving the Text*. In this respect *Glas* becomes a model of future text design: 'Hegel and Genet are given the most sustained analysis and yet the effect remains musical. A deconstructive machine that sings: *Glas*.'[27] Derrida's large-scale textual experiment whose 'nonseriousness' Hartman mentions is, however, much more than a vain play with signs: 'A game that lasts so long must be more than a game. Even if *Glas* were a "self-consuming artefact", we would be left to admire its stylistic sense of the vanity of all things.'[28] In other words, the game with old and new forms does not end in the void but encourages us to extract new meanings from texts and to develop new forms beyond metaphysics or 'true presence'.

However, this serious undertone of Deconstruction turns into a game when it becomes clear that its authors deal with the relations between art, science and contemporary society quite playfully, without being able to analyse them theoretically. For a theoretical analysis of these problems is invonceivable as a textual collage. Only a critical social science can do justice to the complexity of society dealt with by different sociological theories in the past. The relationship between Deconstruction and Critical Theory in the Frankfurt School tradition (Adorno's Negative Dialectic) will be considered in the fourth section and in the last chapter.

3 DECONSTRUCTION AS NEGATIVITY, DELAY AND INDETERMINACY

What has been said so far suggests that Hartman does not conceive Deconstruction as a search for contradictions and aporias inherent in the text. He rather aims at developing its Nietzschean potential in a rhetorical game. In Georg Lukács's work he is fascinated not so much by the systematic aesthetics of the Marxist period but by the collection of essays entitled *Soul and Form* (1913), which he reads as an 'intellectual poem'.[29] In this context one might distinguish two complementary components of Deconstruction: a poststructuralist one geared towards a contradiction which explodes coherence, and a Romantic–Nietzschean one which privileges essayism, the openness of the text and the play of language.

In contrast to Paul de Man and J. Hillis Miller, who tend to focus on formal contradictions, Hartman, the Romantic and Nietzschean, is fascinated less by the dissolution of meaning than by the openness of texts. One could claim that his variant of Deconstruction is closer to Derrida's playful style than to de Man's systematic 'destructuring'. For Hartman pursues *différance* or *dissemination* rather than destructive aporia. His strategy is less rigid than de Man's, but also less radical than Derrida's, and G. Douglas Atkins is probably right when he claims that 'Hartman expresses both admiration and wariness'[30] vis-à-vis Derrida's conceptual and de Man's rhetorical form of Deconstruction.

It seems possible, therefore, to compare not only his aesthetics but also his stylistic approach with the poststructuralist and Nietzschean writings of the later Barthes. Like Barthes he pursues the 'pleasure of the text' in the endless interplay of polysemic signifiers. Like the French essayist he argues polemically against conceptual closure, the *clôture conceptuelle* of the literary and philosophical text and against all attempts to reduce it to a 'structure of signifieds', as Barthes calls it in *S/Z*.[31] Hartman's variant of Deconstruction should therefore be regarded as a pragmatic and essayistic genre which contrasts with Miller's somewhat rigid use of the notion of *iterability*. It is based on three key concepts which will be discussed in more detail below: *negativity, delay* and *indeterminacy*.

G. Douglas Atkins summarizes the key idea of Hartman's approach when he presents the concept of *negativity*. He describes Deconstruction as a 'work of negativity' and as an attempt to save the text by demonstrating continually that 'the issue does not dissolve in the idea. Meaning cannot replace the medium.'[32] This claim is not really new: it dates back to the New Critics who emphasize time and again that the linguistic medium (the 'how') of a literary text cannot be reduced to its meanings. Thus Brooks, for example, remarks that the poem is the *only* medium that communicates the particular 'how' that is mediated.[33] In contrast to the New Critics, Hartman doubts the possibility of an 'objective' or intersubjective description of texts. His commentaries on Wordsworth's poem 'A Slumber Did My Spirit Seal' illustrate his Romantic conviction that the critic's discourse cannot be separated from that of the analysed and criticized text. Both discourses merge in a new unity, a new literary-philosophical-critical work. In *The Fate of Reading* Hartman doubts that we shall ever be able 'to distinguish . . . what is the reader's and what the author's share in "producing" the complex understanding which surrounds a literary work'.[34] An aspect of negativity is therefore the impossibility of clearly distinguishing textual meaning from that of the reader, of defining textual structures clearly, and making them transparent. Hartman's commentaries on Wordsworth's poem show to what extent he makes the *textual horizon* and the *reader's horizon* coincide.

A further aspect of negativity is the ambiguity or ambivalence of the text which make its reduction to conceptual structures – ideologies, for instance – impossible: 'Whatever is being constructed is based on two competing principles: the equivocal and equi-vocal character of words.'[35] At this point a kinship between Hartman and the other Deconstructionists comes to the fore: like theirs, his approach is geared towards Nietzsche's concept of ambivalence and casts doubts on all attempts to reduce the ever-plural text to one meaning.

Hartman's demand that the reader should not prematurely mono-semise the text (reduce it to a concept) but read it with 'doubt and delay' emerges logically from the recognition of such an ambivalence. Only in this way, Hartman claims, an open hermeneutics is guaranteed capable of making the ambivalences and polysemies of texts appear. In his preface to an interview with Hartman, Imre Salusinszky emphasizes the conceptual affinity between Derrida's *différance* and Hartman's *delay*: 'Delay does not lead to eventual determination; meaning does not cease its wanderings, nor criticism its wonderings.'[36] In other words, the debate about a text cannot be concluded, since the 'actual' meaning as presence of meaning never appears. Instead of trying to limit the text's negativity, we ought to question its semantic potential over and over again.

In *Criticism in the Wilderness* Hartman describes the delay as 'a labor that aims not to overcome the negative or indeterminate but to stay within it as long as necessary'.[37] The question 'How long?' is only partly answered by Hartman, for he is not so much concerned with an exact description and interpretation of textual structures as with the process of interpretation, 'the commentary process'.[38] It becomes a goal in its own right for the Deconstructionist, and Hartman thus distinguishes his 'humanistic criticism' from the scientific attempts of certain structuralists, semioticians and phenomenologists who are interested in the relations of structures, thereby neglecting the openness of the text and the impossibility of conceptual closure. He does not want his criticism to dissolve in these disciplines and proclaims: 'We take back from science what is ours.'[39] Here the old rift that already separated New Criticism from science appears once again.

In contrast to the scientific textual analyses of the structuralists, semioticians, phenomenologists, or sociologists who aim at elucidating the text on different levels and explaining it in a context, Hartman sees his own method as a negative hermeneutics. It unmasks the transparency of the object postulated by the rationalists as an illusion and delays the reading process: 'Criticism as a kind of hermeneutics is disconcerting; like logic, but without the latter's motive of absolute internal consistency, it reveals contradictions and equivocations, and so makes fiction interpretable by making it less readable.'[40] The philosophical tradition itself is read against the grain and reinterpreted. While traditional philologists and modern literary *scholars* struggle to develop theoretical models in order to make texts more accessible and their reading easier (one might think of J.-P. Richard's commentaries on Mallarmé; see

Chapter 2, section 4), a Deconstructionist such as Hartman attempts to disrupt the euphoria of transparency and to confront the reader with ambiguities and vagaries: with the opacity of the text.

This approach would be legitimate if Hartman were able to show that semioticians, phenomenologists and sociologists ignore certain textual elements and claim to detect meaningful totalities where polysemy and contradiction prevail. Yet Hartman neither seeks a dialogue with (social) scientists nor does he take into account sociological, semiotic or linguistic analyses of texts. He is content to postulate an unbridgeable gap between his *humanistic criticism* and scientific procedures.

His third concept, *indeterminacy*, is also an abstract postulate rather than a term that can be tested in actual analyses and theoretical debates. Hartman does not explain how 'his' indeterminacy differs from that of Roman Ingarden or Wolfgang Iser and why the theoretical efforts of these scholars are insufficient. In what respect does *indeterminacy* go beyond undefinability in Ingarden's or Iser's sense?

Only G. Douglas Atkins attempts (albeit in three or four sentences) to distinguish Hartman's approach from Iser's aesthetics of and American Reader-Response Theory. 'Rather than on the reader, the reading process, or response as those are (differently) defined by reader-response critics, Hartman stresses, and values, obligation.'[41] Atkins tries to specify this somewhat glossy moral term using expressions such as 'reader's engagement', 'personal involvement', 'accountability' and even 'stress of vocation'. Yet it remains difficult to spot in all these moralizing labels theoretically useful concepts. What are Hartman's own statements on indeterminacy?

In a commentary on Yeats's 'Leda and the Swan' he derives indeterminacy from the impossibility to imagine Leda's face: 'Is it gay, mad, or transfigured: does it "see" in the ordinary sense of the word?' Some lines further he adds as an explanation: 'The ultimate indeterminacy, then, centers on this face that cannot be imagined.'[42] Yet is this not Ingarden's – albeit less dramatic – indeterminacy, which prevents the reader from deciding on the colour of consul Buddenbrook's eyes? Is it not frequently the case that the face of a character remains blank and consequently 'unimaginable'? What does Robbe-Grillet's voyeur look like?

It is very unlikely that other literary scholars have not concerned themselves with this kind of indeterminacy. Hartman's general claims on this subject make one suspect that a magic formula free from the constraints of scientific discourse is to be developed, a formula thriving on vagueness: 'Indeterminacy as a "speculative instrument" should influence the way literature is read, but by modifying the reader's awareness rather than by imposing a method. To methodize indeterminacy would be to forget the reason for the concept.'[43]

It is certainly true that readers ought to read with 'doubt and delay' and ought not to fill points of indeterminacy at random or eliminate them. Yet does one need a revolutionary Deconstructive theory to be reminded of this *desideratum* put forward by the aesthetics of reception and Roman Ingarden? Hartman has failed to explain how his indeterminacy differs from Ingarden's or Iser's much more precisely defined concepts.

4 HARTMAN AND ADORNO

Like Paul de Man's Deconstruction (see chapter 3, section 2), Geoffrey Hartman's criticism has been compared with Adorno's aesthetic theory. Hartman himself claims to spot an affinity between his own position and that of Critical Theory when he says of the Frankfurt School in *Easy Pieces* that it 'reinforced deconstructive thought and sometimes provided a political alternative'.[44] G. Douglas Atkins is even more specific when he compares Adorno's essayism and the paratactic arrangement of his *Aesthetic Theory* with Hartman's use of essay, aphorism and parataxis, reminding us of the fact that Adorno also argued against a strict separation of literature and literary theory (literary criticism). He refers to Gillian Rose who explains in her study on Adorno that he 'called into question the very boundary between criticism and creation, without, however, ever effacing it entirely'.[45]

It is certainly possible and useful to point out similarities between the Deconstructionists and Adorno's aesthetics, especially since Adorno turns against all modes of reading which gloss over the ambiguities of literature. It is well known that he accuses Hegel of his 'intolerance of ambiguity' which entails a devaluation of everything that resists conceptual definition.[46] It is therefore hardly surprising that Hartman invokes somewhat indiscriminately the 'negative thinking' of the Frankfurt School: 'The Frankfurt School, ... though prior to both structuralism and deconstruction, also opposed totalizing explanations.'[47]

All these analogies have one thing in common: they are superficial and *abstract* in a dialectical sense,[48] for they fail to do justice to the many layers of Frankfurt School theory and Deconstruction. They concentrate on that which is *immediately* perceived. In the same way geologists might compare mountain ridges merely because they are covered in snow and therefore white. What remains unaccounted for is the fact that in the different variants of Deconstruction (as in Hartman's), the Nietzschean play of signs is dominant, while in Adorno and Horkheimer's Critical Theory linguistic criticism is part and parcel of a general critique of modern social sciences (sociology, psychology and psychoanalysis) and of a multi-layered critique of late capitalist society. When Adorno comments on various aspects of language and style in Hölderlin's or Eichendorff's poems, he is not merely concerned with linguistic moments, but also with German existentialist philosophy as a 'jargon of authenticity' and with its function in National Socialism. He deals with Eichendorff's conservatism *and* the critical elements of this conservatism which cannot be annexed by contemporary conservative ideologies. His linguistic and aesthetic investigations are not only based on critical analyses of ideology and society, but also on empirical studies such as *The Authoritarian Personality* (1950).[49]

Of course one could object that Hartman also refers to the social context: 'Every work of art, from this point of view, is a criticism of life in terms of a criticism of mediations: of conventions, schematisms, institutions, of art itself, and the way we think or talk about it.'[50] This may be the case. But which conventions, schematisms and institutions are at stake here? How is art being managed in contemporary society? Hartman ultimately fails to answer these questions – unlike Adorno.

At the end of *Criticism in the Wilderness* he sketches in a few sentences the kinship of Stalinism and late capitalism and asks: 'Can any hermeneutics of indeterminacy, any irony however deeply practiced and nurtured by aesthetic experience, withstand either society while they are still distinguishable?'[51] This is certainly a question which also concerns Frankfurt School theory. Yet it is raised in the context of a criticism incapable of describing even approximately the ideologies and social systems to which Hartman *playfully* refers – much less of criticizing them. As a consequence he proves unable to critically engage with the social theories that would allow him to understand art as a *social fact* (Durkheim, Mauss). Yet this is the aspect of art dealt with in Adorno's *Aesthetic Theory* where autonomy and *social fact* are dialectically related: 'Art's double character as both autonomous and *fait social* is incessantly reproduced on the level of its autonomy.'[52] For Adorno Critical Theory was primarily a critical theory of society, despite its orientation towards autonomous art – and not literary or art criticism.

NOTES

1. G. H. Hartman, *Criticism in the Wilderness: The Study of Literature Today* (1980), p. 270.
2. G. D. Atkins, *Geoffrey Hartman: Criticism as Answerable Style* (1990), p. 23.
3. I. Salusinszky, *Criticism in Society* (1987), p. 77.
4. Hartman, *Criticism in the Wilderness*, p. 38.
5. G. H. Hartman, *Easy Pieces* (1985), p. 203.
6. J. H. Miller, *Tropes, Parables, Performatives* (1990), p. 235.
7. G. H. Hartman, *Beyond Formalism: Literary Essays 1958–1970* (1970), p. 307.
8. G. H. Hartman, 'Words, Wish, Worth: Wordsworth', in *Deconstruction and Criticism* (1979), p. 187.
9. Atkins, *Hartman*, p. 58.
10. Quoted in Hartman, *Easy Pieces*, p. 143.
11. Ibid., p. 144.
12. Ibid., p. 149.
13. Ibid., pp. 149–50.
14. Ibid., p. 146. In contrast to Hartman, de Man mentions 'the curious shock of the poem' and talks about 'the very Wordsworthian "shock of mild surprise"'; *Blindness and Insight* (1983), p. 224.
15. See R. Barthes, *S/Z* (1974), p. 4: 'what can be written (rewritten) today: the *writerly*'.
16. Hartman, *Easy Pieces*, p. 41.
17. R. Barthes, *Le Bruissement de la langue: Essais critiques IV* (1984), p. 207.
18. W. Benjamin, *Der Begriff des Kunstwerks in der deutschen Romantik* (1973), p. 72.

19. See Hartman, 'Reflections on French Romanticism', in *Easy Pieces*.
20. G. H. Hartman, *Saving the Text: Literature/Derrida/Philosophy* (1981), p. 28.
21. Hartman, in Salusinszky, *Criticism in Society* (1987), p. 80.
22. Hartman, *Saving the Text*, p. 27.
23. Ibid.
24. Norris, *Deconstruction*, p. 92.
25. Hartman, *Criticism in the Wilderness*, p. 38.
26. Hartman, *Beyond Formalism*, p. 339.
27. Hartman, *Saving the Text*, p. 24.
28. Ibid., p. 25.
29. Hartman, *Criticism in the Wilderness*, p. 196.
30. Atkins, *Hartman*, pp. 19–20.
31. Barthes, *S/Z*, p. 5.
32. Atkins, *Hartman*, p. 167.
33. C. Brooks, *The Well-Wrought Urn: Studies in the Structure of Poetry* (1949), p. 74.
34. G. H. Hartman, *The Fate of Reading and Other Essays* (1975), p. vii.
35. Hartman, *Saving the Text*, p. 14.
36. Salusinszky, *Criticism in Society*, p. 77.
37. Hartman, *Criticism in the Wilderness*, p. 270.
38. Ibid.
39. Ibid.
40. Ibid., p. 32.
41. Atkins, *Hartman*, p. 15.
42. Hartman, *Criticism in the Wilderness*, p. 35.
43. Ibid., p. 269.
44. Hartman, *Easy Pieces*, p. 193.
45. Atkins, *Hartman*, p. 153.
46. Adorno, *Aesthetic Theory* (1997), p. 115.
47. Hartman, *Easy Pieces*, p. 193.
48. On the distinction between 'abstract' and 'concrete' understanding in contemporary dialectics, see K. Kosik, *Dialektik des Konkreten* (1971), pp. 34–59.
49. T. W. Adorno, *The Authoritarian Personality* (1950).
50. Hartman, *The Unremarkable Wordsworth* (1987), p. 191.
51. Hartman, *Criticism in the Wilderness*, p. 283.
52. Adorno, *Aesthetic Theory*, p. 5.

6

HAROLD BLOOM

INFLUENCE AND MISREADING

Although Harold Bloom's work emerged from a similar Romantic–Nietzschean context as that of Hartman and Hillis Miller, it cannot simply be subsumed under the concept of 'Deconstruction'. Bloom himself has continually emphasized the oppositions that divide him from the Yale Deconstructionists, and the distrust with which he regards this group of authors increased when the nationalist and anti-Semitic writings of the young Paul de Man were discovered.

Yet Bloom has distanced himself with humour, and his rejection never turned to bitterness or aggression. Thus he explains in an interview with Imre Salusinszky how his participation in the well-known collection *Deconstruction and Criticism* (1979) came about, in which essays by Derrida, Hillis Miller, Hartman, de Man and Bloom are gathered: 'The title was my personal joke, which no one can ever understand: I meant that those four were deconstruction-ists, and I was criticism.' He added: 'I have no relation to deconstruction.'[1]

While it will emerge that we are faced here with one of the exag-gerations of which Bloom seems to be particularly fond, it is undoubtedly correct that this critic pursues completely different goals from Derrida, de Man or Hillis Miller. Despite all his Romantic and Nietzschean affinities with the Yale theories, Bloom is con-cerned with the historical and psychological relation of individual authors and not with the contradictions of the text.

This is the main reason why Bloom's theory is treated here as an intermezzo or transitional phenomenon that announces critical debates. The aim is, on the one hand, to show that despite his categorical denials a certain affinity between his approach and the Yale theories exists, and, on the other hand, to recognize that the differences that separate his rhetorical and psychoanalytic scheme from these theories fall together with the limits of Deconstruction. They become evident whenever the Deconstructionists refuse to engage with psychological or sociological questions.

1 INFLUENCE AND MISREADING: ROMANTICISM, NIETZSCHEANISM AND PSYCHOANALYSIS

The spiritual affinity between Bloom and the Deconstructionists is primarily of Romantic, Nietzschean and rhetorical origin. In connection with the former's Romanticism and Nietzscheanism, Peter de Bolla remarks that the poetry of English Romanticism 'is (we should not forget) the base for all of Bloom's theoretical work'[2] and that Bloom 'is seen to be one of the inheritors of the Nietzschean tradition, consolidating that playful project of self interpretation in his own fashion'.[3] Almost everything that was stated above about Derrida, de Man, Hillis Miller and Hartman shows that these authors also belong to the literary-philosophical tradition that leads from the Romantics to Nietzsche.

Bloom distinguishes himself essentially from these exponents of Deconstruction, since he considers rhetorical speech not as figurative discourse that is dominated by the untameable trope, but also – and perhaps primarily – as a psychological phenomenon: a defence mechanism in Freud's sense. At the same time he regards it in an historical perspective as part of literary evolution in which poets responded in their works to the writings of other poets.

Bloom's psychoanalytic approach will be the major focus of investigation here, since it produces a concept of rhetoric that differs crucially from de Man's and Hillis Miller's. Bloom is primarily concerned with rhetoric as *power of persuasion* and as an *expression of the Nietzschean will to power*. De Bolla claims that Bloom's concept of rhetoric is governed by the idea of a 'diachronic rhetoric'[4] that presents the polemical dialogue of the poets from an historical perspective and is intended to go beyond the synchronic concept of rhetoric of the Deconstructionists.

In contrast to de Man, who believes to be able to locate an unbridgeable gap or aporia between 'rhetoric as a system of tropes' and 'rhetoric as power of persuasion' in Nietzsche, Bloom attempts to reconcile these two components of rhetoric that had fallen apart in Deconstruction. His response to de Man is: 'What holds together rhetoric as a system of tropes, and rhetoric as persuasion, is the necessity of defense, defense against everything that threatens survival; and a defense whose aptest name is "meaning".'[5]

What is at stake here in a simultanously Nietzschean and Freudian context is the *rhetorical will of the poet to defend the unique and original character of his creation against his paternal precursor, the literary 'father'*. Bloom calls this form of describing and explaining literary development *antithetical criticism*. It is a criticism that aims to be literary criticism rather than literary analysis and is founded on the idea 'that the meaning of a poem can only be a poem, but *another poem – a poem not itself'*.[6] Bloom adds as an explanation: 'And not a poem chosen with total arbitrariness, but any central poem by an indubitable precursor, even if the ephebe *never read* that poem.'[7]

Even if one assumes, in accordance with the Russian Formalists, the Prague Structuralists, and theories of intertextuality,[8] that literary, philosophical, or scientific texts cannot be considered in isolation, but ought to be understood dialogically as responses to other texts, one will notice with astonishment that Bloom's ephebe might not even know the 'central poem' of his precursor and rival. This telepathic view of literary production is on the one hand connected with the Romantic slant of Bloom's theory, and with its Nietzschean rejection of empirical science that would hardly permit such speculative interpretations on the other. The diverse theories of intertextuality indeed imply the possibility of an unconscious processing of spoken or written texts (i.e. an author need not explicitly refer to a text and can still respond implicitly or unconsciously to it); nonetheless they exclude telepathic reactions to completely unknown texts.

In this pre- or post-scientific context, the two key terms *influence* and *misreading* (or *misprision*) must be taken with a grain of salt. According to Bloom, the *strong poet* adapts the texts of his precursor or literary 'father' to his own aesthetic needs in order to escape the paralysing influence of the paternal genius. 'To live', Bloom claims, 'the poet must *misinterpret* the father, by the crucial act of misprision, which is the rewriting of the father.'[9]

Far from being objectively necessary or conforming to the structure of the text, as demanded by Hillis Miller's deconstructive ethics, Bloom's reception is a simultaneously unconscious and deliberate misreading dictated by the needs of the individual poetic psyche. What is true for the poet's psyche is, *mutatis mutandis*, also true for the psyche of the average reader whose reception also follows the principles of misreading. This misreading should not be confused with an erroneous or indeed false reading, for it is a simultaneously personal and partial adaption that one might perhaps compare to Robert Escarpit's 'creative treason' (*'trahison créatrice'*). (Escarpit believes that only texts that can be continually reinterpreted and translated, i.e. betrayed according to the Italian proverb *'traduttore traditore'* (translator traitor), can survive for centuries.)

Bloom calls this creative betrayal of the paternal precursor by the ephebe *revisionism*. Such a revisionism can never be regarded as the completion of the older work, but must always be understood as a rebellious and revolutionary process, as a distortion or deformation. Bloom explains, in *Poetry and Repression*: '*No later poet can be the fulfillment of any earlier poet*. He can be the reversal of the precursor, but whatever he is, *to revise is not to fulfill*.'[10]

In this revisionist context the entire history of literature appears as a linking of Oedipal reactions. The ephebe or apprentice poet responds to the work of a father-figure by dissecting and reinterpreting it in a kind of love-hate relationship. Thus Bloom writes, for instance, about Milton's relationship to his paternal predecessor Spenser: 'Milton rewrites Spenser so as to *increase the distance* between his poetic father and himself.'[11] Something similar is at stake in the relationship between the Romantic poet Shelley and his ephebe Browning: 'Shelley is the Hidden God of the universe created by *Childe Harold to the Dark Tower Came*. His is the presence that the poem labors to void, and his is the force that rouses the poem's force.'[12]

This simultaneously polemical and voluntaristic view of literary history and textual history in general has a long tradition – according to Bloom – that goes back to the Jewish *Kabbalah*, the *gnosis*[13] and the philosophy of Gianbattista Vico (1668–1744), the founder of the philosophy of history and of the psychology of nations. On the Kabbalah Bloom writes: 'Kabbalah misreads all language that is not Kabbalah, and I assert now that belated strong poetry misreads all language that is not poetry.'[14] Peter de Bolla is right in adding that the reinterpretation or misreadings of the poet do not concern poetic language in general, but the language of the admired and hated precursor.[15]

At crucial points in his work Bloom refers to Vico, who strengthens the Kabbalistic and gnostic tendency towards misreading considerably: 'Vico, so far as I know, inaugurated the crucial insight that most critics still refuse to assimilate, which is that every poet is belated, that every poem is an instance of that what Freud called *Nachträglichkeit* or "retroactive meaningfulness".'[16]

At this point a simultaneously Nietzschean and Freudian affinity between Bloom and the exponents of Deconstruction emerges, whose thinking is governed by the *extreme ambivalence* that Nietzsche turns into the starting point of modern philosophy. In Bloom the ambivalence assumes a more psychoanalytic, Oedipal character, since the apprentice poet or ephebe *loves* and *hates* his paternal precursor at the same time.[17] Thus the ephebe Tennyson, for instance, who writes against Keats's influence, assumes an ambivalent attitude towards his predecessor. In *Agon*, Freud appears as the prophet of this Oedipal ambivalence, and in *A Map of Misreading* Bloom explains: 'Initial love for the precursor's is transformed rapidly enough into revisionist strife, without which individuation is not possible.'[18]

What Bloom states about the poet's revisionism also applies to his own apprentice relationship to Freud and other writers. In *A Map of Misreading* he talks about his 'own revisionism in regard to Freud'[19] and points out that Freud had to revise and de-idealize Schopenhauer's work in order to overcome the gap between subject and object and to develop a psychoanalytic theory of the unconscious. Bloom's Freudian revisionism, that has nothing in common with a psychoanalytic literary criticism or a *Psychocritique* in Charles Mauron's sense,[20] produces a simultaneously Nietzschean and psychoanalytic rhetoric whose starting point is the ephebe's first encounter with the paternal precursor. Bloom calls this encounter the *scene of instruction*, analogous to the Freudian primal scene, and defines it in connection with Shelley's relationship to Rousseau and the English Romantics Wordworth and Coleridge as a *primal fixation upon a precursor.*

It is particularly important that Bloom does not conceive this primal scene or primal scene of writing merely negatively and destructively as the incorporation of the ephebe by the established and recognized author, but as an event that is indispensible for the creativity of the younger poet. His description of Shelley's relationship towards Coleridge and Wordworth clearly illustrates this idea: 'Before the winter of 1814–15, Shelley wrote badly; he was a very weak poet. Only after having immersed himself in the works of Wordsworth and Coleridge, especially Wordsworth, he was able to write *Alastor* and the powerful 1816 poems, including *Mont Blanc.* Becoming a poet had meant accepting a primal fixation upon a quasi-divine precursor.'[21]

This example illustrates Bloom's idea of a literary primal scene, yet it also provokes some doubts concerning the strictly Oedipal character of the scene of instruction. Can a diffuse fixation on three poets – Rousseau, Wordsworth and Coleridge – still be understood as a fixation in the psychoanalytic sense? Could more thorough investigations not lead to the insight that Shelley's scene of instruction encompasses much more than these three authors and that one needs to consider the entire linguistic environment of his time (including Godwin's anarchist rhetoric) in order to understand his poetry? It is by no means certain that a poem or the complete works of a poet can be explained through their contrast to a precursor. These problems will emerge in greater detail at the end of the present chapter.

At this point the Romantic slant of Bloom's approach will be emphasized as a form of conclusion. In a completely different context Georges Matoré stresses the importance of individualism and the principle of competition for the French Romantics and the entire literature after 1830.[22] Therefore the question arises if Bloom's theory of literary revisionism or antithetical criticism, as he sometimes calls it, is not of Romantic origin. His pronounced interest in English Romanticism is no coincidence, but can be connected with the fact that Romantic poetry appears to the American critic as a poetry of *Nachträglichkeit* or belatedness that is governed by an 'anxiety of influence'. Bloom himself remarks: 'Romantic tradition is *consciously late*, and Romantic literary psychology is therefore necessarily a *psychology of belatedness*.'[23]

It is likely that the neo-Romantic Bloom has delivered the theoretical framework of this 'psychology of belatedness' with the aid of Nietzsche and Freud. Its notion of competition that is geared towards the individual and its originality is – if one believes Matoré's sociological analysis of French literature – of Romantic origin. Bloom's Romantic individualism might perhaps explain why he conceives the literary process as a competition between individual authors and thus neglects philosophical, scientific and social factors in literature.

2 THE STAGES OF REVISIONISM: PSYCHE AND RHETORIC

In contrast to the Deconstructionists de Man, Hillis Miller and Hartman, who challenge the concept of the subject, Bloom develops a theory of literature that is geared towards the individual subject that aspires to a synthesis of psychological and rhetorical elements. It is no longer concerned with pointing out the contradictions between rhetorical figures – for instance between metaphor and metonymy in Proust (de Man) – and to deconstruct the text, but with an exploration of the psychological function of tropes. This produces a Nietzschean-Freudian concept of rhetorics, as has been pointed out above, that is crucially different from the formal concept of rhetorics of Deconstruction.

Bloom describes the synthesis of psyche and rhetorics to which he aspires in the following way. For him, a rhetorical critic can conceive of a defence mechanism as a hidden trope. A psychoanalytic critic can conceive of a trope as hidden defence. An antithetic critic will learn to use both approaches and not be content to regard the substitution of analogues and the poetic process as one and the same thing.[24]

In *Agon* Bloom complements this synthetical sketch of his theory of revisionism when he accuses the Deconstructionists of not having progressed very far beyond the close reading of the New Critics with their immanent textual procedures. Their practice, he claims, resembles rather 'a refinement upon, but not a break with' Cleanth

Brooks. He adds cautiously – and this is not unimportant for the subsequent outline – that his own conception of trope or figure of speech does not in every aspect coincide with rhetorical definitions of the concept, that it 'goes beyond trope as expounded by any rhetorician, ancient or modern'.[25]

It is crucial that Bloom does not ask for the harmonious or contradictory interplay of these figures in the text, but for their rhetorical and persuasive power: 'Rather than ask again: what *is* a trope? I prefer to ask the pragmatic question: what is it that we want our tropes to do for us?'[26] It is clear that this line of questioning goes far beyond the text and hence beyond the immanent textual interpretations of the New Critics and the Deconstructionists. It targets the author's psyche, that the New Critics attempted to exclude, together with the *intentional fallacy*, and that the Deconstructionists simply ignore as an anachronism. For this reason alone, Christopher Norris is right in remarking: 'At the same time his argument slyly undermines the Deconstructionist position by making the conflict of will appear that is at the heart of the opposition of texts.'[27]

As a summary one can note that Bloom goes beyond the immanent textual approach of the Deconstructionists and the New Critics and that he shifts criticism into the pragmatic realm. He develops a psychoanalytic theory of literature that not so much searches for signals of the unconscious in the text but places an Oedipal scene in the centre of the investigation and makes the love-hate relationship between 'father' and 'son' the driving force of literary development.

Its most important starting point is the literary primal scene or scene of instruction that initiates a long process of differentiation and self-discovery in whose course mechanisms of repression and defence produce six revisionary positions that are equivalent to particular poetic figures. In *The Anxiety of Influence*, where Bloom explains that Nietzsche and Freud were 'the prime influences upon the theory of influence presented in this book',[28] he constructs a system of analogies between revisionary positions, psychological impulses and rhetorical figures. Most of these revisionary positions or attitudes (*revisionary ratios*) are defined with the aid of neologisms – such as *climanen* or *tessera* – that are themselves of philosophical or literary origin.

Clinamen, a term that derives from Lucretius, designates the first revisionary or dissident position that the ephebe assumes towards his precursor: 'A poet swerves away from his precursor, by so reading his predecessor's poem as to execute a *clinamen* in relation to it.'[29] This *clinamen* must therefore be understood as a corrective or departure that the ephebe decides on at a crucial point of the poem in order to replace his initial agreement with his precursor's text by dissent and a creativity of his own. Bloom talks about a 'creative correction'.[30]

The psychological attitude that forms the equivalent of the clinamen is the *reaction-formation*: the ephebe responds to the work of his precursor and simultanously develops his own poetic *self*. The rhetorical figure that accompanies this process is, according to Bloom, the *irony* in relation to the father-figure. From this perspective Thomas Mann's attitude towards Goethe appears as an ironic *clinamen*, when Bloom remarks: 'Mann's swerve away from Goethe is the profoundly ironic denial that any swerve is necessary.'[31] With similar irony Nietzsche encounters his precursor Hegel in the philosophical realm in which also an anxiety of influence reigns.

Tessera, a term that Bloom rediscovers in Mallarmé and Lacan, yet which features already in some antique cults, means as much as complementation or completion. In the literary process it evokes the antithetical completion and complementation of the 'paternal' work by the ephebe who attempts to show that the father 'has not gone far enough'. The analogous mechanism of defence is the role reversal of father and son, in whose course the son turns against himself as a 'paternal force'. The figure of speech characteristic of this process is synecdoche as 'part for the whole'. The precursor appears as a *pars pro toto* of all literary powers that threaten the originality of the young poet.

In this context Bloom can claim that 'Stevens antithetically completes Whitman'.[32] He expands this idea in order to make the difference between British and American poets plausible: 'It seems true that British poets swerve from their precursors, while American poets labor rather to "complete" their fathers.'[33]

Bloom calls the third phase of influence *kenosis* and takes up a biblical term that St Paul employs to describe Christ's renunciation of His Divine nature that He owes to the Father. In an analogous move the ephebe isolates himself from his precursor by renouncing the latter's aesthetics and poetics. The psychological mechanism of defence that dominates in this case is *isolation* or *undoing*. The corresponding rhetorical-poetic figure is *metonymy*.

In the *kenosis* stage of the poetic development the fragment is dominant, and the striving for totality and completion that governed the *tessera* phase is revoked. Together with the admired and hated text of the precursor, the poet's own text is fragmented and 'emptied'. A paradoxical situation is created in which the son's revolt against the father negates the son – or, as Bloom puts it, 'radically undoes the son'.[34] With reference to the father-son relationship between Wordsworth and Shelley he asks: 'Is Shelley's *kenosis* in his *Ode to the West Wind* an undoing, an isolating of Wordsworth or of Shelley?'[35]

When reading Bloom's work terminological questions pose themselves over and over again. Thus one would like to know at this point how 'isolation', 'undoing' or 'retraction' are genetically linked with a figure such as metonymy and other textual features such as 'fullness', 'emptiness' and 'fragmentation'.[36] For one must assume that a multi-faceted and polyvalent figure such as the metonymy can designate many and even contradictory states. Connecting it with the poetic state of isolation does not seem compulsory. Since synecdoche can moreover be conceived as an aspect of metonymy, the simultaneous question emerges of whether metonymy might not also fulfil important functions in the *tessera* stage. Unfortunately Bloom does not engage with these questions.

He labels the ephebe's search for his own uniqueness that radically questions the uniqueness of the precursor *daemonization*. The psychological defence mechanism dominant in this search is the repression of the powerful precursor by the ephebe: a yearning that is supported by the insight into '*the precursor's relative weakness*'.[37]

The equivalent rhetorical figures are *hyperbole* and *litotes*. Although the hyperbole is characterized by strong exaggeration (for example in 'cold as ice' and 'hard as stone'), while the litotes contains an understatement (Greek *litos* = simple), the two figures complement each other. Both emphasize the sublimeness and uniqueness of the ephebe and serve to eclipse the originality of the precursor.

Bloom labels the 'movement of self-purgation'[38] in which the poet renounces a part of himself in order to distinguish himself more clearly from his environment and his precursor *askesis*.

Together with his own poetic self the ephebe also subjects the work of his precursor to a process of purgation that leads to a global simplification and curtailing of this work. It is a process of sublimation that corresponds to Freud's sublimation in so far as it contains an ascetic renunciation: the abandoning of certain procedures and stylistic means (in Freud the renunciation of the sexual object in favour of cultural objects).

Bloom outlines the ascetic sublimation in the context of Browning and Yeats who are dependent, as poets, on their mutual precursor Shelley: 'Browning and Yeats, both dependent heirs of Shelley . . . , perform a massive self-curtailment in their full maturity as poets.'[39] This self-curtailment goes hand in hand with a repression of the precursor, the Other, by the poetic self that is achieved with the rhetorical-poetic means of *metaphor* and *metaphoricity*.

Bloom calls the final phase of poetic revisionism *apophrades* and refers with this expression to the days when the dead were supposed to return to their former homes in classical Athens. The precursor returns, yet is incorporated by the ephebe and deprived of his 'paternal' identity: 'Internalization of the precursor is the ratio I have called *apophrades* . . . .'[40] The new, strong poet can now afford to open himself to the 'paternal' impact without an 'anxiety of influence', since he is capable of transforming this impact into an element of his own creation. In the *apophrades* stage the poet has found his own *self* on the basis of certain psychological processes such as *introjection* and has integrated all alien influences into this *self*.

In this stage the rhetorical figure of *metalepsis* (a particular form of metonymy) forms the centre of the process, since it confirms the reversal of roles: the ephebe becomes the originary and original poet and finally eclipses the precursor. Bloom consequently talks about a 'metaleptic reversal'.

It is important to point out that Bloom's stages of poetic revisionism described here are detected not only in the development of literature as such or that of individual authors, but also in individual texts – especially in poems. In a commentary on Shelley's 'The Triumph of Life' Bloom attempts to sketch all six stages of revisionism and misreading. The poem commences with a *clinamen*, a move 'against Wordsworth's natural piety',[41] then shifts towards the *tessera* governed by the synecdoche, and the *kenosis* dominated by metonymy. In the stage of *daemonization* ruled by repression and hyperbole, Shelley suppresses his desire 'to carry through the Rousseau–Wordsworth dream of natural redemption'.[42] The ascetic phase (*askesis*), for which an aesthetic and stylistic self-curtailment or purgation is characteristic, is followed by the *apophrades* stage in which the precursor Wordsworth returns. Yet he is robbed of his identity and appears 'in Shelley's own colors'.[43]

Two aspects of Bloom's theory are important in the context of Deconstruction: the fact that he stresses again and again that tropes are not merely textual features or rhetorical procedures, but simultaneously fulfil psychological functions, and the idea that poet as well as common reader misunderstand and 'deform' texts according to their own psychological needs.

Not without justification Bloom writes accusingly of de Man that he 'declines to examine the psychological defences that inform Keats's liminal trope'.[44] This discovery of psychological energies that are at the basis of rhetorical procedures leads to the insight that literary, philosophical and perhaps also scientific reading can only be conceived as *misreading*. Each reader – and especially the poet as reader – uses and abuses the text (of the precursor) for his own means, which are dictated by his psyche.

3 CRITIQUE

Bloom's argument also leads to a drastic particularization of theory that (contrary to Derrida's and de Man's) is not connected primarily with the privileging of the level of expression but with a quasi-existentialist orientation towards the individual psyche. A crucial aspect of this tendency of particularization is the theory of *misreading* that not only denies the existence of universally visible textual constants as the starting point of all interpretations, but are also based on the assumption that each interpretation can only be a subjective distortion of the original. This distortion, that leads through all stages from *clinamen* to *apophrades* in the 'ideal case', is not only characteristic of the writer as producer, but also of the 'reproductive' critic and reader. In other words, each reading is a misunderstanding or misreading.

This view may have the advantage of excluding any form of naïve objectivism and of emphasizing the productive (i.e. constructive and constructivist) moment of reading: we do not read with 'disinterested pleasure', but with Freudian passion that must be considered the driving force of our search for identity. Yet it also has the disadvantage of abandoning the theoretical claims of general applicability and plausibility that were upheld by most literary hermeneutics in the past. How can such literary interpretations be judged or criticized at all when there exists only a misreading in the service of the particular search for identity of the poet, critic or reader? The canonization of misreading neither excludes arbitrariness nor relativism.

Just as particularist as the theory of misreading is Bloom's distinction between strong and weak poets, which makes his concept approach the level of literary criticism. Characteristic of it is a passage in *Poetry and Repression*, in which Wordsworth's greatness is serenaded. It states that Wordsworth's particular greatness consists in being the only one to have replaced Milton as ruling genius of the primal scene, and that it is the scandal of modern poetry that no one, not even Yeats or Stevens, has replaced Wordsworth.[45] In whose view? Who talks, who judges, and with what right? In the light of Bloom's regal gesture such questions probably smack of trivial scientism and methodological casuistry.

The literary scholar who still values such debates (despite changing academic fashions) should not overlook the fact that, according to Bloom, 'a theory of strong misreading denies that there is or should be any common vocabulary in terms of which critics can argue with one another'.[46] This answers the question concerning the possibility of a theoretical or scientific dialogue provisionally.

In this context one is reminded of the 'anti-universalist implications of the concept of rhetorics' that Michael Cebulla mentioned in his critique of Paul de Man (see Chapter 3, section 5). Bloom's illustrations of misreading are also anti-universalist in every respect, and it is therefore not surprising that the analogies between psychological states and rhetorical figures that were elaborated above often appear arbitrary. They have to be perceived as subjective, polyvalent and indeed themselves analysable creations of Bloom's own misreading. That this misreading may be creative and stimulating for the reader need not therefore be denied.

What must be denied is its potential of dialogue with respect to theories of literature and its ability to connect with present discussions in the social sciences. In the framework of these discussions one would have to be able to demand from Bloom, among other things, that he not restrict his interpretations of literary production and the behaviour of individual authors to the realm of the individual psyche, but take into account components that are genre-specific, generally linguistic and social.

For literary production is more than a psychological process: it is always also a reaction to aesthetic and extra-aesthetic norms, sociolects, socio-linguistic situations and processes of institutionalization (for example in the realm of genres). Why is the 'anxiety of influence', as Bloom himself remarks, not as strongly pronounced in authors such as Dante, Shakespeare and Goethe as it is in the Romantics?[47] Bloom cannot answer such questions at all in the framework of his approach. For literary evolution cannot simply be understood as a duel between isolated geniuses (such as Wordsworth and Shelley), at least as long as scientific criteria in the most general sense remain valid.

It remains beyond doubt, however, that in the context of Bloom's work scientificity counts for nothing. As Peter de Bolla remarks, 'This theory is anything but a science.'[48] This verdict is also applicable to the theories of the Deconstructionists and forms one of the major themes of the final chapter of the present study.

NOTES

1. H. Bloom, in Salusinszky, *Criticism in Society* (1987), p. 68.
2. P. de Bolla, *Harold Bloom: Towards Historical Rhetorics* (1988) p. 122.
3. de Bolla, *Bloom*, p. 9.
4. Ibid., p. 61.
5. H. Bloom, *Poetry and Repression: Revisionism from Blake to Stevens* (1976), p. 240.
6. H. Bloom, *The Anxiety of Influence: A Theory of Poetry* (1973), p. 70.
7. Ibid., p. 70.
8. The theory of intertextuality, developed by Julia Kristeva from the ideas of the Russian theorist Bakhtin, cannot be reduced to a theory of citation. It implies that an author responds consciously or unconsciously to certain spoken or written texts in his society and transforms these texts in his works in mimetic, ironic, parodic or other ways. See J. Kristeva, *Semeiotikè: Recherches pour une sémanalyse* (1969), p. 144. See also my *Textsoziologie* (1988), pp. 81–5, and my *Ideologie und Theorie* (1989), pp. 250–3. Bloom's problem consists, among other things, in his reduction

of intertextuality to a psychological process and his consequent lack of attention to its discursive, ideological and cultural aspects.

9. H. Bloom, *A Map of Misreading* (1975), p. 19.

10. Bloom, *Poetry and Repression*, p. 88.

11. Bloom, *Map of Misreading*, p. 128.

12. Ibid., p. 116.

13. *Kabbalah*: a collection of mystic writings and Jewish religious tradition. *Gnosis* (Greek: 'understanding'): a theological-philosophical doctrine, originally of ancient Christianity, geared towards an insight into the supernatural world.

14. H. Bloom, *Wallace Stevens: The Poems of Our Climate* (1977), p. 394.

15. de Bolla, *Bloom*, p. 93.

16. Bloom, *Poetry and Repression*, p. 4.

17. See H. Bloom, *Ruin the Sacred Truths: The Charles Eliot Norton Lectures 1987–88* (1989), p. 146.

18. Bloom, *Map of Misreading*, p. 10.

19. Ibid., p. 88.

20. Charles Mauron's *Psychocritique* represents an attempt to apply Freudian psychoanalysis to literature and to determine, with the help of 'obsessive metaphors' ('*métaphores obsédantes*') of a work the 'personal myth' of the author. See C. Mauron, *Des Métaphores obsédantes au mythe personnel: Introduction à la psychocritique* (1983).

21. Bloom, *Poetry and Repression*, p. 105.

22. See G. Matoré, *Le Vocabulaire et la société sous Louis-Philippe* (1951), pp. 22–3.

23. Bloom, *Map of Misreading*, p. 35.

24. Ibid., p. 89.

25. H. Bloom, *Agon: Towards a Theory of Revisionism* (1982), p. 31.

26. Ibid.

27. C. Norris, *Deconstruction: Theory and Practice* (revised edition) (1991), p. 122.

28. Bloom, *Anxiety of Influence*, p. 8.

29. Ibid., p. 14.

30. Ibid., p. 30.

31. Ibid., p. 54.

32. Ibid., p. 68.

33. Ibid.

34. Ibid., p. 90.

35. Ibid.

36. Ibid., p. 36.

37. Ibid., p. 100.

38. Ibid., p. 15.

39. Ibid., p. 128.

40. Ibid., p. 152.

41. Ibid., p. 99.

42. Ibid., p. 100.
43. Bloom, *Poetry and Repression*, p. 100. Bloom confirms here what he states in his book on Yeats: 'The poet, if he could, would be his own precursor . . .'; H. Bloom, *Yeats* (1970), p. 5.
44. Bloom, *Poetry and Repression*, p. 113.
45. Ibid., pp. 81–2.
46. Bloom, *Agon*, p. 21.
47. See Bloom, *Anxiety of Influence*, p. 50: 'Goethe, like Milton, absorbed precursors with a gusto evidently precluding anxiety.'
48. De Bolla, *Bloom*, p. 58.

7

CRITIQUE OF DECONSTRUCTION

Ni ange ni bête noire: the aim of this chapter is neither a wholesale rejection nor a blind exaltation of Deconstruction, for it ought to be preserved from the fate of theoretical schools such as Marxism, psychoanalysis and Existentialism which were used unscrupulously for ideological purposes by friends and foes alike.[1] Paul de Man's juvenile sympathies for nationalism and National Socialism justify neither an equation nor a comparison of Deconstruction with fascism or irrationalism.[2] What has been said so far is meant to foreground the heterogeneity of Deconstruction – Derrida's, de Man's, Hillis Miller's, Hartman's – alluded to in the Preface: a heterogeneity comparable with that of Marxism, psychoanalysis (Freud's and Jung's) and existentialism (Heidegger's and Sartre's). It may have become clear that the notion of aporia underlying de Man's and Miller's investigations is rarely mentioned by Hartman who focuses, like Barthes, on the openness and indeterminacy of texts.

A dialectical and dialogical[3] critique of Deconstruction will not lead to a global rejection of this theory, as proposed by scholars such as John M. Ellis on the basis of an analytical approach (see Chapter 7, section 2) or by David Lehman from a journalistic-political perspective. A dialectical argument which in some respects relies on Critical Theory of the Frankfurt School type will attempt to distinguish the insights of the Deconstructionists from errors and difficulties which in some cases may turn out to be inevitable. For after all, even the theories of the Frankfurt School have produced moments of truth along with contradictions and aporias. Despite its critical distance, *Kritische Theorie* should recognize in Deconstruction a sometimes close, sometimes distant relative.

One of the crucial achievements of Deconstruction is the insight that discourse as a transphrastic structure (as the semioticians would call it) articulates Nietzsche's 'will to power' or Heidegger's 'will to knowledge' (see Chapter 1, section 5). This power aspect of discourse was emphasized time and again by Adorno, while Habermas thinks to exorcize it in his theory of an 'ideal communicative situation' (see Chapter 7, section 4).

Like this critique of discourse which relates Derrida to Adorno, the deconstructive critique of logocentrism confirms Adorno's view that the literary work is not a totality in an Hegelian or Lukácsian sense. It cannot be defined univocally as a structure of signifieds in the context of a Structuralist or hermeneutic approach. By showing us how the text evades the grasp of conceptual thinking, Derrida's, de Man's and Miller's critical arguments make some basic assumptions of rationalism and Hegelian dialectics appear dubious dogmas.

Despite the importance of these arguments, which should not be ignored or explained away, one needs to bear in mind that Deconstruction in its different versions fails to reflect on its own premises in an historical and dialogical context (see Chapter 3, sections 1 and 2). Derrida and his followers seem to observe aporias or forms of iterability and dissemination in almost all texts, and tend to overlook the simple semiotic fact that they themselves – like all their predecessors – project constructions of their own meta-discourses into the texts they comment on. Thus they contribute, without intending it, to the consolidation of absolutist and monological tendencies in philosophy. Like the Hegelian (Lukács for instance) who identifies the text with *his own* totality, like the Structuralist (Greimas for instance), who equates it to *his own* depth structure or *his own* concept of isotopy, de Man confuses it with the aporetic structure that he himself has invented.[4]

When they claim that *all* texts are aporetic and ultimately deconstruct themselves, the Deconstructionists tend to neglect the historical and sociological dimension of their research. For the plurality of texts and of their historical contexts makes such an hypothesis, according to which all works are aporetic constructs, appear rather implausible. In what follows it will be shown that some of these arguments are taken up by various critics of Deconstruction.

1 BOURDIEU'S CRITIQUE OF DERRIDA

Bourdieu's critique is particularly important, since it sheds light on the relationship of Deconstruction to the social sciences and at the same time deals with the function or dysfunction of this strand of philosophy in the *institutions* of a market society. This is why it will be considered first. By describing Deconstruction on a functional level, it observes it 'from the outside' as it were and makes possible an explanation of its discourse in an institutional context. In essence, Bourdieu accuses Derrida of never having left the realm of idealist philosophy and of having failed to consider the actual and possible functions of Deconstruction in the institutions.

In his remarks on Derrida's analysis of the *Critique of Judgement* (see Chapter 1, section 1), Bourdieu points out that Derrida does not go beyond the *intellectual field* (*champ intellectuel*) of the philosophical idealism developed by Kant. 'Because he never withdraws from the philosophical game, whose conventions he respects, even in the ritual transgressions at which only traditionalists could be shocked, he can only philosophically tell the truth about the philosophical text and its philosophical reading.'[5] In other words, Deconstruction's verbal radicalism only deflects attention from its impotence as a critical theory of society and its institutions. Despite Deconstruction's linguistic and terminological subtlety, Derrida appears to be unable to reflect on the function that his philosophy fulfils in the context of an intellectual field and in institutions legitimized by the state: 'The radical questionings announced by philosophy are in fact circumscribed by the interests linked to membership in the philosophical field, that is, to the very existence of this field and the corresponding censorships.'[6] Deconstruction may be a new way of playing the philosophers' game; yet it does not challenge the rules of the game or the game as such. In a similar perspective, American critics view the role of literary Deconstruction in the United States: it is held to be successful, not in spite but because of its radical rhetoric.[7]

Bourdieu compares Derrida's Deconstruction with the experiments of the avant-garde, whose attacks on traditional art ultimately contributed to a strengthening of art as an institution, since they 'have always tuned ... to the glory of art and the artist'.[8] Similarly, the deconstruction of philosophy represents 'the only philosophical answer to the destruction of philosophy'.[9] It is a purely ideal and idealist reaction to the contemporary crisis of philosophy that Marx and his heirs attempted to overcome by a revolutionary practice.

Bourdieu could have added that we are not faced with a simple analogy between Deconstruction and avant-garde literature, but with an institutional link-up. It could be observed in the 1960s and 1970s, when Derrida published his first articles (for instance 'La Double séance') in the avant-garde periodical *Tel Quel*, where contributions by Roland Barthes, Jean Ricardou, Philippe Sollers, Jean-Joseph Goux, Julia Kristeva and others appeared regularly. He published his long essay on 'La Différance' in the well-known volume *Théorie d'ensemble* which contains important contributions by other *Tel Quel* authors: for example Philippe Sollers's essay 'Ecriture et révolution'[10] which starts from Marx's opposition between basis and superstructure and argues for a symbiosis of writing and revolution.

Although Derrida has never made Marxist terminology his own, the critical and revolutionary aims of the *Tel Quel* group and the *mouvements* of 1968 were by no means alien to him. Paradoxically, his later publications such as *Du droit à la philosophie* (1990) and *Spectres of Marx* (1994) emphasize his affinity to the revolutionary groupings of the 1960s more strongly than his critiques of language published in *Tel Quel*. This may be why Bourdieu's critique in *Distinction* does not do justice to Derrida's position in every respect. For the marginality of this position is due, among other things, to the failure of the May revolt and its revolutionary experiments.

In an interview given in 1992 the sociologist explains the importance of French Deconstruction in the institutional realm, referring to the marginality of Deconstruction and its exclusion from official philosophy. Bourdieu accuses Derrida and Foucault of attempting to present their marginal position in academia as a virtue, adding that the two philosophers found themselves obliged 'to turn a social necessity into a virtue and to transform the collective fate of a generation into a conscious decision'.[11] This heroic pose, Bourdieu concludes, is 'disappointing or even a little unappealing . . . .'[12] He may not be completely wrong. However, as a sociologist he might have pondered more critically, more reflexively on the 'collective fate of a generation' to which he himself belongs.

On the whole, it seems precarious to found sociological critcism on resentment. For one could object that Bourdieu fails to notice Derrida's critique of discourse (of particular importance for the *Tel Quel* group), since as a sociologist he is interested more in the institutional functions of collective languages than in their semantic, syntactic and rhetorical structures investigated by Derrida, de Man and Hillis Miller. Despite its originality and its importance for semiotics and socio-linguistics, Bourdieu's study *Ce que parler veut dire* reveals this functional (not functionalist) bias of his sociology which can hardly be said to further a better understanding of Derrida's and de Man's rhetorical analyses. In this study, discourses are primarily considered on an institutional level: as collective languages whose function and authority derive from institutionalized practices.

Moreover, Bourdieu pays no attention to Derrida's deconstructionist critique of insitutionalized philosophy in *Du droit à la philosophie*. In this study, Derrida writes: 'The necessity of Deconstruction . . . did not derive in the first place from philosophical contents, themes or theses, philosophemes, poems, theologemes or ideologemes, but primarily from the global conditions of meaning, institutional structures, pedagogic or rhetorical norms . . . .'[13]

Yet it is hardly possible to explain the social, institutional conditions of meaning as long as one is unwilling to include the experiments and methods of the social sciences which – in contrast to the rhetorics of Deconstruction – are capable of relating discourses to their social, political and institutional contexts.

In *Specters of Marx*, Derrida also argues in favour of a thorough analysis of social and economic phenomena, yet does not carry this analysis through. He is content to list some crucial problems of contemporary societies: unemployment, economic wars (he uses the term very loosely and even speaks of economic wars inside the European Union), the proliferation of nuclear weapons, etc.[14] Yet one hardly requires the subtle and complex rhetoric of a

Deconstructionist philosophy to deal casually with problems which have been thoroughly dissected by sociologists, political and economic scientists.

One of the problems of Derrida's Deconstruction stems from its inability to deal with social and economic processes and from the fact that it ceases to be Deconstruction (in the rhetorical–tropological sense) as soon as it attempts to do so. For Derrida's analysis of some contemporary problems does not even approach the level of a thorough journalistic commentary and has little in common with Deconstruction. The fact that Deconstruction produces a type of text whose compatibility with other discourses and applicability to social problems is very limited, is also confirmed by Niklas Luhmann who, in reading Derrida, is struck by 'the paradox of differentiations which negate themselves'.[15]

By relegating the social sciences indiscriminately to the metaphysical realm – following Heidegger's critique – Derrida bars himself from reflecting critically on the socio-political and historical context of his own theory. His outline of a theory of scientific institutions and of institutionalized philosophy is condemned to failure from the outset because he rejects semiotics, psychology and sociology as forms of metaphysics. In this respect one cannot but agree with Bourdieu: the critical – essentially rhetorical – instruments at the disposal of Deconstruction do not allow for an exploration of the social and economic context from which it has emerged and in which it functions.

2 A CRITIQUE FROM THE STANDPOINT OF ANALYTIC PHILOSOPHY

Analytic philosophy and dialectical Marxism are diametrically opposed, and their immediate succession in the present chapter requires a short explanation. The fact that Deconstruction is rejected by exponents of analytic philosophy as well as by Marxists is certainly no reason to have an analytic critique followed by a Marxist one. More important, more interesting is the fact that the doubts voiced by John M. Ellis in a logical and analytic context are reinforced by some Marxist commentaries (Eagleton, Lentricchia) and seem to confirm Bourdieu's critique at crucial points. Considering these unexpected overlaps, initiating a dialogue on

Deconstruction between heterogeneous yet in some respects complementary theoretical positions appears worthwhile.

Following the analytic tradition of Wittgenstein, Russell and
Ryle, J. M. Ellis attempts to reveal logical contradictions and other
vagaries of Derrida's philosophy. Yet he does not confine himself to
the formal realm, but continually addresses empirical weaknesses of
Deconstruction also commented on by Marxists such as Terry
Eagleton and Frank Lentricchia. These two writers return to the
problems outlined by Bourdieu when they accuse Derrida and the
American Deconstructionists of glossing over political issues and
rejecting the social sciences.

In these debates Christopher Norris defends Deconstruction by
emphasizing its analytic accuracy in response to Ellis's critique and
by highlighting its political engagement in response to Marxist
criticism. The dialogue between Norris, Ellis and the Marxists
envisaged here develops into a dialogue between Deconstruction
and Critical Theory towards the end of this chapter. In the course
of this dialogue, the author articulates his own stance vis-à-vis
Deconstruction.

The arguments put forward by Ellis against Deconstruction
deserve closer scrutiny not merely because they converge with
Bourdieu's sociological critique and some Marxist objections, but
also because they expose crucial weaknesses of Derrida's
philosophy.

Ellis is probably right in doubting Derrida's basic distinction
between *parole* and *écriture* when he insists on the impossibility of
proving the pre-eminence of the written word: 'Even in admitting
that speech cannot exist until writing is *possible*, Derrida is conced-
ing the *logical* priority of speech, since it is speech's *existence* that
makes writing *possible*.'[16] In other words, writing presupposes the
functioning of oral communication.

At this point one could object with Derrida that Deconstruction
is not primarily concerned with establishing priorities but with
demonstrating how writing highlights the mechanisms of *différance*
and *dissemination* which are obliterated and repressed by privileging the spoken word. The fact that a text can be repeated and
interpreted in various contexts could then be quoted as evidence
of a continual shift: a non-presence of the written sign. Unfortunately this argument does not reinforce Derrida's position, for it is

reversible: one only needs to refer to the common sense phrase *verba volant* and to claim that only the word written according to certain rules and conventions (for instance those of lawyers) provides a reliable check on semantic proliferation. The objection that legal texts are also ambivalent and can become inexhaustible sources of controversy is not helpful, since it is well known that oral agreements are even more controversial and lead to endless quarrels.

All things considered, any attempt to prove the primacy of *écriture* as *archi-écriture* and to demonstrate that it is more prone to ambiguities than the spoken word, when the spoken word is constantly threatened by misunderstanding, false retelling, grammatical faults and malfunctions in everyday life, appears to be extremely risky. Hence the hierarchical distinction of *parole* and *écriture* remains a metaphysical weakness of Deconstruction which Habermas has also remarked on (see section 4).

This may be one of the reasons why Derrida turns the diference between *parole* and *écriture* into a banality in *Points de suspension* where he mentions their 'somewhat trivial opposition' ('*opposition un peu triviale entre la parole et l'écriture*').[17] However, the attentive reader of *Grammatology* will certainly remember that Derrida adorns *archi-écriture* with euphoric connotations, while condemning *parole* as an instrument of logocentrism.

Ellis develops his criticism of the term *écriture* when he accuses Derrida of conceiving language and *écriture* as synonyms: 'Language does *not* mean writing, and if we use "writing" to substitute for "language" we have misspoken.'[18] Derrida's tendency to derive the problems of language from an *archi-écriture* or original writing not only produces a flaw in the discourse of Deconstruction, but also widens the gap which separates this discourse from linguistics, a science concerned with the particularities of the written and the spoken work in different communicative contexts.[19]

Another argument raised by Ellis against Derrida also concerns (albeit indirectly) the rift between Deconstruction and the social sciences. Thus Ellis questions the thesis that *all* texts can be deconstructed and that *every* language eventually undermines what it states. He explains: 'If we say only that a text *often* signifies on different levels then we are back in the province of traditional criticism.'[20] In order to distinguish itself from this philology, Ellis claims, Deconstruction must assume an extreme position in the 'intellectual field' (Bourdieu) and declare that *all* texts can be deconstructed or deconstruct themselves.

It was shown that Derrida, Paul de Man and J. Hillis Miller assume this extreme and ahistorical position starting from the assumption that all texts are ambivalent and aporetic. Their formalism, which abstracts from the social, ideological and psychological dimensions of the text, harbours certain risks noted by Ellis as well as David Lehman.

Lehman wonders, for example, what kind of result a deconstructive reading of Adolf Hitler's *Mein Kampf* would yield. Could one not emphasize the fact that Hitler rejects religious anti-Semitism?, he asks in *Signs of the Times*.[21] One might develop Lehman's criticism remembering the ambivalent and contradictory character of *Mein Kampf*. In this situation a deconstructive reading of the text might absurdly reveal that its author secretly implies the opposite of what he declares 'openly'. Should one imagine Hitler as a democrat *malgré lui* or as a friend of the Jews who represses his sympathies? Like every formalism, Deconstruction, marked by Nietzsche's extreme ambivalence, contains imponderables and risks.

In view of such risks it seems important to insist with Greimas and Bertil Malmberg (see Chapter 1, section 3) on the importance of textual constants, depth structures and actant models in a text such as *Mein Kampf* and on the impossibility of dissolving them by shifts, contradictions and polysemies, whose existence, however, should not be denied either. Deconstructionists all too often lose sight of the interplay of determinacy and indeterminacy, univocity and polysemy and forget that a text must display constants in order to be identifiable as a particular text.

This idea is also taken up by M. H. Abrams when he remarks that Derrida can only *deconstruct* that which he has previously *constructed* in a very conventional manner: 'He cannot demonstrate the impossibility of a standard reading except by going through the stage of manifesting its possibility; a text must be read determinately in order to be disseminated into an undecidability that never strikes completely free of its initial determination; deconstruction can only subvert the meanings of a text that has always already been construed.'[22] This is correct in so far as a text can never be perceived by the subject as a text, a 'thing-in-itself', but only ever as a construct (of this very subject).

Another aspect of deconstructive formalism is revealed by Ellis in a sociological perspective, when he points out that American Deconstruction only succeeded in establishing itself and surviving in an institutional setting by continually attacking the tradition of American criticism without ever suggesting concrete alternatives: 'Deconstruction and conservatism are in a kind of symbiosis in which the two feed on each other; and thus ideas that deserve to die will not be allowed to do so.'[23] In other words, Deconstruction's ceaseless fight against logocentrism and conservatism guarantees the survival of conservative ideologies *and* of Deconstruction. At this point Ellis's analytic argument converges with Bourdieu's sociological critique: Deconstruction thrives on the dominant conservative tradition which marginalizes it and condemns it to an heroic struggle against the institutions.

In a detailed response to Ellis and other critics, Christopher Norris defends Deconstruction by emphasizing the 'analytical' and rigorous character of Derrida's and de Man's argument. On Deconstructionists in general he writes: 'they engage in a close and critical reading of texts, drawing out the various orders of meaning (logical, grammatical and rhetorical) that organise those texts, and only then – with the strictest regard for such protocols – locating their blind spots of naïve or uncritical presupposition'.[24] Norris is right in so far as the exponents of Deconstruction tend to dissect established meanings and received ideas by an hypercorrect analysis of rhetorical and semantic patterns. One may also agree with his claim that 'Deconstruction is indeed susceptible to reasoned argument and counter-argument'.[25] Yet he should have considered the fact that the diverse variants of Deconstruction are indebted to the dialectical tradition of Hegel, the Young Hegelians and Nietzsche. These philosophers start from the unity of opposites, a figure of thought that excludes analytic patterns of reasoning based on a propositional logic which has always been at loggerheads with dialectics. It makes little sense therefore to praise the analytic advantages of Deconstruction(s).

By ignoring the Nietzschean and dialectical context of Deconstruction at crucial points, Norris overlooks the essentially *ambivalent* character of this kind of thinking which combines analytic (logical) rigour with rhetorical (Nietzschean) word play. He is of course right when he points out in his study on Derrida that

Deconstruction is a call to think 'through the paradoxes in the nature of reason'.[26] Fortunately or unfortunately, Deconstruction is a lot more, since Derrida, de Man and Hartman frequently sacrifice formal (propositional) logic in favour of a rhetoric of subjective association (see Chapter 2, section 5) and an essayism located beyond right and wrong. If the Deconstructionists had remained content to reflect on the paradoxes of reason, their problems would be comparable to those of Wittgenstein or analytic philosophy. The impossibility of aligning Deconstruction with analytic thinking is mainly due to its dialectical origin.

This dialectical origin is also neglected by Samuel C. Wheeler in his otherwise stimulating study on *Deconstruction as Analytic Philosophy*. According to Wheeler, both Derrida and Donald Davidson reject the metaphysical idea of language: the idea that meaning is spontaneously present in language which is a non-problematical manifestation of the Platonic *nous*. 'The fundamental point of agreement between Derrida and Davidson, as well as other thinkers in the analytic tradition such as Quine and Wittgenstein', Wheeler explains, 'is their denial of what I call the "magic language". This is the language of *nous*, a language that is, in Wittgenstein's terms, self-interpreting.'[27] One might also say that some thinkers in the linguistic (rather than analytic) tradition reject the idea of an objectively given meaning in language which to them appears as a permanent interaction between the *content plane*, the *expression plane* and an always open context of communication. It is one of their basic aims to analyse this interaction with utmost precision – and one might say in defence of Derrida that he is no less precise than the analytic philosophers. In this respect it is certainly meaningful to seek for affinities between Deconstruction and analytic philosophy.

However, as Wheeler himself points out, such affinities yield to divergencies as soon as the concept of truth is introduced. While an analytic philosopher like Davidson believes that truth is fundamental to our thought, Derrida turns out to be far more sceptical in this respect: 'Derrida, on the other hand, holds that, while the notion of truth is indeed central to our thought, we must abandon the hope of making strict sense of that notion.'[28] It is not by chance that divergencies between the two philosophers become visible in conjunction with 'truth'. While analytic philosophers such as Davidson are sufficiently rationalist to hold on to this notion, Derrida considers it in a Nietzschean perspective: as a rhetorical interplay of metonymies and metaphors organized and safeguarded by social convention. Here it becomes clear why it is so important to understand Derrida as an heir of the Young Hegelian and Nietzschean tradition. Far from being an analytic philosopher, he is – like Nietzsche and Adorno – a dialectical thinker who has turned against dialectics.

3 DECONSTRUCTION, MARXISM AND MARXIST CRITICISM

Michael Ryan might have had this origin in mind when, in *Marxism and Deconstruction*, he attempted a synthesis of Derrida's Deconstruction and a brand of humanist Marxism. Like some earlier attempts to combine Marxism with psychoanalysis or existentialism, Ryan's model suffers – despite its originality – from a schematism that occasionally produces unacceptable simplifications. The author might have avoided them if he had reflected on the relationship between Derrida's (pseudo-)dialectics and the post-Hegelian philosophies of the Romantics, the Young Hegelians and Nietzsche. He might have discovered an irreconcilable antagonism between Romantic, Young Hegelian, Nietzschean and pro-anarchic Deconstruction and an Hegelian Marxism whose historicism and logocentrism Derrida radically criticizes in *Glas*. Even if he had opted in favour of Althusser's non-Hegelian interpretation of Marx's writings, Ryan would have had to notice that his intended synthesis was doomed to fail. For it is well-known that Althusser attempted to prove that the author of *Capital* laid the foundations of a new exact science by making the continent called 'history' accessible to scientific thought – after Galileo had done the same for the 'mathematical continent'. It is obvious, however, that Althusser's scientistic reading of Marx is as irreconcilable with Deconstructive interpretations as the Hegelian brands introduced by Lukács and Goldmann.

In order to make his synthesis of Marxism and Deconstruction appear plausible, Ryan is obliged to imagine a third model of Marxism based on a diffuse humanism which draws heavily on American feminism and various ecological ideologies. To Ryan this

Marxism appears as an open and interpretable theory: 'Marxism, as an historical mode of theory and practice, is from the outset undecidable, that is, open to extension according to what history proffers.'[29] It is by no means certain that 'Marxism' in the singular (the expression 'Marx's works' would be more precise) is so undecidable and open to all and sundry.

Nor is it certain that the analogies between Marxism and Deconstruction postulated by Ryan are real (genetic or typological) affinities. In order to justify his attempt at synthesis Ryan proposes four core arguments: 1. Like Marx, Derrida criticizes Western metaphysics. 2. Deconstructive criticism strengthens the anti-conservative, differential and pluralist tendencies in Marxism (one has to bear in mind that Ryan's book appeared in 1982). 3. It favours a radical critique of capitalist-patriarchal institutions within the framework of Marxism. 4. Finally, Deconstruction strengthens the egalitarian and non-hierarchical tendencies in the development of Socialist society (here the politically aware reader might ask what part Deconstruction could have played in the scientific or academic life of the Soviet Union or the GDR).

If one considers these four programmatic points in the light of recent developments, one is reminded of psychoanalytic or existentialist efforts to 'humanize' Marxism on an individual and psychological plane. Like Ryan's synthesis, Sartre's *Critique of Dialectic Reason* of 1960 (particularly the introductory 'Questions of Method') also emphasized the 'individualist' and 'democratic' orientation of Marx's early writings, relating the whole of Marxism to the situation of the individual. Like the existentialist and psychoanalytic critiques in their days, Ryan's reinterpretation leads to an anti-Hegelian particularization of Marxism (or Marx's philosophy) – which certainly has the merit of being more humane than all types of Hegelianism.

However, it also produces superficial analogies: for example that between Marx's and Derrida's critique of metaphysics. This analogy has the disadvantage of obscuring the difference between an historical and materialist critique directed against the chimera of idealism and an Heideggerian Deconstruction aiming to subvert the principle of domination (the 'will to will') on an ontological and discursive level. Marx would have had no use for this kind of Deconstruction, since he never intended to criticize domination in general. The target of his critique was social class domination in capitalism. Bill Martin also overlooks this point when he mentions a 'deconstructive side' of Marx's thinking with reference to Ryan.[30]

Since Derrida and Heidegger refuse to engage in a serious dialogue with the social sciences, the two critiques of metaphysics Ryan would like to combine could turn out to be incompatible. Ryan himself touches on this problem when he realizes 'that deconstruction lacks a social theory'.[31] Of course this lack is not due to chance, but to Derrida's rejection of the social sciences which, in contrast to most Marxists,[32] he derives from the heritage of 'metaphysics or onto-theologies',[33] without differentiating between critical and uncritical types of social science. For this reason it also appears futile to compare Derrida's critique of individual or subjective identity with Marx's attack on the idea of an homogenous society: 'Marxism thus adds a missing dimension to deconstruction by extending it into social and political-economic theory.'[34] It is hardly possible to make Deconstruction expand into spheres which Derrida subsumes globally under Western metaphysics.[35]

Until recently it seemed possible to speculate about the question of how Derrida himself assessed the relationship between Deconstruction and Marxism, and how he would criticize Marxism as Hegelianism (Lukács, Goldmann), scientism (Althusser) or logocentrism. It was also possible to wonder to what extent he might agree with Ryan's attempt at a synthesis. Since the publication of *Specters of Marx* (1993) this situation has changed fundamentally.

The author of this somewhat polemical work attempts to argue against the grain and to refute the ideological cliché of 'the end of Marxism'. Beginning with the first sentence of the *Communist Manifesto*, 'A spectre haunts Europe – the spectre of communism', Derrida claims that the contemporary enemies of Marxism try once again to exorcize the phantom of communism. One of their manifestos is Francis Fukuyama's book *The End of History and the Last Man* (1992) which Derrida considers the gospel of a neo-Hegelian and Christian liberalism: 'The model of the liberal State to which he explicitly lays claim is not only that of Hegel, the Hegel of the struggle for recognition; it is that of a Hegel who privileges the "Christian vision".'[36] In short, Fukuyama's book is a manifesto of liberal and Christian ideologies which jointly proclaim the death of Marxism and the advent of a market economy-driven millennium.

It is hardly surprising that Derrida cannot believe in this Christian liberal and neo-Hegelian prophecy. He quite rightly evokes the large number of worldwide conflicts and the fact that most inhabitants of the Earth are far from enjoying the advantages of democracy and a social market economy, since they are plagued by famine, wars and violent regimes. As a counterpoint to Fukuyama's positive utopia he quotes Shakespeare's tragedy *Hamlet* which proclaims that 'the world is out of joint'. Just as he confronted Hegel's texts with those of Jean Genet in *Glas*, in *Specters of Marx* he systematically relates a tragedy which announces chaos to a self-admiring liberal utopia which insinuates that we live in the best of all possible worlds.

Faced with this ideological challenge, Derrida attempts – still in the spirit of the Frankfurt School – to revive a particular Marxism that might appear to the ideologues of the *status quo* as a phantom, yet is interpreted by critical thinkers as an *emancipatory promise* (*promesse émancipatoire*). Derrida may seek to accomplish the impossible when he locates this emancipatory promise, for him the core of Marxism, beyond deconstructive criticism: 'What remains irreducible to any deconstruction, what remains as un-deconstructible as the possibility itself of deconstruction is, perhaps, a certain experience of the emancipatory promise.'[37] Beyond all rhetorical word play Derrida seems to believe in a system of values which remains unquestioned and is in some respects reminiscent of Frankfurt School theory, for instance of Adorno's hope for emancipation.

Yet it remains unclear what exactly Derrida means by this promise of emancipation. In *The Other Heading*, a book to which he alludes in *Specters of Marx*, he underlines the necessity to accept 'differences, idioms, minorities, singularities',[38] argues in favour of the universal application of human rights and a self-critical assessment of Enlightenment which acknowledges the limits of reason, yet fails to explain how all these goals can be achieved. Very much like Adorno he continues to hold out in the negativity and irreconcilability of the existing world.

Derrida mentions Michael Ryan's book in *Specters of Marx*, yet does not comment at all on the synthesis suggested by Ryan. Considering what has been said so far, one might assume that he would agree with some components of this synthesis – women's emancipation, the rights of minorities, the protection of the environment and of animals. Yet despite this agreement one should not overlook Derrida's critique of Marxism. This critique has a number of aspects which are complementary within the framework of the Deconstructionist project. Like Ernst Bloch and the members of the Frankfurt School,[39] Derrida rejects Marxist historical teleology. He declares his critique of the notion of history in Hegel and Marx to be a 'deconstructive procedure' ('*démarche déconstructrice*').[40]

Derrida contrasts this teleological notion of history propounded by the Hegelians Marx and Engels with an historical openness which replaces the 'onto-theo- but also archeo-teleological concept of history – in Hegel, Marx . . .'[41] by the promise. Derrida confronts this teleology propounded by Hegelians such as Marx and Engels with an historical openness and replaces the 'onto-theological' and 'teleo-eschatological'[42] programme by his utopian *promesse*. In other words, the emancipatory promise or desire ('*désir émancipatoire*') is meant to explode the teleological framework which is formed by the modern state in Hegel and by the dictatorship of the proletariat in Marx. Announced in a modified form by Camus's *L'homme révolté* (1951) this idea is not really new. What is new is Derrida's attempt to relate it to concepts such as *heterogeneity*, *undecidability*, *différance* and *iterability*. These concepts not only evoke the openness or impossiblity of closure ('*clôture*') of the historical process, but also refer to the alterity and heterogeneity inherent in this process. Both factors can bring about unexpected realignments and reorientations.

Derrida is determined to foreswear a certain positivism from which the Marxists never quite managed to detach themselves and to foreground the phantom effects ('*effets de phantôme*') or 'haunting quality' of Marxism. For not only the neo-liberal bourgeoisie feels haunted by the phantoms of Marxism. Marx himself, according to Derrida, continually had to face phantoms and spectres. And the Young Hegelian Stirner, whom Derrida quotes several times, addressed his reader thus: 'Man, your mind is haunted!', in order to demystify oppressive abstractions such as political authority and the state. Derrida claims that one should view Marx's struggle against the phantom of commodity fetishism and the spectres of ideology or reification. 'The spectres of Marx are also his.'[43] Marx was beleaguered by the spectres that he himself called into being: 'More than others, perhaps, Marx had ghosts in his head and knew without knowing what he was talking about ("Mensch, es spukt in deinem Kopfe!", one might say to him in a parody of Stirner).'[44] In the context of the *German Ideology* Derrida speaks of the 'most gigantic phantomachia in the whole history of philosophy'.[45] Marx's spectres, he continues, never granted Marxism peace, especially in its totalitarian phases: ideology, state, dictatorship and reification were continually invoked, yet were never mastered or banished. 'The theory of ideology', he explains, 'depends in many of its features . . . on this theory of the ghost.'[46]

The final chapter of *Specters of Marx* makes the Young Hegelian context of Derrida's arguments apparent.The spectres in Marx can be traced back to the *Geister* of Hegel's philosophy, reappear in the writings of Young Hegelians such as Feuerbach, Stirner, Hess, Bauer and continue to haunt Marxism. For the difference between spirit (*Geist*) and spectre, Derrida continues his interpretation, 'is a differ*a*nce'.[47]

The reader who decides to take this seriously and finish reading this book as a critical philosophy or history of Marxism is reminded of Robert Tucker's *Philosophy and Myth in Karl Marx*. Would it not have been possible to analyse the myths and ideologies underlying Marx's discourse from the perspectives of the social sciences (sociologically or semiotically) without resorting to ghost stories, without indulging in analyses of Marx's 'exorcism' and his 'spectrology'? Derrida would probably brush aside such questions and claim that the term *spectre* assumes a key function and that his *spectrology* is part and parcel of Deconstruction (in the same way as, for instance, grammatology). One might accept this objection for argument's sake – a theory of ghosts not being verifiable in any case.

Yet how would true Marxists (if there are any) deal with this new science and Derrida's remarks on the common features of Marxism and Deconstruction? Instead of guessing, one should turn to some Marxist critiques of Deconstruction. In a commentary on Michael Ryan's synthesis, the British Marxist Terry Eagleton continues his critique of Deconstruction which he began in *The Function of Criticism*. He questions Ryan's crucial thesis according to which Marxism as well as Deconstruction are opposed to hierarchical order. Eagleton reminds us of the fact that Marxism is a revolutionary doctrine which cannot give up concepts such as organization and discipline without ceasing to exist: 'For discipline, power, unity, and authority are the utterly indispensable characteristics of any revolutionary movement with the faintest hope of success.'[48] This remark can also be read as a possible response to *Specters of Marx*. What is the use, the Marxist might ask, of invoking an emancipatory promise when the groups or organizations that might *realize* such an emancipation are not even mentioned?

Elsewhere Eagleton accuses Deconstruction of frustrating all revolutionary hopes by radically criticizing the concept of subject. For only 'the subjective agency' in history is capable of acting 'politically rather than textually'[49] against the ideological systems which Deconstruction aims to dissolve. This objection is shared by Lukács's pupil István Mészáros who writes about Derrida's claim that Deconstruction will one day enter a positive phase in *The Power of Ideology*: 'However, it would be most unfair to blame Derrida for the non-arrival of the positive phase. For it is very difficult to be positive in an intellectual enterprise without the sustaining ground of an emancipatory social movement.'[50] Similar arguments were put forward by Marxists such as Lucien Goldmann against the Frankfurt School.[51]

At this point the Marxist critique converges with that of Ellis, who accuses Deconstruction of only being able to fill its social and political vacuum by ceaselessly attacking conservative logocentrism without actually wishing to destroy it. By contrast, Eagleton's Marxism appears as inseparable from political practice. It focuses on the reversal of the status quo and of those institutions which conservative and logocentric discourses tend to justify.

Nonetheless, a reader sympathetic to Derrida could ask whether Deconstruction cannot also be read as a response to the kind of Marxism whose logocentric, monologic and repressive character comes to the fore whenever disciplined and blindly obedient revolutionaries seize power. Those who are willing to take seriously the Marxist's objections to the idealist and ahistoric character of Deconstruction should not overlook the critical insights of Deconstruction which, especially in *Specters of Marx*, expose the Marxist-Hegelian tendency towards totalitarianism. This tendency is also criticized by Adorno in *Negative Dialectics*, where he reminds us that the Hegelian historicism in Marx and Engels is directed against the anarchists. Some of his arguments would sound familiar to Derrida.

In contrast to Derrida's critical philosophy, which in recent years has rediscovered the emancipatory promise, de Man's rhetorical theory of the text is politically ambiguous. Eagleton is perhaps right in criticizing the political conservatism of American Deconstruction for excluding the possibility of social change by dissolving historical discourse: 'It is because de Man consistently reduces historicity to empty temporality that he displaces the dilemma of the liberal intellectual under late capitalism into an irony structural to discourse as such.'[52] De Man is presented here as the 'anti-humanist deconstructor' who turns even the self-ironic humanist heritage of Eliot, James and Forster against itself.

This critique of American Deconstruction is echoed by Frank Lentricchia who remarks on Paul de Man's ahistoricism: 'De Man can know what he knows because in his theory of history there is no future'.[53] There is none, because historical action and historical discourse which could open up perspectives for the future founder on the deconstructive aporia that prevents a knowledge of reality: 'He (de Man) means the paralysis of action, underwritten by an aporia "between trope and persuasion" which will deny lucidity to the intellect and guarantee in the end that no mind knows what it is doing – no mind, apparently, except de Man's, which lucidly knows that no lucidity is possible.'[54]

Lentricchia believes that the decline of historical reason staged by de Man is due to the fact that the Deconstructionist identifies historical with literary discourse: 'He is saying that history is an imitation of what he has defined as the literary.'[55] This interpretation is confirmed in a different context (outside Marxism and the social sciences) by Jürgen Fohrmann who claims: 'De Man does not completely banish history from the humanities, but turns it into a secondary phenomenon consisting of linguistic figures. Language and not history is the sovereign granted constitutive power.'[56] 'Granted' is the correct term, since it reveals the decisionist element at the heart of most theories: when I decide that polysemic language is the basis of all my thought, then an interpretation of reality comes about which differs substantially from interpretations geared towards the 'unconscious', 'class struggle' or 'ethnic affiliation'.

Whenever this simple fact is not taken into account by the subject of discourse, the result is often ideological monologue and not a self-reflecting theory.

If the literary and the linguistic spheres are subject to the rules of aporia, as described by de Man, history as historical text will not escape the effect of these laws either. Both de Man and Hillis Miller are therefore inclined to believe that the discursive representation of historical facts or events can be relegated to the realm of literary illusion. Miller goes one step further when he replaces the historicity of the rationalists, Hegelians and Marxists by Nietzsche's 'eternal return' (see Chapter 4, section 5).

Although it would be unfair to consider Deconstruction globally as a new irrationalism because of its ahistorical bias, it makes sense to have a closer look at the affinity between de Man's radical agnosticism and the fascist sympathies of his early years. If such an affinity exists at all, then it cannot be understood within a continuum ('from fascism to deconstructivist irrationality'), but rather as a reaction to the disappointments of his youth. The individual who is forced to distance himself from the ideology which shaped his subjectivity for many years[57] has the choice between converting to a different ideology or accepting implicitly or explicitly the indifference of market society as a negation of all ideologies. Along with ideology such an individual will tend to renounce subjectivity. De Man decided in favour of this solution. He thus differs fundamentally from Derrida, whose Deconstruction also tends towards indifference, yet without submitting to it entirely (see Chapter 7, section 5).

Less ambiguously than Derrida, who criticizes the institutions of society (especially its academic ones), de Man postulates an irreparable break between literature (rhetorics) and the social sciences. The next section will show how this attempt to reduce the social to the literary sphere is contested by Habermas.

4 DECONSTRUCTION AND FRANKFURT SCHOOL CRITICAL THEORY

Adorno's and Horkheimer's Critical Theory (*Kritische Theorie*) of the postwar era, whose basic orientations and arguments have been developed in this study, owes many of its tenets to the works of

Karl Marx – although it should not be labelled 'Marxist'. Having rejected Marx's demand for a unity of theory and practice, of historical immanence and an identity between the revolutionary subject and the historical process, it exiled itself from the realm of materialist dialectics as defined by Marx and Engels. Its Kantian demand for a non-identity of subject and object, its radical critique of Hegel's system as well as its individualist essayism draw it closer, within a 'Young Hegelian' context, to Kierkegaard or Sartre's existentialism – and to Deconstruction. Yet this social and linguistic affinity justifies neither an identification with Deconstruction as 'negative thinking' (see Chapter 5, section 4) nor attempts at synthesis.

One can share Michael Ryan's view, who emphasizes that Adorno and Derrida are in agreement when they 'attack the idealist privilege of identity over non-identity':[58] a rationalist and Hegelian form domination associated by both critical philosophers with the idealist and metaphysical domination of the subject over the object and nature. Yet Ryan is lead astray by fashion when he interprets Adorno's negative dialectic as an attempt to revaluate the rhetorical dimension of language: 'Negative dialectic', he writes, 'rescues rhetoric from being a mere flaw and promotes the necessary link between thought and language.'[59] This statement is too vague. It is true that Adorno analyses discursive forms and argues that a systematic discourse (of rationalist or Hegelian origin) tends to articulate the interests of a dominant subject; but nowhere does he sacrifice conceptual critique to a rhetoric of tropes.

In this crucial point he differs radically from Derrida, Hillis Miller and de Man who implicitly and explicitly proclaim that conceptual truth is inaccessible. Unlike the Deconstructionists, Adorno and Horkheimer are anxious to *rescue* conceptual thought from its involvement in systems of domination by orienting it towards artistic mimesis. This does not mean that they renounce the notions of truth and theory. *Against* Hegel Adorno insists in the non-conceptual character of art: 'This is why art mocks verbal definition.'[60] *With* Hegel and the Marxists, however, he attempts to describe the *truth content* of art. In this point he differs from Derrida, as H. M. Briel has rightly pointed out: 'Starting from the impossible conclusion of interpretation Derrida cannot and does not want to decide on a truth content of the work of art.'[61]

The extreme ambivalence from which negative dialectics – in this respect similar to Deconstruction – sets out cannot be reduced to Derrida's or de Man's aporia. When Adorno emphasizes the ambivalence of Stefan George's poetry and shows how some of the poet's texts combine an elitist ideology and an archaic style with a critical language which resists all ideological rhetorics of the inter-war years, he by no means declares the texts to be aporetical and truth to be inaccessible. Rather, he reminds us of the fact that truth and ideology interact dialectically and that a critique of ideology as *conceptual* search for the literary truth content is therefore indispensable. He would certainly disagree with Derrida who advocates the Deconstruction of all meanings in the realm of philosophical *logos* and '[p]articularly the signification of truth'.[62] Adorno and Horkheimer do not share the Deconstructionist view that the concept of truth is wedded willy-nilly to logos. They search for a theoretical truth situated beyond the principle of domination.

In contrast to Derrida, de Man and Hillis Miller, the Frankfurt theorists have always sought a dialogue with the social sciences (especially sociology and psychoanalysis) in order to highlight their critical components and moments of truth. Horkheimer's critique of Mannheim's sociology of knowledge[63] and Adorno's critique of Erich Fromm's conformist psychoanalysis[64] do not aim at a global rejection social science. They rather ask what a critical sociology or psychoanalysis might look like. Adorno's, Horkheimer's and Habermas's empirical studies – especially Adorno's comprehensive study of the authoritarian character[65] – show that the attitudes and aims of these authors differ substantially from Derrida's, de Man's and Hillis Miller's negative stance.

Despite these differences and incompatibilities, the affinity of Adorno's and Derrida's philosophy which has been mentioned repeatedly in the preceding chapters should not be overlooked. The first sentence of *Negative Dialectic* reads: 'Philosophy, which once seemed obsolete, lives on because the moment to realize it was missed.'[66] It could also introduce Derrida's work which, like Adorno's theory, is condemned to negativity since it lacks the historical subject capable of translating the emancipatory promise into revolutionary practice. The disappearance of this subject causes the critical-philosophical discourse to become reflexive and to question its own organization.

This explains why Adorno, while not turning his back on those social sciences which analysed the *development* of society after the Second World War, relegated them to the periphery of *Kritische Theorie*[67] and turned towards aesthetic problems. At the same time he began experimenting with essayistic writing, theoretical models and paratactic (non-linear, non-hypotactic) forms of discourse in order to strengthen the individual's autonomy in a totally administered society. He thus projects the critique of society into discourse itself and departs from a Marxism which has always relied on the unity of theory and practice and on historical immanence. Adorno thus resembles the artist of whom he claims: 'The artist who is the bearer of the work of art is not the individual who produces it; rather, through his work, through passive activity, he becomes the representative of the total social subject.'[68] This also applies to Adorno's theory which turns towards the realm of aesthetics after the Second World War, after the disappearance of the historical subject.

It thereby moves closer to Derrida's Deconstruction which also has to make do with the negativity of an emancipatory promise. For it also lacks an historical subject and the corresponding notion of social practice, as Mészáros and, in a very different context, Stuart Sim[69] correctly remark. Like Adorno, Derrida eventually has to sublimate aesthetically the utopian-revolutionary yearning that still echoes in some of his articles published in the *Tel Quel* of the 1960s.[70] His essayistic style and his associative, paratactic way of writing arise from a similar social situation as Adorno's, yet lack the critical engagement of Adorno's *Aesthetic Theory*.[71]

This is where Habermas's critique of Adorno and Derrida sets in. Without losing sight of the differences between Adorno's critique of ideology and Derrida's Deconstruction, he insists on the common problematic of Deconstruction and negative dialectics: 'Adorno and Derrida are sensitized in the same way against definitive, totalizing, all-incorporating models, especially against the organic dimension in works of art. Thus, both stress the primacy of the allegorical over the symbolic, of metonymy over metaphor, of the Romantic over the Classical. Both use the fragment as an expository form; they place any system under suspicion.'[72] Both are accused by Habermas of subjecting discourse to aesthetic criteria, thus ignoring the communicative aspects of theory and neglecting the critical-communicative potential of contemporary social science.

Moreover, Habermas reminds us, in his critique of Adorno and Horkheimer's *Dialectic of Enlightenment* (1947), of the fact that modern social sciences cannot be identified with the production of technologically useful knowledge: 'I am thinking here of the specific theoretical dynamic that continually pushes the sciences, *beyond* merely engendering technically useful knowledge.'[73] Derrida also disregards the critical potential of these sciences when he dismisses them as metaphysical in the Heideggerian sense. Habermas accuses Derrida and de Man of being hostile to science and conceptualization, thereby producing a discourse which breaks down the boundaries between literature and philosophy (theory) and subsumes both types of text under the label 'rhetorics': 'Derrida wants to expand the sovereignty of rhetoric over the realm of the logical . . . .'[74] Elsewhere he adds: 'Derrida can only attain Heidegger's goal of bursting metaphysical thought-forms from the inside by means of his essentially rhetorical procedure if the philosophical text is *in truth* a literary one – if one can *demonstrate* that the genre distinction between philosophy and literature dissolves upon closer inspection.'[75]

But even this 'literarization' of philosophy and the concomitant revaluation of writing do not represent a victory over metaphysics, according to Habermas. Plato's pure form and Heidegger's Being are replaced by writing as *archi-écriture*; yet their origin-bound thought is not overcome, but merely renews its claim to truth.[76] Derrida's critique confirms the rejection of the social sciences by idealism and reinstates the idealist myth of origin, now poetically renamed *archi-écriture*.

Habermas might have a point when he criticizes Derrida's (and Adorno's) dismissal of the social sciences. However, his assertion that Derrida and de Man dissolve philosophy in literature and rhetorics is debatable. Derrida has responded to it in several interviews with his own characteristic verve: 'Those who accuse me of reducing philosophy to literature or logic to rhetoric (see, for example, the latest book of Habermas, *The Philosophical Discourse of Modernity*) have visibly and carefully avoided reading me.'[77] Derrida explains that he has 'never assimilated a so-called philosophical text to a so-called literary text', and adds 'the two types seem to me irreducibly different'.[78]

If one pleads in earnest (and not only rhetorically) for a dialogue of theories, then one must attempt to understand these statements deconstructively: Derrida assumes that the difference between literature and theory cannot easily be determined (one might think of Pascal, Bergson, Nietzsche, among others), and that each attempt at defining it leads to the well-known *différance*. In fact the possibility of distinguishing the two types of text depends on a stable definition or construction of the literary and the philosophical. Every literary scholar, every philosopher, knows only too well that such a definition cannot be obtained – yet. Derrida might add that it is not even desirable, since the 'language of art', as H. M. Briel remarks,[79] makes an aesthetic critique of philosophical discourse possible, a critique undertaken by Derrida in *Glas* and *Specters of Marx*.

Moreover, Habermas does not really deal with Derrida's work in *The Philosophical Discourse of Modernity*, as Bill Martin rightly remarks: 'The version of Derrida that Habermas presents is almost completely inaccurate and self-serving.'[80] His idea that Deconstruction breaks down the genre distinction between literary and philosophical texts is applied indiscriminately to Derrida, de Man and Hillis Miller and obliterates the critical potential of Derrida's writings. It is, however, an idea which seems less relevant with respect to Derrida's work than in the context of American Deconstruction which Habermas, who repeatedly misspells Hartman as Hartma*nn*,[81] seems to be less familiar with. A dialogue between Deconstruction and the Frankfurt School is not made easier by the fact that Habermas relies heavily on Jonathan Culler's (in part questionable) interpretations for his critique of Derrida. He quotes Derrida exclusively in German or even English translation.[82] In the extreme case, which for Deconstruction is the normal case, Derrida could object that Habermas has not taken account of his works at all, since a translation is a different text.

On three points, however, one can agree with Habermas as a representative of the Frankfurt School. 1. The ambivalent attitude towards conceptual thought and the rejection of 'truth' which is common to all Deconstructionists prevents them from developing the social and critical potential of their theories. 2. Moreover, this attitude vitiates a meaningful dialogue between Deconstruction and the social sciences without which an adequate and up-to-date critical theory of society is impossible. 3. Finally, one will agree with Habermas when, as an alternative to Derrida's Deconstruction and Adorno's parataxis, he suggests a theory geared towards communication: 'But they [the participants in a debate] can never be wholly absolved of the idea that wrong interpretations must in principle be criticizable in terms of consensus to be aimed for ideally.'[83] In other words, even Deconstruction cannot renounce its claim to truth. According to Habermas, this claim can only be assessed with respect to an *ideal speech situation*.

At this point, however, one could object that the ideal speech situation postulated by Habermas 'in a contrafactual manner' within the tradition of Kant, Apel and American Speech Act Theory is an idealist abstraction. For it presupposes that those who take part in dialogue ('participants of discourse' for Habermas) overcome their psychological, political and ideological prejudices, that they are able to exchange their roles, and that they agree on an homogenous use of language. Habermas writes on this issue: 'Different speakers must not use the same expression with different meanings.'[84]

But who should prevent them from doing so? Even if one considers Habermas's central assumption that we are dealing with an ideal, contrafactually assumed, not a *real speech situation*,[85] one will not wish to forget three basic insights of socio-semiotics: 1. That the subject becomes a subject through its discourse (as a semantic and narrative structure); 2. That it cannot abandon this discourse with its phrases, its lexical repertory, its taxonomies and its narrative processes, without giving up its identity; and 3. That this discourse (as a collective phenomenon or sociolect) is always modelled by culture and ideology.[86]

Derrida will always associate the terms *signifier* and *signified* with different meanings from Greimas, and he is perfectly entitled to do so. The author of this book will always define the concept of discourse differently from Habermas and thereby refer to Adorno and Derrida who, in contrast to Habermas, hold on to the realist assumption that each discourse harbours a striving for power which cannot be neutralized by relying on an ideal speech situation. On the contrary, the ideal speech situation exhibits – like Habermas's entire project – repressive features which are inseparable from the commendable moral demand for equal rights of the communication partners. They must be able to switch roles; they must not use the same expression with different meanings, and so on. Is this not an idealist suppression of subjective freedom or indeed of subjectivity as such? Faced with this attempt to decree an homogenous (and probably tedious) use of language, Michael Ryan might not be far off the mark when he points out: 'Absolutely undistorted truth is possible only on the basis of absolute constraints.'[87]

In order to escape such constraints it is necessary to start from the insights of socio-semiotics referred to above and to consider the fact that subjects are formed in heterogeneous discourses as psychological, cultural and ideological agents and hence cannot submit to an ideal speech situation that presupposes linguistic homogeneity. Theoretical dialogue can only be envisaged as a real communication situation between heterogeneous subjects and their discourses.

The idea that this real communication situation cannot be idealistically avoided or overcome does not mean a renunciation of understanding. Rather, understanding is not envisaged as a mere search for consensus (Habermas), but as a dialectic of consensus and dissent in the course of which heterogeneous positions are confronted with one another. Such a dialogue can only be successful on three conditions: 1. The subject of discourse must be willing and able as a speaking subject (*sujet d'énonciation*) to reflect on its linguisic and social contingency (particularity) as well as on the particular semantic and syntactic structure of its discourse. 2. It must be prepared to renounce a monological identification of its discourse with its objects (reality). 3. Only a rejection of monologue and identification ('Identitätsdenken', Adorno, Horkheimer) makes a theoretical dialogue between heterogeneous subjects and discourses possible: a dialogue based on the acknowledgement of the alterity of the Other in the sense of Adorno, Derrida and Levinas.[88]

A fourth, and not completely irrelevant factor may be the self-irony of the interlocutors, a self-irony illustrated by Robert Musil's posthumously published comments on his great novel: 'Irony is: to portray a conservative in such a way that the Bolshevik next door could also be meant. To portray an idiot in such a way that the author suddenly feels: that could also be me. This kind of irony – constructive irony – is quite unknown in contemporary Germany.'[89]

Constructive irony in a theoretical sense could mean to present Deconstruction in such a way that a Frankfurt School theorist would suddenly feel that his own approach is involved *in some respects*. This affinity between Deconstruction and Critical Theory has been highlighted here, as well as the differences without which no dissent and no dialogue would exist.

5 FEMINIST DECONSTRUCTION AND FEMINIST CRITIQUES: THE PROBLEM OF SUBJECTIVITY

Critical Theory, Deconstruction and feminism are related by their common rejection of social domination, logocentrism and metaphysical notions of subjectivity. This is probably the main reason why some feminist authors keep referring to the thinkers of the Frankfurt School,[90] while others develop a feminist Deconstruction which goes well beyond the boundaries of literary criticism, aiming at a subversion of established gender roles and of the notion of subject (cf. Chapter 2, section 4). Like Marxism, however, feminism is far from being an homogeneous ideology or theory, and it will be shown that its deconstructive tendencies are being challenged by feminists for whom concepts such as meaning, structure and subject are by no means obsolete.

The central argument of feminist Deconstruction sounds plausible in the light of Derrida's critique of metaphysics and even in the light of Adorno's and Horkheimer's Critical Theory. Applying deconstructive procedures to the dominant gender structures, feminists set out to show that dichotomies such as male/female or masculine/feminine are part and parcel of the male-dominated social order which can be subverted by notions such as *différance*, indeterminacy and decentering (*décentrement*).

Penelope Deutscher establishes several links between Deconstruction and feminism: 'Deconstruction has been crucial to the formulation of feminisms of sexual difference, and to the rejection by some of essentialism and identity politics. It has been seen as a methodology for destabilising dichotomous oppositions, for decentring masculinity in relation to an "othered" femininity, decentring heterosexuality in relation to an "othered" homosexuality and decentring natural, normalised gender in relation an "othered" artificiality, as seen in the works of Judith Butler and Eve Sedgwick.'[91]

Discussing 'Le Doeuff, Kofman and Irigaray as Theorists of Constitutive Instability',[92] Penelope Deutscher develops Luce Irigaray's thesis according to which the male subject only exists by virtue of contrasting himself with the female element, by virtue of using 'Woman' narcissistically as his negative reflexion.[93] 'Masculine identity, contrasted with femininity as a negative other, is all the more associated with positive qualities',[94] Deutscher points out in conjunction with Irigaray's theories. Following Irigaray, she attempts to decentre male identity by showing to what extent it depends on its 'negative Other': it would cease to exist if this Other disappeared. In other words, this Other has always been present in the One which is inseparable from the Other, and attempts to reduce *all others to the economy of the Same*'[95] by opposing a positive male to a negative female principle are doomed to failure, to a process of *différance* which reveals the difference and interdependence of the sexes along with the impossibility of separating the One from the Other.

This critique of male subjectivity and identity which Irigaray develops in her analyses of European metaphysics from Plato to Freud by detecting, for example, Freud's propensity for representing woman as the negative Other of man, eventually leads to a wholesale rejection of the notion of subject. Adopting a post-modern rather than a deconstructive stance, Nancy Fraser and Linda Nicholson elect to dispense with the metaphysical (Hegelian) 'subject of history'.[96]

Representatives of feminist Deconstruction go even further when they reject *individual subjectivity*, arguing that it is a male construction which women should refuse to have imposed upon them. Adopting Derrida's point of view, Diane Elam reminds us of the fact that both men and women are born into certain social structures such as power relations, social role-sets and linguistic conventions and become seemingly autonomous subjects by being *subjected* to these structures. The latter articulate male interests, and women are only recognized as subjects by submitting to male domination and its preconstructed patterns: 'The achievement of a definitive or calculable subjectivity is, as Derrida points out, not solely liberatory. Indeed, the constraint of subjectivity, even when subjectivity seems to offer agency, is clear when we realize that women become subjects only when they conform to specified and calculable representations of themselves as subjects.'[97]

Having thus defined subjectivity as submission, Elam is weary 'of the subject as a cause of celebration'.[98] She considers with critical impatience all attempts by feminist organizations and movements to deliver women from their roles as objects of male action by turning them into agents, into subjects. For socially defined subjectivity is a construction of the male order and being a subject within this order means submitting to it.

Like Deutscher, Irigaray and other Deconstructionists, Elam warns us against taking the socially preconstructed role of the subject for granted. Without simply rejecting the notion of subject, we ought to deconstruct it by revealing the mechanisms which make subjectivity possible on a linguistic, psychic and social level. Only a critical analysis in the deconstructive sense, she believes, will enable women to take effective precautions against their unwitting integration into established patterns of interaction.

This is also Judith Butler's stance. To begin with, she reminds us of the fact (pointed out by Althusser, Pêcheux and Lacan)[99] that the individual 'I' does not position itself freely within a social context, but is positioned within a system of power structures: 'It is clearly not the case that "I" preside over the positions that have constituted me, shuffling through them instrumentally, casting some aside, incorporating others, although some of my activity may take that form. The "I" who would select between them is always already constituted by them.'[100]

In this situation, subjectivity as a preconstructed social position or role-set (in the functionalist sense) or as a male 'fantasy of autogenesis'[101] which disavows its dependence on the maternal feminine is clearly unacceptable to Butler. Like Elam, she pleads in favour of a critical analysis of subjectivity which questions its linguistic, psychic and social origins. Her approach is deconstructive rather than destructive in as much as she envisages a radical 'structural analysis' ('analyse de la structure', Derrida).[102] 'The critique of the subject', she explains, 'is not a negation or repudiation of the subject, but rather a way of interrogating its construction as a pregiven or foundationalist premise.'[103] From this point of view subjectivity appears as a key element of metaphysics and 'phallogo-centrism' which cannot simply be continued, but must be radically questioned and subverted.

The problems which crop up within this kind of deconstructive feminism are similar to those of Adorno's and Horkheimer's Critical Theory. Like Derrida, Elam and Butler, the Frankfurt critics adopted a critical and sceptical attitude towards socially precon-structed subjectivity: towards the subjectivity of the ideologues, the rationalist philosophers, the Hegelians and Marxists. Like the Deconstructionists they believed that the idealist and Marxist notions of subject merely served to mobilize individuals for ideo-logical goals and to justify man's domination over nature, over other men and women. They nevertheless refused to renounce the concept of subject, but associated individual subjectivity (after the Second World War) with critique, negativity and non-identity. The postulate of non-identity in particular led to a dissolution of the Marxist nexus between theory and practice and to a disavowal of historical action, or *agency*. In much the same way as feminist Deconstruction, Critical Theory thus tended to replace historical action with criticism and negativity. Time and again it was attacked by Marxists for acquiescing to the status quo by repudiating revolutionary action. Similarly, feminist Deconstruction is being criticized for subverting subjective agency, thus thwarting feminist action.

One of the critics of a post-modern renunciation or a deconstruc-tive weakening of the subject is Sabina Lovibond. In her reappraisal of post-modernism she rejects all attempts to discard the notion of subject and pleads in favour of feminine subjectivity and agency. 'The pursuit of a fully integrated subjectivity', she argues, 'takes the form of an attempt to rise above our present mental limitations.'[104] Unfortunately, Lovibond does not deal critically with one of the fundamental post-modern and deconstructive arguments put for-ward by feminists such as Butler and Elam: that subjectivity as a preconstructed role-set is a product of the established order.

In this respect, the American feminist Honi Fern Haber is a lot more explicit. Although she identifies post-modernism somewhat one-sidedly with Post-structuralism ('post-modernism is correlative to Post-structuralism'),[105] she confirms the idea (discussed in Chapter 2, section 4) that Post-structuralism and Deconstruction lead to a negation of the individual subject and to a disintegration of agency: 'The field of language, to use Derrida's terminology, becomes the field of play, that is, the field of infinite substitutions.'[106] This infinite process of *différance* or *iterability* undermines the subject by impeding its linguistic (discursive) constitution: 'All this bears on our understanding of the subject. Semiotic analysis decenters the subject. In the linguistic world the author of meaning disappears without identity into the field of differential play; the author of meaning becomes a "trace" in the linguistic act. The epistemological subject is therefore declared dead, or at least unknowable.'[107]

To this deconstructive trend (which she oddly identifies with 'semiotic analysis') Honi Fern Haber opposes women's solidarity and female subjectivity. She even reintroduces the concept of structure which she considers indispensable for female subjectivity and female agency. Post-modernism and Post-structuralism, as she understands them, hamper women's efforts to act individually or collectively and to co-ordinate their policies. Pleading in favour of 'coherent *subjects*'[108] she considers Deconstruction – in its widest sense, which tends to be co-extensive with Post-structuralism – as an obstacle on the road to emancipation: 'To summarize: the danger lies in reading the law of difference as demanding the *universalization* of difference, as demanding the deconstruction of any and all centers including the deconstruction of a unified, coherent subject. This is sometimes joyfully described as the Nietzschean or aesthetic view of the self. However, such an aesthetic view of the self and its world is problematic for the purposes of empowerment.'[109] This argument, which is not only directed against Derrida and Deconstruction but also aims at Lyotard, Rorty and Foucault, contains the feminist theory of *agency* in a nutshell. It starts from the premise that a radical critique of subjectivity is detrimental to the feminist movement because it undermines 'empowerment'.

The arguments presented so far seem to warrant a clear-cut distinction between feminists who favour a liberating deconstruction of the masculine metaphysical concept of subject and feminists for whom subjectivity is an indispensable prerequisite of agency, of collective and individual action. However, this kind of dualistic approach obliterates the fact that deconstructive feminism, far from being apolitical, insists on the political character of Deconstruction.

Quoting Barbara Johnson's dictum that 'the undecidable is the political',[110] Diane Elam explains 'that a politics which does not have a notion of the subject as its founding principle is a politics best understood as a politics of the undecidable'.[111] Unfortunately, this kind of politics is a contradiction in terms: for the political is that which can be decided and acted on. Politics without decisions and actions only exist in modernist novels such as Musil's *The Man without Qualities*. Elam herself gives support to this argument when she attempts to introduce the undecidable in the deconstructionist sense into the debates on abortion. 'To win the debate on abortion', she argues, 'would be to allow the *undecidable* in so far as abortion would be neither a decision which could be made in advance or made once and for all for all women.'[112] Although it goes without saying that no universally valid rule can be applied to each individual case, it is also clear that basic decisions and (collective) demands have to be made if the 'debate on abortion' is to be won from a feminist point of view. It has to be *decided* as a matter of principle, for example, that the individual woman is to have the last word. In this case, introducing deconstructive 'indeterminacy and undecidability'[113] simply destroys agency and foils political action. In this respect Sabina Lovibond's and Honi Fern Haber's scepticism towards Deconstruction and its political practice is justified.

However, as was pointed out earlier, the Deconstructionists also have a case: following Adorno, they could argue that the insistence on agency and political action has a blinding effect on theory and theoretical reflection. 'Those who act without detecting and deconstructing the power structures underlying subjectivity', they could argue, 'continue to play the masculine game.' To this the feminist advocates of agency could answer that you condemn yourself to passive contemplation if you spend your time deconstructing what enables you to act.

It is not easy to break this stalemate, which in many respects reproduces the stalemate prevailing between Marxism and Critical Theory in the late 1960s. The Marxists who insisted on the unity of theory and practice were told that their theory had long since degenerated into ideology; at the same time, the thinkers of the Frankfurt School were blamed for withdrawing into an ivory tower built on negativity and non-identity.

On a more general level, both stalemates are due to the fundamental contradiction between ideology and theory: unlike ideology which makes action possible by monologically identifying with the real, by dualistically distinguishing friends from foes, theory presents its reality as a *possible* construction marked by contingency and ambivalence. Always tentative, self-critical and self-conscious, theory may enlighten, but does not encourage, action. The feminists cannot be blamed for not having overcome this ancient antagonism. The final section of this investigation will show that critical theories of society not only oscillate between theory and practice, but also between a post-modern status quo and a modern *utopia*.

6 EPILOGUE: DECONSTRUCTION BETWEEN MODERNITY AND POST-MODERNITY

It is not easy to do justice to a problem which might be the object of a comprehensive study in an epilogue. However, the aim is not to introduce a completely new topic, but to project the critique of Deconstruction onto an historical plane in order to make it more concrete. The question is: how far can Deconstruction still be understood as a modern theory because of its affinity to the Frankfurt School and to what extent does it break with modernity as a post-critical and post-modern theory? Or should one go even further and speak with Christopher Norris of 'the deep (though problematical) project of enlightened critique set forth by Kant and taken up – albeit with significant modifications – by Jürgen Habermas'?[114]

The first question has a teleological character in as much as the aim is to explain Deconstruction as a heterogeneous whole which has its roots in modernity, but announces the post-modern problematic in some respects. This hypothesis can only be made plausible if a minimal definition of modernity and post-modernity is offered.

Definitions of post-modernity are so disparate that only a long and thorough investigation could disentangle their incongruities and contradictions. Uwe Japp reminds us of the fact that the distinctive features frequently associated with post-modernity are too unspecific and also applicable to modernity. While David Lodge observes in post-modernity 'the staging of conscious and irreconcilable *contradictions*', Ihab Hassan constructs an opposition between an 'authoritarian' and 'aristocratic' modernity and a 'subversive' and 'anarchist' post-modernity. 'With such a wide range of criteria',

Japp comments, 'one is not surprised to find that Joyce, for instance, is simultaneouly modern and post-modern, or rather, is meant to be.'[115] In this situation it is important to refine the criteria and to reduce complexity – at the risk of simplifying in some instances.

If one starts from Jean François Lyotard's well-known definition of post-modernity as an era of scepticism towards meta-narratives,[116] one soon notices that not only Deconstruction, but also the Frankfurt School and writers such as Kafka, Musil, Gide and Italo Svevo can be categorized as post-modern. Even Joris-Karl Huysmans's *A Rebours* (1884) can be read as a post-modern text, since it questions the narrative principle as such along with the narrative structure of traditional novels. In the second half of the nineteenth century some of the Young Hegelians and Nietzsche refused to take narrative seriously.

Wolfgang Welsch attempts a clarification of this problem with his thesis 'that post-modernity continues modernity, indeed fulfils it in radicalised form'.[117] He develops Lyotard's project, adding that modern authors lament the loss of wholeness (of holistic meta-narratives), while the exponents of post-modernity welcome it: 'As long as the dissolution of wholeness is experienced as loss, we are still within modernity. Only when a positive perception of this loss prevails do we move into post-modernity.'[118] In this perspective, however, the European avant-gardes (Dada, Surrealism, Italian and Russian Futurism) which cannot be associated with a yearning for lost totalities appear as post-modern movements: along with Albert Camus who was among the first to reject Christian and Marxist teleologies. Umberto Eco, on the other hand, aligns the avant-garde with modernity: 'But the moment comes when the avant-garde (the modern) can go no further . . . .'[119]

This contradiction is less crucial here than the question of how the Frankfurt School and Deconstruction relate to Lyotard's and especially Welsch's definitions of modernity and post-modernity. It would certainly be dangerous to read Adorno and Horkheimer as modern authors who lament the loss of an harmonious totality. In contrast to Lukács and Goldmann, whose aesthetics are marked by an Hegelian yearning for identity and totality, Adorno's *Aesthetic Theory* must be read as a clear rejection of Hegel's notion of wholeness: 'The mistake of traditional aesthetics is that it exalts the relationship of the whole to the parts to one of entire wholeness, to totality, and hoists it in triumph of the heterogeneous as a banner of illusory positivity.'[120] Adorno foregrounds the contradictory, unreconciled and heterogeneous elements in the work of art.

Unlike the Deconstructionists, however, he neither abandons the concept of aesthetic truth nor the social concept of utopia.[121] The aim of literary and art criticism is the discovery of truth in the critical sense: 'The truth content of artworks is the objective solution of the enigma posed by each and every one. By demanding its solution, the enigma points to its truth content. It can only be achieved by philosophical reflection. This alone is the justification of aesthetics.'[122] Critique and truth cannot be separated: 'Grasping truth content postulates critique.'[123]

For critique creates a link between truth and utopia which implies the realization of the historical subject and the reconciliation of subject and object: 'Also intended in this kind of representation of the total social subject, of the whole, undivided human being which Valéry's idea of the beautiful invokes, is a state of affairs that would cancel out the fate of blind isolation, a state of affairs in which the total subject would finally be realized socially.'[124] This passage in which the 'dissolution of wholeness' in the modern sense is 'experienced as a loss' (Welsch) also evokes a utopia situated beyond pure negativity. It confirms Habermas's remark that Adorno has 'unreservedly subscribed ... to the spirit of modernity'.[125] At the same time it reminds us of the fact observed by Hauke Brunkhorst[126] that in Frankfurt School theory the core concepts of *truth*, *subject* and *historical utopia* are inseparable. They express the solidarity of this theory with metaphysics – 'at the time of its fall'.[127]

Such a solidarity is incompatible with deconstructive theories. They not only reject the concepts of truth and subject which have come under attack in Nietzschean modernity, but also tend to abandon the concept of utopia which they associate with metanarratives. This concept is perceived as part and parcel of modernity by some authors: 'But unlike in aesthetic modernity, in post-modern thinking a pronounced scepticism towards utopian concepts becomes dominant ...'[128] This interpretation by Paul Michael Lützeler is confirmed by Klaus R. Scherpe: 'The post-modern consciousness seems to have lost the aesthetic imagination of a "different state" that develops explosive force.'[129]

This diagnosis applies very pointedly to the deconstructive theories of Paul de Man and J. Hillis Miller. These theories exclude the kind of utopian teleology underlying Frankfurt School philosophy or a late modern novel such as Musil's *The Man without Qualities*, because they focus on aporia defined as irreconcilable contradiction. For Paul de Man not only literary history ('a history of an entity as self-contradictory as literature'[130]) is wrecked by this contradiction, but historical writing in general. Even Adorno's meta-narrative, which reveals the negativity and irreconcilability of the great works of art, must crumble when it is subjected to rhetorical analysis and reduced to an interplay of contradictory tropes, as in de Man.

How the historical discourse, along with that of literary history, falls victim to deconstructive tropology can be observed in some commentaries by J. Hillis Miller on periodization, where the very possibility of a theoretical discourse on literature is called into question (see Chapter 4, section 5). In Chapter 4 it was shown how Hillis Miller tends to replace the linear or dialectical conception of history by the Nietzschean principle of the 'eternal return'. It is in accordance with this principle that he and Paul de Man interpret the concept of modernity: 'as Paul de Man's discussion of "Modernism" shows it to be a concept by no means unique to a single period but a recurrent ever-repeated self-subverting move in each period's sense of itself in relation to previous periods. If de Man is right the term "post-Modernism" is a tautology or an oxymoron, since no writer or critic ever reaches the modern, in the sense of the authentically self-born, much less goes beyond it.'[131] If we accept this idea of an 'eternal return' of modernity, utopias in a positive or negative sense cannot exist, since an overcoming in the sense of the Marxists or a *dépassement* in the sense of the early *Tel Quel* group is inconceivable.

In so far as they abandon the metaphysical concepts of truth, subject and utopia, the Deconstructionists, in contrast to the Frankfurt School, no longer belong to modernity. They are post-modern. Derrida's approach, however, does not fully align itself with this kind of Deconstruction, since the emancipatory promise discussed above entails a vocabulary (*Enlightenment, democracy, reason, justice*) which is modern in all respects and can be related to the vocabulary of the Frankfurt School. There seems to be a crucial philosophical and political difference within Deconstruction between Derrida on one side and de Man and Hillis Miller on the other. In this context Hartman is closer to Derrida than to his American colleagues (see Chapter 5, section 4).

In view of these distinctions the general ambivalence of Deconstruction comes to the fore. Although it is related to the critical philosophy and literature of late modernity (only in this way can Derrida's and de Man's interest in Benjamin, Adorno, Celan and Kafka be explained), it can no longer accept their values such as truth, subject, reconciliation and utopia. It may have its roots in the problematic of modernity, yet it points beyond its limits towards a post-modernity (denied by Paul de Man), in which notions such as *truth*, *subject*, *autonomy* and *utopia* are declared obsolete or considered to belong to an 'ancient European thinking' (Luhmann).[132] In this context Derrida's utopian emancipatory promise can most plausibly be interpreted as a modern, avant-garde and Marxist inheritance of the *Tel Quel* years. It is no coincidence that this promise of happiness is situated by Derrida himself beyond the sphere of deconstructive analysis (see Chapter 7, section 3).

The transition from modernity to post-modernity mapped out here is no more than a provisional and hypothetical *construction*. Nevertheless, it requires an explanation. Why does modernity point beyond its limits, if one is to believe Eco, Lyotard and some others? In addition to the well-known answers to this question, a socio-semiotic explanation will be proposed by way of conclusion which might shed new light on the historical context of Deconstruction.

The preceding chapters were meant to show that the late modern and deconstructive problematic marked by Nietzsche's philosophy is structured by extreme ambivalence, the irreconcilable unity of opposites (see Chapter 1, section 4). Hence it is impossible to detect in modernist novels whether a goal is just or unjust (Kafka), whether a character is good or evil ('*ero io buono o cattivo?*', Svevo), whether an action leads to peace or war (one may think of Musil's 'parallel action' in this context).

The radicalization of this ambivalence in late capitalism is due to the mediation by the exchange value which tends to translate all cultural values into the economic value, thus making them ambivalent. However, it is also due to the ideological conflicts which bring about a destructive encounter of opposites. Jean-Paul Sartre illustrates this phenomenon in a particularly vivid commentary on Brice Parain's linguistic theory: 'It deals with the language of the sick words in which "peace" means aggression, "freedom" oppression, and "Socialism" a regime of inequality.'[133] The market- and ideology-driven ambivalence turns into indifference or exchangeability of word-values as soon as a situation develops which makes it difficult or impossible to prefer one value to another and to decide in favour of specific values such as freedom, truth or Socialism. While it still seemed meaningful to defend certain problematical values within the framework of late modernity ('Individualism is coming to an end ... Yet its moments of truth ought to be preserved', Musil), in post-modernity a radical pluralism emerges which both Bill Martin and William Corlett correlate with Deconstruction.[134] Its global tendency is a destructive and dangerous merger of universal tolerance (radical pluralism) with indifference as exchangeability of values.

One aspect of this exchangeability is deconstructive aporia which replaces the late modern search for a truth content. It brings together two contradictory readings of a text which, far from converging in an Hegelian synthesis or an Adornian moment of truth, mutually destroy each other, since their truth claims are undecidable: 'The two readings have to engage each other in direct confrontation, for the one reading is precisely the error denounced by the other and has to be undone by it.'[135] Hillis Miller adds: 'The heterogeneity of a text (and so its vulnerability to deconstruction) lies rather in the fact that it says two entirely incompatible things at the same time. ... It is "undecidable".'[136] This undecidability ought to be read as an aspect of exchangeability, of indifference: the two meanings outbalance each other, are 'of equal value', and we do not know which is valid.

The interest of Deconstruction to so many readers is ultimately due to the fact that they consider Sartre's modern *engagement* to be as anachronistic as Adorno's attempts to rescue truth and the autonomous subject. Luhmann, the founder of a post-modern sociological system and apparently Derrida's antipode, confirms their belief that concepts such as reason, utopia and subject belong to an 'ancient-European' tradition whose decline accompanies that of the grand meta-narratives. Yet the renewal of ideological *meta-narratives* is possible at any time. And this possibility makes a concomitant renewal of Critical Theory which turns against both ideology and post-modern indifference seem more urgent than ever.

NOTES

1. See, for instance, M. Burnier, *Les Existentialistes et la politique* (1966), pp. 27–61.
2. In this respect, D. Lehman's critique in *Signs of the Times* (1991), pp. 240–3, is a simplification.
3. On the relation of dialogue and dialectic, see my *Ideologie und Theorie* (1989), ch. 10, 'Ambivalenz und Dialektik'.
4. The term 'invented' does not carry negative connotations here, but refers to a claim by radical constructivists according to which we do not perceive objects as such, but only as constructed ones. See P. Watzlawick (ed.), *Die erfundene Wirklichkeit: Wie wissen wir, was wir zu wissen glauben? Beiträge zum Konstruktivismus* (1984).
5. P. Bourdieu, *Distinction: A Social Critique of the Judgment of Taste* (1984), p. 495.
6. Ibid., p. 496.
7. See Lehman, *Signs of the Times*, p. 37.
8. Bourdieu, *Distinction*, p. 496.
9. Ibid.
10. P. Sollers, 'Ecriture et révolution', in *Théorie d'ensemble* (1968), p. 78: 'Writing and revolution work together, mutually providing each other with their recharges of meaning, and working out, as their weapon, a new myth . . .'
11. P. Bourdieu (with L. J. D. Wacquant), *Réponses: Pour une anthropologie réflexive* (1992), p. 46.
12. Ibid.
13. J. Derrida, *Du droit à la philosophie* (1990), p. 452.
14. J. Derrida, *Specters of Marx* (1994), p. 81.
15. N. Luhmann, *Die Wissenschaft der Gesellschaft* (1990), p. 93.
16. J. M. Ellis, *Against Deconstruction* (1989), p. 23. A counter-position, partly geared towards Freudian psychoanalysis, can be found in C. Johnson, *System and Writing in the Philosophy of Jacques Derrida* (1993).
17. J. Derrida, *Points . . . Interviews, 1974–1994* (1995), p. 199.
18. Ellis, *Against Deconstruction*, p. 24.
19. In conjunction with glossematics, one could, for instance, ask if *speech* and *writing* do not belong together as forms of use (of performance): 'And all that which displays "substance" (spoken, written language, etc.) is "use", i.e. realisation of language, of "parole".' E. Coseriu, *Einführung in die Allgemeine Sprachwissenschaft* (1988), p. 123.

20. Ellis, *Against Deconstruction*, p. 73.
21. Lehman, *Signs of the Times*, p. 238.
22. M. H. Abrams, 'Construing and Deconstructing', in Rajnath (ed.), *Deconstruction: A Critique* (1989), p. 44.
23. Ellis, *Against Deconstruction*, p. 89.
24. C. Norris, 'Limited Think: How Not to Read Derrida', in *What's Wrong with Postmodernism: Critical Theory and the Ends of Philosophy* (1990), p. 140.
25. Norris, 'Limited Think', p. 148.
26. C. Norris, *Derrida* (1987), p. 163.
27. S. C. Wheeler, *Deconstruction as Analytic Philosophy* (2000), p. 3.
28. Ibid. p. 7.
29. M. Ryan, *Marxism and Deconstruction: A Critical Articulation* (1982), p. 21.
30. B. Martin, *Matrix and Line: Derrida and the Possibilities of Postmodern Social Theory* (1992), p. 168.
31. Ryan, *Marxism and Deconstruction*, p. 35.
32. Although the exponents of Marxism and Leninism always displayed an ambivalent attitude towards the 'bourgeois' social sciences, Western European Marxists, such as Henri Lefebvre and Lucien Goldmann, have always proved responsive to them.
33. Derrida, *Points . . .* , p. 284.
34. Ryan, *Marxism and Deconstruction*, p. 63.
35. Derrida, *Memoirs – For Paul de Man* (1986), pp. 14–15.
36. Derrida, *Specters of Marx*, p. 60.
37. Ibid., p. 59.
38. J. Derrida, *The Other Heading: Reflections on Today's Europe* (1992), p. 78.
39. See, for example, E. Bloch, *Über Methode und System bei Hegel* (1975), pp. 80–5.
40. Derrida, *Specters of Marx*, p. 74.
41. Ibid.
42. Ibid., p. 75.
43. Ibid., p. 98.
44. Ibid., p. 106.
45. Ibid., p. 120.
46. Ibid., p. 127.
47. Ibid., p. 136.
48. T. Eagleton, *Against the Grain: Essays 1975–1985* (1986), p. 84.
49. T. Eagleton, *The Function of Criticism: From the Spectator to Post-Structuralism* (1984), p. 99.
50. I. Mészáros, *The Power of Ideology* (1989), p. 57.
51. See L. Goldmann, 'La Mort d'Adorno', *La Quinzaine littéraire*, 78 (1–15 September 1969).
52. Eagleton, *Function of Criticism*, p. 100.

53. F. Lentricchia, *Criticism and Social Change* (1984), p. 42.

54. Ibid., p. 43.

55. Ibid., p. 49.

56. J. Fohrmann, 'Misreadings revisited: Eine Kritik des Konzepts von Paul de Man', in *Ästhetik und Rhetorik*, p. 87.

57. This problem can best be explained with the help of Althusser's idea of the ideological constitution of subjectivity: '*All ideology has as its function . . . the "constitution" of concrete individuals as subjects*'; L. Althusser, *Positions* (1976), p. 123. This means that an individual who parts with his or her ideology, or is forced to abandon it, simultaneously abandons his or her subjectivity and becomes obliged to search for a new one. This subjectivity can be a new ideology or the paradoxical attempt to deconstruct all ideologies and to deny one's own subjectivity.

58. Ryan, *Marxism and Deconstruction*, p. 75.

59. Ibid.

60. T. W. Adorno, *Aesthetic Theory* (1997), p. 176.

61. H. M. Briel, *Adorno und Derrida: Oder wo liegt das Ende der Moderne?* (1993), p. 121.

62. J. Derrida, *Of Grammatology* (1974), p. 10. M. H. Kramer outlines the paradoxical attitude of the Deconstructionists towards truth in a particularly poignant way: 'They realize that the ideal of Truth will have continued to haunt their writing even when (or especially when) Truth appears to have been eliminated'; M. H. Kramer, *Legal Theory, Political Theory and Deconstruction: Against Rhadamantus* (1991), p. 259. The paradox consists in the absolute impossibility to *argue* in a deconstructive or anti-deconstructive manner without *presupposing* a concept or criterion of truth.

63. See M. Horkheimer, 'Ein neuer Ideologiebegriff?', in *Der Streit um die Wissenssoziologie* (ed. V. Meja and N. Stehr), vol. 2 (1982).

64. T. W. Adorno, 'Die revidierte Psychoanalyse', in *Sociologica II: Reden und Vorträge* (1973).

65. T. W. Adorno, *The Authoritarian Personality* (1950).

66. T. W. Adorno, *Negative Dialectics* (1973), p. 3.

67. Adorno continued to pursue questions of the social sciences after the Second World War. Evidence of this are, in particular, the methodological writings in T. W. Adorno, *Gesellschaftstheorie und Kulturkritik* (1975).

68. T. W. Adorno, *Notes to Literature*, vol. I. (1991), p. 107.

69. See S. Sim, 'Derrida and the Destruction of Metaphysics', in *Beyond Aesthetics: Confrontations with Post-Structuralism and Postmodernism* (1992), pp. 43 and 52: 'At this point doubts again begin to surface concerning the direction of Derrida's practico-political programme'; 'It is when we move from the objections (the negative critique) to the programme for subsequent critical action that the doubts begin to crowd in.'

70. On the relation of *Tel Quel*, avant-garde and philosophy, see R. Brütting, *'Ecriture' und 'texte': Die französische Literaturtheorie 'nach dem Strukturalismus'* (1976); and M. Charvet and E. Krumm, *Tel Quel: Un'avanguardia per il materialismo* (1974).

71. See H. M. Briel, *Adorno und Derrida* (1993), p. 123: 'While Adorno views literature as a critique of society, Derrida regards it as a pure critique of text.'

72. J. Habermas, *Philosophical Discourse of Modernity* (1987), p. 187.

73. Ibid., p. 113.

74. Ibid., p. 188.

75. Ibid., p. 189.

76. 'Writing counts as the absolutely originary sign, abstracted from all pragmatic contexts of communication, independent of speaking and listening subjects' (*ibid.*, p. 178).

77. Derrida, *Points . . .* , p. 218.

78. Ibid., p. 217. Cf. also J. Derrida, *Passions* (1993), where the author refuses to subordinate philosophy to literature (p. 63), but at the same time associates literature with democratic freedom: 'Thus literature links its destiny to the rejection of censorship, to the realm of democratic freedom (freedom of press, opinion, etc.).'

79. Briel, *Adorno und Derrida*, p. 107.

80. Martin, *Matrix and Line*, p. 107. Martin remarks on the difference between philosophy and literature in Derrida: 'Derrida not only accepts that philosophy is "literary", he further accepts that there are different genres within philosophy. He often practices these different genres in the same text' (p. 126). Christopher Norris argues in a similar way in *What's Wrong with Postmodernism* (1990), p. 71.

81. Habermas, *Philosophical Discourse of Modernity*, p. 141.

82. See Habermas, *Der philosophische Diskurs der Moderne* (1985) (2nd ed.), p. 214, where Derrida's *Positions*, Paris, Minuit, 1972, is quoted as follows: J. Derrida, *Positions*, Chicago, 1981.

83. Habermas, *Philosophical Discourse of Modernity*, p. 198.

84. J. Habermas, *Moral Consciousness and Communicative Action* (1990), p. 87.

85. See J. Habermas, 'Entgegnung', in *Kommunikatives Handeln: Beiträge zu Jürgen Habermas' 'Theorie des Kommunikativen Handelns'* (1986), pp. 346, 368, 372–3.

86. On the definition of the subject in relation to discourse and sociolect, see my *Ideologie und Theorie* (1989), ch. 11–12.

87. Ryan, *Marxism and Deconstruction*, p. 113.

88. On the problem of *alterity*, see Critchley, *The Ethics of Deconstruction* (which has already been commented on in Chapter 3); Martin, *Matrix and Line*, p. 170; and J. Derrida and P.-J. Labarrière, *Altérités* (1986), p. 10, in which Labarrière explains: 'Throughout Levinas' exemplary struggle to re-establish the rights of the Other against the imperialism of

the Self, Derrida detects the "dream of a purely *heterological* thinking at its source. A pure thinking of pure difference".' The close relation between Deconstruction and Critical Theory with regard to the idea of alterity cannot be denied.

89. R. Musil, *Der Mann ohne Eigenschaften*, 1952, p. 1603.
90. See for example N. Fraser 'What's Critical about Critical Theory? The Case of Habermas and Gender', in *Feminism as Critique: Essays on the Politics of Gender in Late-Capitalist Societies* (eds S. Benhabib and D. Cornell) (1987).
91. P. Deutscher, *Yielding Gender: Feminism, Deconstruction and the History of Philosophy* (1997), p. 42.
92. Ibid., p. 59.
93. See L. Irigaray, *Speculum of the Other Woman* (1985).
94. Deutscher, *Yielding Gender*, p. 76.
95. Irigaray in P. Deutscher, *Yielding Gender*, p. 77.
96. N. Fraser and L. Nicholson, 'Social Criticism without Philosophy: An Encounter between Feminism and Postmodernism' (1988), p. 391.
97. D. Elam, *Feminism and Deconstruction: Ms. en abyme* (1994), p. 29.
98. Ibid.
99. See M. Pêcheux, *Les Vérités de La Palice* (1975).
100. J. Butler, 'Contingent Foundations: Feminism and the Question of Postmodernism', in *Feminists Theorize the Political* (eds J. Butler and J. W. Scott) (1992), p. 9.
101. Ibid.
102. Derrida, *Points . . .*, p. 212.
103. Butler, 'Contingent Foundations', p. 9.
104. S. Lovibond, 'Feminism and Postmodernism', in *Postmodernism and Society* (ed. R. Boyne and A. Rattansi) (1990), p. 159.
105. H. Fern Haber, *Beyond Postmodern Politics: Lyotard, Rorty, Foucault* (1994), p. 6.
106. Ibid., p. 12.
107. Ibid.
108. Ibid., p. 120.
109. Ibid.
110. D. Elam, *Feminism and Deconstruction* (1994), p. 82.
111. Ibid., p. 81.
112. Ibid., p. 84.
113. Ibid.
114. C. Norris, *Deconstruction and the 'Unfinished Project of Modernity'* (2000), p. 2.
115. U. Japp, 'Kontroverse Daten der Modernität' (1986), pp. 133–4.
116. J.-F. Lyotard, *The Postmodern Condition: A Report on Knowledge* (1984), pp. 27–37.
117. W. Welsch, *Unsere postmoderne Moderne* (1991), p. 189.
118. Ibid., p. 175.

119. U. Eco, 'Reflections on The Name of the Rose' (1985), p. 17.
120. Adorno, *Aesthetic Theory*, p. 157.
121. See also Briel, *Adorno und Derrida*, pp. 112–13.
122. Adorno, *Aesthetic Theory*, pp. 127–8.
123. Ibid., p. 128.
124. Adorno, *Notes to Literature*, vol. I, pp. 107–108.
125. J. Habermas, *Die Moderne – ein unvollendetes Projekt: Philosophisch-politische Aufsätze 1977–1990* (1990), p. 32.
126. H. Brunkhorst, *Theodor W. Adorno: Dialektik der Moderne* (1990), p. 144: 'Adorno's idea of a *cultural modernity* rises above the broad glittering stream formed by postmodern, neo-conservative, and deconstructionist sources, all of which converge in an affect against utopian thinking, through its *modernism*, its *autonomism*, and its *utopia of truth*.' That Deconstruction cannot be classified in such simple terms was meant to be demonstrated in the present study.
127. Adorno, *Negative Dialectics*, p. 408.
128. P. M. Lützeler, 'Einleitung: Von der Spätmoderne zur Postmoderne', in *Spätmoderne und Postmoderne: Beiträge zur deutschsprachigen Gegenwartsliteratur* (1991), p. 20.
129. K. R. Scherpe, 'Dramatisierung und Entdramatisierung des Untergangs – zum ästhetischen Bewußtsein von Moderne und Postmoderne', in *Postmoderne: Zeichen eines kulturellen Wandels* (eds A. Huyssen and K. R. Scherpe) (1989), p. 272.
130. P. de Man, *Blindness and Insight* (1983), p. 162.
131. J. H. Miller, *Theory Now and Then* (1991), p. 210.
132. N. Luhmann, 'Systemtheoretische Argumentation: Eine Entgegnung auf Jürgen Habermas', in *Theorie der Gesellschaft oder Sozialtechnologie – Was leistet die Systemforschung?* (eds J. Habermas and N. Luhmann) (1971), p. 401.
133. J.-P. Sartre, 'Aller et retour', in *Critiques littéraires I* (1946), p. 236.
134. See Martin, *Matrix and Line*, p. 162; and W. Corlett, *Community without Unity: A Politics of Derridean Extravagance* (1989), pp. 155–8.
135. P. de Man, *Rhetoric of Romanticism* (1984), p. 12.
136. Miller, *Theory Now and Then*, p. 106.

BIBLIOGRAPHY

Adorno, T. W., *The Authoritarian Personality: Studies in Prejudice*, New York, Harper, 1950.

Adorno, T. W., *The Jargon of Authenticity* (trans. K. Tarnowski and F. Will), London, Routledge & Kegan Paul, 1973.

Adorno, T. W., 'Die revidierte Psychoanalyse', in *Sociologica II: Reden und Vorträge* (ed. M. Horkheimer and T. W. Adorno), Frankfurt am Main, Europäische Verlagsanstalt, 1973.

Adorno, T. W., *Gesellschaftstheorie und Kulturkritik*, Frankfurt am Main, Suhrkamp, 1975.

Adorno, T. W., *Notes on Literature*, vol. 1, New York, Columbia University Press, 1991.

Adorno, T. W., *Aesthetic Theory* (trans. R. Hullot-Kentor; ed. G. Adorno and R. Tiedemann), London, Athlone, 1997.

Albert, H., *Treatise on Critical Reason*, Princeton, Princeton University Press, 1985.

Althusser, L., *Positions*, Paris, Ed. Sociales, 1976.

Angehrn, E. *et al.* (eds), *Dialektischer Negativismus*, Frankfurt am Main, Suhrkamp, 1992.

Anonymous, 'Derrida Derided', *The Economist* (16 May 1992).

Apel, F., *Sprachbewegung: Eine historisch-poetologische Untersuchung zum Problem des Übersetzens*, Heidelberg, Winter, 1982.

Atkins, G. D., *Reading Deconstruction, Deconstructive Reading*, Lexington, University of Kentucky Press, 1983.

Atkins, G. D., *Geoffrey Hartman: Criticism as Answerable Style*, London, Routledge, 1990.

Bakhtin, M. M., *Problems of Dostoevsky's Poetics*, Manchester, Manchester University Press, 1984.

Barthes, R., *S/Z* (trans. R. Miller), New York, Hill & Wang, 1974.

Barthes, R., *Le Bruissement de la langue: Essais critiques IV*, Paris, Seuil, 1984.

Baudelaire, C., *Oeuvres complètes*, Paris, Gallimard, Bibliothèque de la Pléiade, 1975.

Behler, E., *Derrida-Nietzsche/Nietzsche-Derrida*, Paderborn, Schöningh, 1988.

Belgardt, R., *Romantische Poesie: Begriff und Bedeutung bei Friedrich Schlegel*, The Hague and Paris, Mouton, 1969.

Bell, R. T., *Translation and Translating*, New York, Longman, 1991.

Benhabib, S. and D. Cornell (eds), *Feminism as Critique: Essays on the Politics of Gender in Late-Capitalist Societies*, Oxford, Polity/Blackwell, 1987.

Benjamin, W., *Der Begriff des Kunstwerks in der deutschen Romantik*, Frankfurt am Main, Suhrkamp, 1973.

Benjamin, W., *Gesammelte Schriften* (eds R. Tiedemann *et al.*), Frankfurt am Main, Suhrkamp, 1977.

Bennet, E. T., 'The Scene of Translation: After Jakobson, Benjamin, de Man, and Derrida', *New Literary History*, 24 (1993).

Bennington, G., *Le Passage des frontières: Autour du travail de Jacques Derrida*, Paris, Galilée, 1994.

Bense, M., *Aesthetica* (2nd ed.), Stuttgart, Deutsche Verlagsanstalt, 1965.

Bloch, E., *Auswahl aus seinen Schriften*, Frankfurt am Main, Fischer, 1967.

Bloch, E., *Über Methode und System bei Hegel* (2nd ed.), Frankfurt am Main, Suhrkamp, 1975.

Bloom, H., *Yeats*, Oxford, Oxford University Press, 1970.

Bloom, H., *The Anxiety of Influence: A Theory of Poetry*, Oxford, Oxford University Press, 1973.

Bloom, H., *A Map of Misreading*, Oxford, Oxford University Press, 1975.

Bloom, H., *Poetry and Repression: Revisionism from Blake to Stevens*, New Haven, Yale University Press, 1976.

Bloom, H., *Wallace Stevens: The Poems of Our Climate*, Ithaca and London, Cornell University Press, 1977.

Bloom, H., *Agon: Towards a Theory of Revisionism*, Oxford, Oxford University Press, 1982.

Bloom, H., *Ruin the Sacred Truths: The Charles Eliot Norton Lectures 1987–88*, Cambridge, Harvard University Press, 1989.

Bloom, H. *et al.* (eds), *Deconstruction and Criticism*, London, Routledge & Kegan Paul, 1979.

Bohn, V. (ed.), *Romantik: Literatur und Philosophie*, Frankfurt am Main, Suhrkamp, 1987.

Bohrer, K. H. (ed.), *Ästhetik und Rhetorik: Lektüren zu Paul de Man*, Frankfurt am Main, Suhrkamp, 1993.

Bolz, N. W. and W. Hübener (eds), *Spiegel und Gleichnis: Festschrift für Jacob Taubes*, Würzburg, Königshausen und Neumann, 1983.

Bourdieu, P., *Distinction: A Social Critique of the Judgment of Taste* (trans. R. Nice), London, Routledge & Kegan Paul, 1984.

Bourdieu, P. (with L. J. D. Wacquant), *Réponses: Pour une anthropologie réflexive*, Paris, Seuil, 1992.

Boyne, R. and A. Rattansi (eds), *Postmodernism and Society*, London, Macmillan, 1990.

Bras, G., *Hegel et l'art*, Paris, PUF, 1989.

Briel, H. M., *Adorno und Derrida: Oder wo liegt das Ende der Moderne?*, New York, Peter Lang, 1993.

Brooks, C., *The Well-Wrought Urn: Studies in the Structure of Poetry*, New York, Harcourt Brace Jovanovitch, 1949.

Brunkhorst, H., *Theodor W. Adorno: Dialektik der Moderne*, Munich, Piper, 1990.

Brütting, R., *'Ecriture' und 'texte': Die französische Literaturtheorie 'nach dem Strukturalismus'*, Bonn, Bouvier, 1976.

Burnier, M., *Les Existentialistes et la politique*, Paris, Gallimard, 1966.

Burwick, F. and W. Pape (eds), *Aesthetic Illusion: Theoretical and Historical Approaches*, Berlin, de Gruiter, 1990.

Butler, J. and J. W. Scott (eds), *Feminists Theorize the Political*, London, Routledge, 1992.

Cebulla, M., *Wahrheit und Authentizität: Zur Entwicklung der Literaturtheorie Paul de Mans*, Stuttgart, M & P Verlag, 1992.

Charvet, M. and E. Krumm, *Tel Quel: un'avanguardia per il materialismo*, Bari, Dedalo, 1974.

Choi, M.-G., 'Frühromantische Dekonstruktion und dekonstruktive Frühromantik: Paul de Man und Friedrich Schlegel', in *Ästhetik und Rhetorik: Lektüren zu Paul de Man* (ed. K. H. Bohrer), Frankfurt am Main, Suhrkamp, 1993.

Cometti, J.-P., 'Situation herméneutique et ontologie fondamentale', in *Etre et temps de Martin Heidegger*, *Sud* (May 1989).

Corlett, W., *Community without Unity: A Politics of Derridean Extravagance*, Durham, Duke University Press, 1989.

Coseriu, E., *Einführung in die Allgemeine Sprachwissenschaft*, UTB, Tübingen, Francke, 1988.

Critchley, S., *The Ethics of Deconstruction. Derrida and Levinas*, Oxford, Blackwell, 1992.

Critchley, S. and Dews, P., *Deconstructive Subjectivities*, Albany, State University of New York Press, 1996.

Culler, J., *On Deconstruction: Theory and Criticism after Structuralism*, Ithaca, Cornell University Press, 1982.

Culler, J., *Framing the Sign: Criticism and its Institutions*, Oxford, Blackwell 1988.

Currie, M., 'The Voices of Paul de Man', *Language and Literature*, 3 (1993).

de Bolla, P., *Harold Bloom: Towards Historical Rhetorics*, London, Routledge, 1988.

de Man, P., 'Reply to Raymond Geuss', *Critical Inquiry*, 10 (December 1983).

de Man, P., *Blindness and Insight: Essays in the Rhetoric of Contemporary Criticism* (2nd ed.), London, Routledge, 1983.

de Man, P., 'Sign and Symbol in Hegel's *Aesthetics*', *Critical Inquiry*, 8 (1982).

de Man, P., 'Phenomenality and Materiality in Kant', *Hermeneutics: Questions and Prospects* (ed. G. Shapiro and A. Sica), Amherst, University of Massachusetts Press, 1984.

de Man, P., *The Rhetoric of Romanticism*, New York-London, Columbia University Press, 1984.

de Man, P., *The Resistance to Theory*, Minneapolis, University of Minnesota Press, 1986.

de Man, P., *Allegories of Reading: Figural Language in Rousseau, Nietzsche, Rilke, and Proust*, New Haven, Yale University Press, 1988.

de Man, P., *Critical Writings 1953–1978* (ed. Lindsay Waters), Theory and History of Literature, 66, Minneapolis, University of Minnesota Press, 1989.

de Saussure, F., *Course in General Linguistics* (trans. W. Baskin), London, Peter Owen, 1960.

Deleuze G., *Empirisme et subjectivité: Essai sur la nature humaine selon Hume*, 2nd ed., Paris, PUF, 1973.

Deleuze G., *Empirism and Subjectivity. An Essay on Hume's Theory of Human Nature* (trans. C. V. Bandas), New York, Columbia University Press, 1991.

Deleuze, G., *Difference and Repetition* (trans. P. Patton), London, Athlone, 1994.

Deleuze, G. and C. Parnet, *Dialogues*, Paris, Flammarion, 1977.

Derrida, J., *La Voix et le phénomène*, Paris, PUF, 1967.

Derrida, J., *et al.*, *Théorie d'ensemble*, Paris, Seuil, 1968.

Derrida, J., *Of Grammatology* (trans. G. C. Spivak), Baltimore, Johns Hopkins University Press, 1974.

Derrida, J., *Spurs: Neitzsche's Styles* (trans. B. Harlow), Chicago, University of Chicago Press, 1978.

Derrida, J., *Writing and Difference* (trans. A. Bass), London, Routledge & Kegan Paul, 1978.

Derrida, J., *Dissemination* (trans. B. Johnson), Chicago, University of Chicago Press, 1981.

Derrida, J., *Positions* (trans. A. Bass), London, Athlone, 1981.

Derrida, J., *Margins of Philosophy* (trans. A. Bass), London, Routledge & Kegan Paul, 1982.

Derrida, J., *The Ear of the Other: Otobiography, Transference, Translation* (trans. P. Kamuf; ed. C. V. McDonald), New York, Schocken Books, 1985.

Derrida, J., *Glas* (trans. J. P. Leavey Jr., and R. Rand), Lincoln, University of Nebraska Press, 1986.

Derrida, J., *Memoirs – For Paul de Man*, trans. C. Lindsay, J. Culler and E. Cadava), New York, Columbia University Press, 1986.

Derrida, J., *Parages*, Paris, Galilée, 1986.

Derrida, J., *The Archaeology of the Frivolous: Reading Condillac* (trans. J. P. Leavey Jr.), Lincoln, University of Nebraska Press, 1987.

Derrida, J., *The Post-Card: From Socrates to Freud and Beyond* (trans. A. Bass), Chicago, University of Chicago Press, 1987.

Derrida, J., *Psyché: Inventions de l'autre*, Paris, Galilée, 1987.

Derrida, J., *The Truth in Painting* (trans. G. Bennington and I. McLeod), Chicago, University of Chicago Press, 1987.

Derrida, J., *Geschlecht (Heidegger): Sexuelle Differenz, ontologische Differenz, Heideggers Hand*, Edition Passagen, Vienna, Böhlau, 1988.

Derrida, J., *Limited Inc.*, Evanston, Northwestern University Press, 1988.

Derrida, J., *Du droit à la philosophie*, Paris, Galilée, 1990.

Derrida, J., *Donner le temps 1. La Fausse monnaie*, Paris, Galilée, 1991.

Derrida, J., *Given Time. 1. Counterfeit Money* (trans. P. Kamuf), Chicago, University of Chicago Press, 1992.

Derrida, J., *The Other Heading: Reflections on Today's Europe* (trans. P. A. Brault and M. B. Naas), Bloomington, University of Indiana Press, 1992.

Derrida, J., *Passions*, Paris, Galilée, 1993.

Derrida, J., *Specters of Marx* (trans. P. Kamuf), New York, Routledge, 1994.

Derrida, J., *Points . . . Interviews, 1974–1994* (ed. E. Weber), Stanford, Stanford University Press, 1995.

Derrida, J., *Monolingualism of the Other or The Prosthesis of Origin*, Stanford, Stanford University Press, 1998.

Derrida, J. and Labarrière, P. J., *Altérités*, Paris, Editions Osiris, 1986.

Deutscher, P., *Yielding Gender: Feminism, Deconstruction and the History of Philosophy*, London, Routledge, 1997.

Dubarle, D. and A. Doz, *Logique et dialectique*, Paris, Larousse, 1972.

Eagleton, T., *Literary Theory: An Introduction*, Oxford, Basil Blackwell, 1983.

Eagleton, T., *The Function of Criticism: From the Spectator to Post-Structuralism*, London, Verso, 1984.

Eagleton, T., *Against the Grain: Essays 1975–1985*, London, Verso, 1986.

Eco, U., 'Reflections on The Name of the Rose', in *Encounter*, vol. 64, 4, April 1985.

Elam, D., *Feminism and Deconstruction: Ms. en abyme*, New York, Routledge, 1994.

Eliot, G., *Adam Bede*, London, Penguin, 1980 (first published in 1859).

Ellis, J. M., *Against Deconstruction*, Princeton, Princeton University Press, 1989.

Eßbach, W., *Die Junghegelianer: Soziologie einer Intellektuellengruppe*, Munich, Fink, 1988.

Falk, W., *Leid und Verwandlung: Rilke, Kafka, Trakl und der Epochenstil des Impressionismus und Expressionismus*, Salzburg, O. Müller, 1961.

Felperin, H., *Beyond Deconstruction*, Oxford, Clarendon Press, 1985.

Fohrmann, J., 'Misreadings Revisited Eine Kritik des Konzepts von Paul de Man, in *Ästhetik und Rhetorik: Lektüren zu Paul de Man* (ed. K. H. Bohrer), Frankfurt am Main, Suhrkamp, 1993.

Forget, P. (ed.), *Text und Interpretation*, Munich, Fink, 1984.

Foucault, M. *et al.* (eds), *Théorie d'ensemble*, Paris, Seuil, 1968.

Frank, M., *Der unendliche Mangel an Sein: Schellings Hegelkritik und die Anfänge der Marxschen Dialektik* (2nd ed.), Munich, Fink, 1992.

Fraser, N. and L. Nicholson, 'Social Criticism without Philosophy: An Encounter between Feminism and Postmodernism', in *Theory, Culture and Society*, no. 2–3 ('Postmodernism'), 1988.

Giovannangeli, D., 'Mauss entre Sartre et Derrida', in *Le Passage des frontières: Autour du travail de Jacques Derrida* (ed. G. Bennington), Paris, Galilée, 1994.

Goldmann, L., 'La Mort d'Adorno', *La Quinzaine littéraire*, 78 (1–15 September 1969).

Goldmann, L., *The Hidden God* (trans. P. Thody), London, Routledge & Kegan Paul, 1970

Goldmann, L., *Towards a Sociology of the Novel* (trans. A. Sheridan), London, Tavistock, 1975.

Goth, J., *Nietzsche und die Rhetorik*, Tübingen, Niemeyer, 1970.

Gottsched, J. C., *Ausgewählte Werke* (ed. P. M. Mitchell), vol. 7, 2, Berlin, de Gruyter, 1975.

Graeff, O. de, *Serenity in Crisis: A Preface to Paul de Man, 1939–1960*, Lincoln, Nebr., University of Nebraska Press, 1993.

Greimas, A. J., *Sémantique structurale*, Paris, Larousse, 1966.

Greimas, A. J., *Structural semantics: An Attempt at a Method* (trans. D. McDowell, R. Schleifer and A. Velie) Lincoln, Nebr.-London, University of Nebraska Press, 1983.

Greimas, A. J., *Du sens II: Essays sémiotiques*, Paris, Seuil, 1983.

Greimas, A. J. and J. Courtés, *Semiotics and Language: An Analytical Dictionary* (trans. Larry Crist *et al.*), Bloomington, University of Indiana Press, 1982.

Haar, M., 'Le Jeu de Nietzsche dans Derrida', *Revue philosophique*, 2 ('Derrida') (1990), 215.

Haber, H. Fern, *Beyond Postmodern Politics. Lyotard, Rorty, Foucault*, New York, Routledge, 1994.

Habermas, J. and N. Luhmann, *Theorie der Gesellschaft oder Sozialtechnologie – Was leistet die Systemforschung?*, Frankfurt am Main, Suhrkamp, 1971.

Habermas, J., 'Entgegnung', in *Kommunikatives Handeln: Beiträge zu Jürgen Habermas' 'Theorie des Kommunikativen Handelns'*, Frankfurt am Main, Suhrkamp, 1986.

Habermas, J., *The Philosophical Discourse of Modernity: Twelve Lectures* (trans. F. Lawrence), Studies in Contemporary German Social Thought, Cambridge, MIT Press, 1987.

Habermas, J., *Die Moderne – ein unvollendetes Projekt: Philosophisch-politische Aufsätze 1977–1990*, Leipzig, Reclam, 1990.

Habermas, J., *Moral Consciousness and Communicative Action* (trans. C. Lenhardt and S. W. Nicholsen), Cambridge, Polity, 1990.

Hamacher, W. (ed.), *Nietzsche aus Frankreich*, Frankfurt am Main, Ullstein, 1986.

Hamacher, W., 'Unlesbarkeit', in P. de Man, *Allegorien des Lesens* (trans. W. Hamacher and P. Krumme), Frankfurt am Main, Suhrkamp, 1988.

Hartman, G. H., *Beyond Formalism: Literary Essays 1958–1970*, New Haven, Yale University Press, 1970.

Hartman, G. H., *The Fate of Reading and Other Essays*, Chicago, University of Chicago Press, 1975.

Hartman, G. H., 'Words, Wish, Worth: Wordsworth', in *Deconstruction and Criticism*, London, Routledge & Kegan Paul, 1979.

Hartman, G. H., *Criticism in the Wilderness: The Study of Literature Today*, New Haven, Yale University Press, 1980.

Hartman, G. H., *Saving the Text: Literature/Derrida/Philosophy*, Baltimore, Johns Hopkins University Press, 1981.

Hartman, G. H., *Easy Pieces*, New York, Columbia University Press, 1985.

Hartman, G. H., *The Unremarkable Wordsworth*, London, Methuen, 1987.

Hatim, B. and I. Mason, *Discourse and the Translator*, London, Longman, 1990.

Haug, Walter and Wilfried Barner (eds), *Ethische contra ästhetische Legitimation von Literatur/Traditionalismus und Modernismus. Kontroversen um den Avantgardismus*, Acts of the 7th International Congress of Scholars of German Literature, Göttingen, 1985, Tübingen, Niemeyer, 1986.

Hegel, G. W. F., *Die Wissenschaft der Logik*, vol. 1, Frankfurt am Main, Suhrkamp, 1969.

Hegel, G. W. F., *Science of Logic* (trans. A. V. Miller), London, Allen & Unwin, 1969.

Hegel, G. W. F., *Aesthetics: Lectures on Fine Art*, vol. 1 (trans. T. M. Knox), Oxford, Clarendon Press, 1975.

Heidegger, M., *Identity and Difference* (trans. J. Stambaugh), New York, Harper & Row, 1969.

Heidegger, M., *Nietzsche* (trans. F. A. Capuzzi, ed. D. F. Krell), San Francisco, Harper & Row, 1982.

Heidegger, M., *On the Way to Language* (trans. P. D. Hertz), Perennial Library, New York, Harper & Row, 1982.

Heidegger, M., *Gesamtausgabe*, Frankfurt, Klostermann, 1985.

Heidegger, M., *Vorträge und Aufsätze* (6th ed.), Pfullingen, Neske, 1990.

Heidegger, M., *Being and Time* (10th ed.) (trans. J. Macquarrie and E. Robinson), Oxford, Blackwell, 1992.

Henrich, D. (ed.), *Kant oder Hegel? Über Formen der Begründung in der Philosophie*, Stuttgart, Klett-Cotta, 1983.

Honneth, A. and H. Joas (eds), *Kommunikatives Handeln: Beiträge zu Jürgen Habermas' 'Theorie des Kommunikativen Handelns'*, Frankfurt am Main, Suhrkamp, 1986.

Horkheimer, M., 'Ein neuer Ideologiebegriff?', in *Der Streit um die Wissenssoziologie* (ed. V. Meja and N. Stehr), vol. 2, Frankfurt am Main, Suhrkamp, 1982.

Husserl, E., *Philosophie als strenge Wissenschaft*, Frankfurt, Klostermann, 1965.

Husserl, E., *Phenomenology and the Crisis of Philosophy* (trans. Q. Laver), New York, Harper & Row, 1965.

Huyssen, A. and K. R. Scherpe (eds), *Postmoderne: Zeichen eines kulturellen Wandels*, Reinbek, Rowohlt, 1989.

Irigaray, L., *Speculum of the Other Woman* (trans. by G. C. Gill). Ithaca, Cornell University Press, 1985.

Japp, U., 'Kontroverse Daten der Modernität', in *Ethische contra ästhetische Legitimation von Literatur/Traditionalismus und Modernismus: Kontroversen um den Avantgardismus*, Acts of the 7th International Congress of Scholars of German Literature, Göttingen, 1985, Tübingen, Niemeyer, 1986.

Johnson, B., 'Rigorous Unreliability', *Critical Inquiry*, 11 (1984).

Johnson, C., *System and Writing in the Philosophy of Jacques Derrida*, Cambridge, Cambridge University Press, 1993.

Johnson, P. and M. Wigley, *Deconstructivist Architecture*, New York, Museum of Modern Art, 1988.

Jurainville, A., *Lacan et la philosophie*, (2nd ed.) Paris, PUF, 1966.

Kant, I., *Critique of Aesthetic Judgement* (trans. J. C. Meredith), Oxford, Clarendon Press, 1911.

Kant, I., *The Critique of Pure Reason, The Critique of Practical Reason, The*

Critique of Judgement (no translator given), Chicago, Encyclopaedia Britannica, 1952.

Kofman, S., *Lectures de Derrida*, Paris, Galilée, 1984.

Kosik, K., *Dialektik des Konkreten*, Frankfurt, Suhrkamp, 1971.

Kramer, M. H., *Legal Theory, Political Theory and Deconstruction: Against Rhadamantus*, Bloomington, University of Indiana Press, 1991.

Kristeva, J., *Semeiotikè: Recherches pour une sémanalyse*, Paris, Seuil, 1969.

Lacan, J., *Le Séminaire, livre II. Le Moi dans la théorie de Freud et dans la technique de la psychanalyse*, Paris, Seuil, 1978.

Lacoue-Labarthe, P. and J.-L. Nancy, *The Literary Absolute: The Theory of Literature in German Romanticism* (trans. P. Barnard and C. Lester), New York, State University of New York Press, 1988.

Lakatos, I. and A. Musgrave (eds), *Criticism and the Growth of Knowledge*, Cambridge, Cambridge University Press, 1970.

Lange, W.-D. (ed.), *Französische Literaturkritik in Einzeldarstellungen*, Stuttgart, Kröner, 1975.

Lehman, D., *Signs of the Times: Deconstruction and the Fall of Paul de Man*, London, André Deutsch, 1991.

Lentricchia, F., *Criticism and Social Change*, Chicago, University of Chicago Press, 1984.

Lohmann, G., 'Fragmentierung, Oberflächlichkeit und Ganzheit individueller Existenz: Negativismus bei Georg Simmel', in *Dialektischer Negativismus* (ed. E. Angehrn et al.), Frankfurt am Main, Suhrkamp, 1992.

Löwith, K., *Von Hegel zu Nietzsche: Der revolutionäre Bruch im Denken des neunzehnten Jahrhunderts* (9th ed.), Hamburg, Meiner, 1986.

Löwith, K., *From Hegel to Nietzsche: The Revolution in Nineteenth-Century Thought* (trans. D. E. Green), London, Constable, 1984.

Luhmann, N., *Die Wissenschaft der Gesellschaft*, Frankfurt am Main, Suhrkamp, 1990.

Lützeler, P. M., (ed.), *Spätmoderne und Postmoderne: Beiträge zur deutschsprachigen Gegenwartsliteratur*, Frankfurt am Main, Fischer, 1991.

Lyotard, J.-F., *The Postmodern Condition: A Report on Knowledge* (trans. G. Bennington and B. Masumi), Theory and History of Literature, 10, Manchester, Manchester University Press, 1984.

Macherey, P., *Hegel ou Spinoza?*, Paris, Maspero, 1979.

Mallarmé, S., *Oeuvres complètes*, Bibl. de la Pléiade, Paris, Gallimard, 1945.

Malmberg, B., 'Derrida et la sémiologie: quelques notes marginales', in *Semiotica*, 11, 2 (1974).

Martin, B., *Matrix and Line: Derrida and the Possibilities of Postmodern Social Theory*, Albany, State University of New York Press, 1992.

Matoré, G., *Le Vocabulaire et la société sous Louis-Philippe*, Geneva and Lille, Droz, 1951.

Mauron, C., *Des métaphores obsédantes au mythe personnel: Introduction à la Psychocritique*, Paris, Corti, 1983.

Meja, V. and N. Stehr (eds), *Der Streit um die Wissenssoziologie*, vol. 2, Frankfurt am Main, Suhrkamp, 1982.

Mészáros, I., *The Power of Ideology*, New York, Harvester-Wheatsheaf, 1989.

Meyer, T., *Nietzsche und die Kunst*, UTB, Tübingen-Basel, Francke, 1993.

Miller, J. H., *Fiction and Repetition: Seven English Novels*, Cambridge, Harvard University Press, 1982.

Miller, J. H., *The Linguistic Moment: From Wordsworth to Stevens*, Princeton, Princeton University Press, 1985.

Miller, J. H., *The Ethics of Deconstruction*, New York, Columbia University Press, 1987.

Miller, J. H., *The Ethics of Reading: Kant, de Man, Eliot, Trollope, James, and Benjamin*, The Wellek Library Lectures at the University of California, Irvine, New York-Guildford, Columbia University Press, 1987.

Miller, J. H., *Tropes, Parables, Performatives: Essays in Twentieth-Century Literature*, New York, Harvester-Wheatsheaf, 1990.

Miller, J. H., *Victorian Subjects*, New York, Harvester-Wheatsheaf, 1990.

Miller, J. H., 'Geneva or Paris: George Poulet's "Criticism of Identification"', in *Theory Now and Then*, New York, Harvester-Wheatsheaf, 1991.

Miller, J. H., *Hawthorne and History: Defacing It*, Oxford, Blackwell, 1991.

Miller, J. H., *Theory Now and Then*, New York, Harvester-Wheatsheaf, 1991.

Miller, J. H., *Ariadne's Thread*, New Haven, Yale University Press, 1992.

Musil, R., *Der Mann ohne Eigenschaften*, Reinbek, Rowohlt, 1952.

Nietzsche, F., *The Gay Science* (trans. W. Kaufmann), New York, Vintage, 1974.

Nietzsche, F., *Werke* (ed. K. Schlechta), Munich, Hanser, 1980.

Nietzsche, F., *Friedrich Nietzsche on Rhetoric and Language* (ed. and trans. S. L. Gilman, C. Blair and D. J. Parent), Oxford, Oxford University Press, 1989.

Nietzsche, F., *Human, All Too Human* (trans. R. J. Hollingdale), Cambridge, Cambridge University Press, 1996.

Nietzsche, F., *Beyond Good and Evil: Prelude to a Philosophy of the Future* (trans. and ed. M. Faber), Oxford, Oxford University Press, 1998.

Norris, C., *The Deconstructive Turn: Essays in the Rhetoric of Philosophy*, London, Methuen, 1984.

Norris, C., *Derrida*, London, Fontana, 1987.

Norris, C., *Paul de Man: Deconstruction and the Critique of Aesthetic Ideology*, London, Routledge, 1988.

Norris, C., 'Limited Think: How Not to Read Derrida', in *What's Wrong with Postmodernism: Critical Theory and the Ends of Philosophy*, New York, Harvester-Wheatsheaf, 1990.

Norris, C., *What's Wrong with Postmodernism: Critical Theory and the Ends of Philosophy*, New York-London, Harvester-Wheatsheaf, 1990.

Norris, C., *Deconstruction: Theory and Practice* (2nd ed.), London, Methuen, 1991.

Norris, C., *Deconstruction and the 'Unfinished Project of Modernity'*, London, Athlone, 2000.

O'Malley, J. J., K. W. Algozin and F. G. Weiss (eds.), *Hegel and the History of Philosophy: Proceedings of the 1972 Hegel Society of America*, The Hague, Nijhoff, 1974.

Pêcheux, M., *Language, Semantics and Ideology*, London, Macmillan, 1982.

Pêcheux, M., *Les Vérités de La Palice*, Paris, Maspero, 1975.

Prieto, L. J., 'Entwurf einer allgemeinen Semiotik', *Zeitschrift für Semiotik*, 1 (1979).

Proust, M., 'A propos du "style" de Flaubert', *Contre Sainte-Beuve* (ed. P. Clarac), Bibliothèque de la Pléiade, Paris, Gallimard, 1971.

Rajnath (ed.), *Deconstruction: A Critique*, London, Macmillan, 1989.

Ransom, J., *The New Criticism*, Norfolk, Conn., New Directions, 1941.

Rastier, F., *Essais de sémiotique poétique*, Paris, Larousse, 1972.

Richard, J.-P., *L'Univers imaginaire de Mallarmé*, Paris, Seuil, 1961.

Rorty, R., 'Deconstruction and Circumvention', *Critical Inquiry*, 11 (September 1984).

Rousseau, J.-J., *The Social Contract and Discourse on the Origin of Inequality* (trans. G. D. H. Cole), London, Dent, 1967

Ryan, M., *Marxism and Deconstruction: A Critical Articulation*, Baltimore, Johns Hopkins University Press, 1982.

Salusinszky, I., *Criticism in Society*, New York, Methuen, 1987.

Sartre, J.-P., 'Aller et retour', in *Critiques littéraires I*, Paris, Gallimard, 1946.

Sartre, J.-P., 'L'Univers singulier', in *Kierkegaard vivant: Colloque organisé par l'Unesco à Paris du 21 au 23 avril 1964*, Paris, Gallimard, 1966.

Searle, J. R., 'Reiterating the Differences: A Reply to Derrida', *Glyph*, 1 (1977).

Schlegel, F., *Kritische Ausgabe*, Paderborn, Schöningh, 1967.

Schmitt, H.-J. (ed.), *Einführung in Theorie, Geschichte und Funktion der DDR-Literatur*, Stuttgart, Metzler, 1975.

Shapiro, G. and A. Sica (eds), *Hermeneutics: Questions and Prospects*, Amherst, University of Massachusetts Press, 1984.

Sim, S., *Beyond Aesthetics: Confrontations with Post-Structuralism and Postmodernism*, New York, Harvester-Wheatsheaf, 1992.

Smith, R., *Derrida and Autobiography*, Cambridge, Cambridge University Press, 1995.

Sollers, P., 'Ecriture et révolution', in *Théorie d'ensemble*, Paris, Seuil, 1968.

Stirner, M., *Kleinere Schriften und seine Entgegnungen auf die Kritik seines*

Werkes 'Der Einzige und sein Eigentum', Stuttgart, Frommann-Holzboog, 1976.

Störig, H.J (ed.), *Das Problem des Übersetzens*, Darmstadt, Wissenschaftliche Buchgesellschaft, 1973.

Taminiaux, J., 'La Présence de Nietzsche dans Sein und Zeit', in *Etre et temps de Martin Heidegger, Sud* (May 1989).

Vischer, F. T., *Das Schöne und die Kunst: Einführung in die Ästhetik* (2nd ed.), Stuttgart, Verlag der J. G. Cottaschen Buchhandlung, 1898.

Vischer, F. T., *Kritische Gänge*, Munich, Meyer & Jessen, 1922.

Warning, R. (ed.), *Rezeptionsästhetik*, Munich, Fink, 1975.

Watzlawick, P. (ed.), *Die erfundene Wirklichkeit: Wie wissen wir, was wir zu wissen glauben? Beiträge zum Konstruktivismus*, Munich, Piper, 1984.

Welsch, W., *Unsere postmoderne Moderne* (3rd ed.), Weinheim, VCH, 1991.

Wheeler, S. C., *Deconstruction as Analytic Philosophy*, Stanford, Stanford University Press, 2000.

Wiehl, R., 'Prozesse und Kontraste', in *Kant oder Hegel? Über Formen der Begründung in der Philosophie* (ed. D. Henrich), Stuttgart, Klett-Cotta, 1983.

Zima, P. V., *L'Ambivalence romanesque: Proust, Kafka, Musil* (2nd ed.), Frankfurt, Peter Lang, 1988.

Zima, P. V., *Textsoziologie*, Stuttgart, Metzler, 1988.

Zima, P. V., *Ideologie und Theorie: Eine Diskurskritik*, Tübingen, Francke, 1989.

Zima, P. V., *Literarische Ästhetik: Methoden und Modelle der Literaturwissenschaft*, UTB, Tübingen, Francke, 1991.

Zima, P. V., *Komparatistik. Einführung in die Vergleichende Literaturwissenschaft*, Tübingen, Francke, 1992.

Zourabichvili, F., *Deleuze: Une philosophie de l'événement*, Paris, PUF, 1994.

INDEX